'Raw, absorbing, stomach-punchingly funny. As I've seen first-hand, where Kris goes, chaos follows. He's the master of the blag and king of riding his luck, capturing his extraordinary and calamitous life on the road to F1 perfectly in this sensational tale. A much-needed feel-good book that will have you in stitches one minute and feeling his pain another. An awesome human being, with an incredible life story.'

Lawrence Barretto
Formula One writer, presenter and broadcaster

'It's often said that in Formula One you meet a better class of person at the back of the grid. For all that Kris makes out he's the Mr. Bean of the paddock, he's actually a solid bloke and much appreciated. If you want a different take on the mad, mad world that is F1, this is the book for you.'

James Allen
President, Motorsport Business & F1 Liaison
Motorsport Network Media

'I first encountered Kris at BSkyB in London when his career was on a terminal downhill trajectory, so it was a huge surprise to meet him again in the Formula One paddock. Like a durable (but blistered and slow) hard compound tyre, he somehow kept going when he should have been black-flagged long ago. This book is an exhaustive compendium of how not to make sports television. Read it at your peril.'

Craig Slater
Formula One News reporter, Sky Sports UK

'Kris may claim to have no idea what he's doing, but he somehow lasted this long, so I have my suspicions. This book shows that many of the F1 paddock's weird and wonderful personalities have hilarious failings and, like Kris, needed more than a few lucky breaks to make it. This book provides a unique angle on the glamorous, intriguing and outlandish world of Formula One.'

Chris Medland
Formula One journalist and broadcaster Racer/Motor Sport Magazine/SiriusXM

'Formula One is a travelling circus with hundreds of people making the show happen. Having taken time to think back over the many characters I have met in the sport, I have no hesitation in saying that Kris, unequivocally, is one of them!'

Will Buxton
Formula One digital presenter, author, journalist and reporter,
Liberty Media/FOM

'Kryslexia: a learning difficulty that drastically impairs the skills required for the accurate reading, writing and speaking of Spanish, resulting in a hilarious vocabulary.'

Diego Mejía
Motorsport broadcaster, Fox Sports LatAm

'TV crews in the F1 paddock work under extreme pressure and every second counts. When I am preparing my technical demonstrations, I am often working against the clock to get ready for the live broadcast. It's a relief to know that Kris is there solving problems with a smile and positive energy, even if he seems to be running around like a headless chicken. I hope you enjoy the book.'

Albert Fabrega,
Formula One presenter, technical expert and broadcaster

'Kris is hard to keep up with as he zooms round the paddock at warp speed, but on the rare occasions when the job allows, he's outstandingly cool company too!'

David Tremayne
Formula One writer and author

'Kris, the man with the cap, is one of the friendliest and most helpful people in the paddock. He always has time for everyone. No matter how hectic or stressful the situation, he is always calm and kind.'

Mervi Kallio
Formula One host, reporter and news anchor, Viaplay TV

'Had I known half of what I learned reading these hilarious, hair-raising stories, I would have fired Kris years ago!'

Juan Fossaroli
Formula One presenter, producer and reporter, ESPN Disney

STARTING FROM THE BACK OF THE

GRID

MISADVENTURES INSIDE FORMULA ONE'S FLYING CIRCUS

CO-WRITTEN BY
KRIS HENLEY & IAN HENLEY
FOREWORD BY GUENTHER STEINER

First published by Pitch Publishing, 2023

Pitch Publishing
9 Donnington Park,
85 Birdham Road,
Chichester,
West Sussex,
PO20 7AJ
www.pitchpublishing.co.uk
info@pitchpublishing.co.uk

© 2023, Kris Henley and Ian Henley

Every effort has been made to trace the copyright.
Any oversight will be rectified in future editions at the
earliest opportunity by the publisher.

All rights reserved. No part of this book may be reproduced,
sold or utilised in any form or transmitted in any form or by
any means, electronic or mechanical, including photocopying,
recording or by any information storage and retrieval system,
without prior permission in writing from the Publisher.

A CIP catalogue record is available for this book
from the British Library.

ISBN 978 1 80150 647 2

Typesetting and origination by Pitch Publishing

Printed and bound in Great Britain by TJ Books, Padstow

Contents

Foreword by Guenther Steiner 8
Latin America, We Have a Problem! 9
Red Bull Gives Me Wings 14
A Clown in the Formula One Circus 24
How (not) to Become a Formula One TV Producer 29
Searching for a Seat 32
Why We Can't Be Formula One Drivers 41
Useless Business Cards 48
Diamond Geezer at Silverstone 54
Paddock Survival Skills 61
Track Slide Camera 68
Joker in the Hole 76
Money, Money, Money! 80
Creative Writing Crash Course 88
Finding the Fun in Formula One 92
Cowboy Meets Cowgirl 97
The Engineering Edge 105
Prime Time 112
Charlie and Walter 117
Black-Flagged 126
Racing's In My Blood 133
F! 138
Crash Test Dummy 143
Four Steps to Heaven 150
Snappers 153
Monte Carlo or Bust 162
In a Different Dimension 166
Moroccan Black 173
Crashgating the Party 180

Restricted Access	184
The Pride of Venezuela	193
Animal Farm	198
Gooshbumpsh on the Grid	204
The Art of Silence	212
Lost in Lewis's Eyes	216
Rubbish Performance	222
Sebastian's Slowest Lap	227
Nousnous Violet	230
Away with the Fairways	235
Liar, Liar, Car's on Fire	239
Sky Dive	244
Careering Around	257
Ulises the God of Love	265
Batigol	272
Electric Dreams	277
Run For Your Lives!	289
Never Lift, Never Give Up	295
Frankenstein's Baby	304
'We're Going to Need a Miracle'	310
The Ace and the Joker	317
Acknowledgements	320

To our mother, Stella Elizabeth Henley, who made us what we are and so has plenty to answer for.

WLYLS&CP

Foreword

AS READERS of my own book *Surviving to Drive* know, my life is dedicated to motorsport. Since *Drive to Survive* first aired in March 2019, Formula One has enjoyed a surge in interest around the world, especially in the United States, which is the best possible news for everyone who loves the sport.

Starting from the Back of the Grid builds on the fabulous success of Formula One by telling another hilarious story of how a most unlikely character somehow succeeded in our crazy world, introducing us to many of the characters behind the scenes and providing another unique perspective on how the Flying Circus really works. I hope you enjoy reading the book as much as I did.

Guenther Steiner
Team Principal, Haas Formula One Team

Latin America, We Have a Problem!

Abu Dhabi 2021, Race Day

FIVE MINUTES and 18 seconds before we started broadcasting the last Grand Prix of the thrilling 2021 season to Spanish-speaking America, I knew a disaster was imminent.

The enthralling Formula One season had reached a thrilling climax. The eyes of tens of millions of fans were locked on two drivers: the up-and-coming pretender, supremely talented and intensely ambitious Dutchman Max Verstappen, in hot pursuit of his maiden Formula One World Championship; and the all-business, undisputed master of his craft, British superstar Sir Lewis Carl Davidson Hamilton, MBE and Honorary Fellow of the Royal Academy of Engineering. Having won every other conceivable honour in the sport, Lewis Hamilton was striving to surpass racing legend Michael Schumacher by winning his eighth Formula One drivers' title.

Astonishingly, the fierce rivals were tied on 369.5 points after 21 closely fought races throughout a contentious season. Tens of millions of seasoned Formula One fans and newcomers alike were restlessly anticipating the finale of a sporting epic that would be talked about for decades.

Our onsite production crew, charged with bringing this mouth-watering action to Latin America, however, scarcely seemed to match the importance of the occasion. Covid-19 had reduced our numbers to just two. Our dynamic duo consisted of the youthful-looking, 57-year-old, blond-haired, ruggedly handsome Argentinian Juan Fossaroli, a superstar in his own right as presenter, principal interviewer, commentator and pit reporter for millions of Latin American motorsport fans and, as a partner of the production company attached to Fox Sports, my boss. And then there was me. A less-eye-catching, somewhat balding 54-year-old from Jersey with, as we shall see, some serious challenges in presenting the same aura of suave sophistication. Oh, and that's Jersey, the tiny island just off the coast of France, by the way. Which is nothing like the place where Tony Soprano built his various dubious businesses.

The job title on my F1 season pass boasts 'producer' which certainly sounds good, suggesting an authoritative figure strutting around in mirror shades, dishing out orders to cowering subordinates. The reality is not always so impressive. My duties do include interviewing the racing drivers, team principals,[1] engineers, mechanics and other F1 team members (as well as passing celebrities); and I edit features for the motorsports programmes which air across Latin America. But I can also be seen performing more mundane tasks, such as clearing the way for our regular cameraman, the affable Ulises Panizza (Uli to his many friends), as he tracks backwards during a walking interview; sprinting up the paddock[2] searching frantically for a new battery; fetching Juan's jacket from the press room, or an umbrella from my locker to protect the camera when it rains; or begging another TV crew to lend us a forgotten cable; and then returning a few moments later to beg the same crew for the microphone that goes with the cable. In short, I get to do the jobs that Juan, the star of the show, is too busy to do.

It is also my pleasure to grovel to the FIA[3] for not filling in the appropriate paperwork for a parking pass and then to be haughtily reprimanded because they have nothing to do with such mundane

---

1 I optimistically hope this book will be of interest to relative newcomers to Formula One as well as seasoned fans, so I will explain F1 terminology in footnotes as we go. Team principals are the F1 team bosses.
2 The paddock is the area that the drivers walk through as they make their way from the teams' hospitality suites to their garages and is where the press do most of the driver interviews.
3 Fédération Internationale de l'Automobile, the governing body for world motorsport.

matters and say that I should instead apply to FOM.[4] And, by the way, I really should know the difference by now. Cue: more grovelling.

Indeed, whatever job needs doing, however much kowtowing is required, I do what has to be done to bring the action to our audience. And right now, what had to be done was to stand in for Uli, whose Chinese CanSino Covid-19 vaccine had been insufficient to satisfy officialdom that he was safe to travel to the Middle East. Which left us short-handed. So heroically, if somewhat diffidently, I accepted the mission to save the day.

Under my sole supervision was the hi-tech Sony PMW-300 XDCAM camera that would provide millions of Latin American F1 fans with an intimate, insider's perspective, up close and personal with the superstars of this elite sport. Our viewers would experience the febrile atmosphere in the paddock, hear the roar of the engines on the chaotically coordinated grid, snatch glimpses of, and maybe even a sound bite from, their heroes as they strode purposefully to their cars. And they would hear the latest fevered speculation and sensational developments from Juan, their beloved correspondent.

The ever-so-tiny flaw in this plan was that handling a production grade camera is skilled work and I was, more or less, a novice. There are many features on a modern video camera, but the only ones I had really mastered were the on/off switch, the focus, the zoom, the iris (sort of) and the record button. Which is not necessarily to say I always pressed it at the right time.

So, just two guys with a big responsibility, working on a shoestring. There were no back-ups, no additional support staff and no spares. The all-important camera was perched on top of its tripod to take a final shot of FOM's promotional poster 'Lewis vs Max – Winner Takes All', which was affixed to the wall between the back entrances of the Mercedes and Red Bull garages. The drivers appeared to be staring one another down like prize fighters and I thought I could use the image in the following week's highlights

---

4 Formula One Management, the operating company that controls the broadcasting, organisation and promotional rights of Formula One.

magazine, dramatically zooming out to reveal the protagonists in a montage of victorious, celebratory, reflective and pensive poses. And to be honest, I was feeling quite smug about how good my seventh attempt at the Tarantino-inspired reverse crash-zoom shot looked.

The feed was already streaming from the LiveU video transmission pack on my back to our studios in Buenos Aires and Mexico City for recording and broadcast. I would not touch the record button again until the race was over. The studio-based producers were no doubt wondering why they were seeing repeated crash-zooms of a poster instead of our presenter, Juan. It was past time to get going.

My job for the half-hour pre-show, the race itself and the hour-long post-show was simple. I just had to point and focus the camera either on Juan, or on the drivers, as they rushed through the paddock to their garages, climbed over their halos,[5] pulled in their elbows and slithered into their specially moulded carbon fibre seats in their cockpits, before turning right out of their garages and roaring off down the pit lane on to the anti-clockwise circuit.

Or perhaps I would shoot nervous-looking team principals, suavely unruffled former world champions, excited celebrities, or one of the many other voracious attention-seekers, of which there is a plentiful supply at this sort of sporting spectacular. Some interviews I had arranged weeks before. Others would be done as the opportunity presented.

I might pan from Juan to the #44 Mercedes in the pits and then zoom in slowly on to Lewis's helmet as Juan pointed out an intriguing design detail. Or maybe I would follow Max with a dramatic whip pan (if perhaps not perfectly in frame) as he emerged from the garage in his #33 Red Bull and cruised on to the circuit to perform final checks before taking pole position,[6] the rest of the field slotting neatly into place behind.

---

5   The horseshoe-shaped titanium tube above the driver's head that provides crash protection.
6   The front of the starting grid.

Or after crossing over from the pits to the grid, I might capture the moment they pushed Lando Norris in his McLaren-Mercedes into third place and film him climbing out of his car; and then walk inelegantly backwards ('moonwalking' as Uli likes to call it) to keep Lando in frame as he made his way to the front of the grid for the national anthem. Doubtless I would stumble over a wheel gun or tyre cover in the absence of anyone to clear my way, but I might create a compelling, if shaky, travelling shot of the British driver. My job was just to follow whatever action Juan chose to highlight while he confided the latest buzz to our viewers or bantered with the hosts in our studios in Buenos Aires and Mexico City.

I checked the time on my wristwatch again. 16:24:40. The second hand was racing around the clock face and I was running out of time. The heavy, cumbersome tripod would not be required again until the post-race interviews, so I planned to switch the camera to a lightweight monopod that I could fasten to my belt clip.

So, all I had to do was lift the camera and tripod and carry the vital but fragile equipment ten metres up the paddock to the meeting point with Juan and make the swap. Five minutes and 18 seconds before we went on air, I began to lift.

Perhaps it was a subtle shift in the weight above me, or the slight sound of metal sliding against metal. But whatever it was, I knew for sure that there was nothing I could do to prevent a catastrophe.

Red Bull Gives Me Wings

Monaco 2022

I ATTENDED my first ever Grand Prix in Monaco[7] in 1994. Humiliating though that experience was (as I shall shortly explain) the Principality has ever since had a special place in my heart. Though the streets of Monte Carlo are too narrow for the most exciting racing with modern day Formula One cars, Monaco is far more than sparkling sunshine, flashy boats, Lamborghinis, Porsches and Ferraris, although there is no shortage of those. As a venue for a Grand Prix, the Principality stands defiantly and effortlessly above them all, steeped in the history of Formula One. Here we rub shoulders with the rich and famous and imagine, just for a while, that we are part of an untouchable world.

I am on the top deck of the Red Bull Energy Station[8] looking down at the team's colourful logo emblazoned on the bottom of the swimming pool; two red bulls, combatant,[9] in front of a golden solar disc. The water is calm, but the image still undulates and for a moment has me mesmerised. The sun is setting and the myriad lights in the streets, luxury apartments, swanky yachts and ritzy cruise liners will soon shine out, making the panoramic views, if anything, yet more spectacular.

---

7   The race at Monaco is often referred to as Monte Carlo because it mostly takes place in the Monte Carlo neighbourhood.
8   At all Grands Prix, F1 teams have 'hospitality suites' to entertain their guests and sponsors and provide office facilities, changing rooms etc. The 130-tonne Red Bull Energy Station is the most flamboyant of them all, a luxury barge built in Italy that is floated up the Mediterranean coast to the Monaco harbour.
9   Charging one another. It's a heraldic term, you know!

But for now, it's still bright enough to record so I put the camera light into Uli's rucksack and let him know where it is. Thankfully Uli has now had the necessary vaccinations and has been restored to our team, so I can revert to my usual role of producer.

I spot my friend Vladimir Rys, the affable and talented Red Bull team photographer crouching poolside, swapping a wide-angled lens into one of his cameras. His task today, and every working day, is to add to Red Bull's catalogue of spectacular Formula One photographs.

'Well at least you won't have to work this evening if Ferrari get their way,' I joke and Vlad looks up at me and laughs. 'Did you hear any news?'

'Nothing yet,' he says, after checking his phone.

Ferrari have protested against Red Bull's first and third place, alleging they breached a technical regulation crossing the yellow line at the pit exit. We are waiting to hear the stewards' decision and, as a Red Bull team member, Vlad will be one of the first to know.

He turned his attention back to his camera, adjusting the settings before looking for the best position to capture the creative images that are his trademark. So far it was Red Bull's day and we were in prime position to scoop the anticipated celebrations. Sergio 'Checo' Pérez had taken the chequered flag. His team-mate and world champion Max Verstappen crossed the line in third. Tears rolled down the Mexican's face as he stood on the podium in the Royal Box, the Monaco brass band below him on the starting grid playing his national anthem 'Himno Nacional Mexicano'.[10]

Meanwhile, I had messaged Checo's press officer, Alice, and arranged the exclusive interview that Juan did with Checo when he arrived back at the Energy Station. It was later that rumours began to circulate that the victory was subject to a formal protest. Further festivities would have to wait until the F1 stewards' final decision.

Most Monaco Red Bull Energy Station celebrations are chaotic, packed with all sorts of photographers, freelance journalists,

---

10 'Mexicans, at the cry of war!'

cameramen, bloggers, presenters, guests, crew members and even the odd opportunist fan who has somehow managed to sneak on board. But on this occasion, as no one knew when the result would be finalised, the crowd had been slimmed down to 'just' 150 or so. Unless you were a selected VIP, part of the Red Bull team, or a member of the press who could take photographs or video of the upcoming celebration and beam them around the world (so ensuring the widest possible visibility of the Red Bull brand and those of their sponsors) you were politely escorted to dry land.

Among the remaining TV crews were Sky UK. Martin Brundle and Paul Di Resta were looking at a mobile monitor showing replays of Red Bull's supposed rule violation. I leaned in to watch. It seemed to my far-from-expert eye that the 'Prancing Horse'[11] was clutching at straws. Ferrari were no doubt seething, as they had thrown away a race they certainly should have won. After heavy rain on a drying track, they didn't switch Charles Leclerc, the home driver and pole-sitter, from wet to intermediate tyres quickly enough, which gave Checo enough of a speed advantage for four laps to cost Charles a much-coveted victory.

I felt for Charles, but Checo's third Grand Prix victory was fantastic for Mexico and welcome news for the Latin American sports channels I was working for. His win, should it stand, would surely cement his place in one of the top teams in Formula One, giving him a genuine chance of winning each time he climbed into the car. Sports fans in our region would be guaranteed a Latin American driver to root for. So my fingers were crossed for Checo.

I sent a WhatsApp to Alice, thanking her for arranging the interview, empathising with the frustration she was no doubt feeling and asking if she had any news. Alice replied immediately, 'Decision soon.'

We waited. The Sky team left the Energy Station, presumably to wrap up their show elsewhere. Sky News presenter Craig Slater and a cameraman took their place.

---

11 The Prancing Horse is the symbol and so nickname of Ferrari and Scuderia Ferrari, its racing arm.

Long minutes later, Vlad looked up from his phone and casually relayed the all-important news that Checo's win was confirmed and he was on his way to the pool. Max was also confirmed in third place. Carlos Sainz would have to wait a little longer for his first Grand Prix victory,[12] his second place providing meagre consolation for the disappointed Ferrari team.

I let Juan and Uli know that Checo would soon be with us. Juan nodded and Uli put his camera on his shoulder and moved into position at the top of the terrace stairs, ready to record. Worried expressions on the faces of Team Red Bull turned to happy smiles as the news spread. Caterers, press officers, engineers and mechanics, some dressed in high viz fluorescent yellow-green T-shirts, but most in the deep 'Red Bull blue' team colours, took their cue to line up on one side of the pool, while the cameramen, photographers and presenters jostled for the best positions on the other three sides.

The cheers from the crowds outside the Energy Station announced the arrival of the star of the show a few seconds before he appeared at the top of the stairs. Alice was smiling by his side and the rest of his entourage pumped their fists behind him as the roars of approval gradually escalated in volume until every team member was chanting the Mexican's name.

'Checo! Checo! Checo! Checo!'

How would he choose to immortalise himself in the videos and photos that would be beamed all over the world? Would he strip off and jump into the pool naked, wearing only a red superman-style cape as Christian Horner[13] had done in 2006 when David Coulthard claimed the team's first ever podium? Or would he backflip in, as Mark Webber had done in 2010 and 2012? Webber then went one better after his first victory, jumping – with his team-mate Sebastian Vettel – the full ten metres from the second floor of the Energy Station into the harbour.

---

12 In fact he only had to wait a month before winning the British Grand Prix at Silverstone.
13 The Red Bull team principal.

Or perhaps Checo would try something unexpected, as Daniel Ricciardo had done in 2016, and produce a comical slow-motion belly flop in the crucifix position?

All heads turned to the newly crowned king of Monaco as Uli tracked backwards to capture the euphoric scenes. Checo did not disappoint. Sporting his Red Bull racing uniform and cap, he was careful not to forget his roots, wrapping himself in the Mexican flag. Smiling as widely as when he won his first go-kart race in Guadalajara at the age of six, and without hesitation, he skipped happily to the edge of the pool and executed a tidy forward somersault into the water, not an easy acrobatic feat, but no great challenge for a super-fit Formula One driver. Okay, it would have been great to see a couple of twists and a pike, but had there been judges present to give marks for execution, eight-point-fives or nines would have shown across the board. Except, of course, from the Mexican judge, who would be forgiven for awarding a perfect ten.

Checo's hat floated on the surface of the pool as he climbed out to join his team as the chants of 'Checo! Checo! Checo!' reached a crescendo. The sodden hat was speedily retrieved and thrown back to the winning driver to ensure the logo of his main sponsor, Telcel, would clearly be seen in all the photos and videos. Checo had good reason to make sure his sponsor got full value from his greatest moment in the spotlight. Without their financial backing, his career could never have played out the way it has.

But this was not the moment to think about sponsorship. Getty Images' photographer Mark Thompson gamely tried to direct the excited team for the official photograph from poolside and one of his colleagues looked for a different angle from the top of a stepladder. Max showed up to congratulate his team-mate and join in the celebration. But this day belonged to Checo and Max soon disappeared.

With the more formal photos snapped and videos recorded, the Mexican and his team went crazy, offering plenty more photo opportunities as they screamed, jumped, dived and bombed into the pool, hugging each other and savouring the precious, glorious moments of the hard-earned victory.

'Déjà vu!' I said to Vlad as he snapped away. He winked and laughed as always. We had both been here many times before, so we knew what came next. Celebrations on the tethered palace never ended with just the victorious driver and a few willing members of the team going into the pool. They would shortly be joined by various members of the press, with scant consideration for whatever expensive equipment they might be carrying. Some went in willingly, but others were given no choice by manic mechanics, working in twos or threes, who used brute force to claim their victims. Less muscled team members used cunning techniques, sneaking up behind the unsuspecting to push them in, but often following their victims into the water when even sneakier colleagues crept up behind them.

I watched Craig Slater become the first victim as Christian Horner pushed the Scottish Sky reporter into the pool during his interview. Craig backstroked to the side of the pool and pulled himself out, taking back the microphone he had deftly offloaded to his cameraman before hitting the water.

'Today was about going from dries to wets,' Craig quipped to camera.

I watched from what I hoped was a safe distance. Juan, who was recording a piece, had to be closer to the action. It wasn't long before Checo himself crept up behind Juan and sent him flailing into the water. As the face of motor racing in Latin America and someone who has spent hundreds of hours interviewing Checo from his early days in the lower formulae, there was no way Juan was staying dry. A stray red sponge microphone-cover floated on the surface before someone fished it out. Checo went after Uli and nearly pushed him in too, but a friendly fellow cameraman, knowing the damage that would be caused to Uli's camera, pulled him back to safety.

Felipe McGough, the representative of Fox Sports Mexico, put up a good fight, but in the end was overpowered and went the same way as the rest. I smiled broadly watching the happy chaos, stage managed though it was. Red Bull had changed the Monaco celebration ritual forever.

When the poolside celebration wound down, Uli followed Checo as he descended the wooden steps and posed for photos with the delighted crowd. At last Checo waved 'goodbye' to his adoring fans and went inside the Energy Station where private celebrations would continue into the night.

The temperature was dropping and Juan and Felipe stood dripping and shivering beside the pool, checking to see if their phones were still working. Uli gave me the footage on a camera card and winked, a gesture I knew to mean he had recorded some great material.

I looked out over La Condamine, Monte Carlo and beyond as many memories of Monaco flooded back. I remembered the rush of adrenaline I felt when Juan first handed me the white tabard that allowed me access to the pit lane, making me one of the few people permitted to get close to a racing Formula One car. But I was completely unprepared for the deafening sound of the V8 engine, and the shock when Lewis Hamilton's Vodafone McLaren Mercedes came hurtling into the pits towards me so fast that I braced for impact, imagining his front wing slicing through my shins.

But I had no need to be alarmed. He effortlessly swerved past before gliding to a halt, his mechanics immediately surrounding the car to push him back into the garage. Of course, Lewis's speed in the pits was slow motion compared to what he does on the track (and to this day I am still shocked by the speed of the cars as they tear down the main straight) but it still scared the hell out me the first time I experienced an incoming F1 car.

Then I recalled my first encounter with Fernando Alonso, who was sitting in a comfy red chair at the back of the Ferrari garage, the cooling fan usually used on the car brakes aimed at his face, causing his long hair to stream behind him like some sort of Greek god. I turned to Juan and asked, wide-eyed, 'Is that Alfonso?'

'Alfonso!? Alfonso!?' Juan laughed out loud, without correcting me, although this faux pas (and countless others) would resurface many, many times in the years to come.

From my vantage point on the Energy Station, I looked towards the media centre as I had done briefly in 2012 after a suspicious package was found outside the entrance and the words 'bomb scare' spread quickly through the Red Bull party. But the ladies and gentlemen of the press had just got their hands on their free Thursday evening cocktails, so it would have taken more than a bomb blast to get their attention. Luckily for everyone, it turned out to be a false alarm.

It was time for the mechanics to make their way back towards the garage to resume the work of dismantling their equipment and packing it into the huge articulated lorries, a logistical challenge in itself in the narrow streets of the Principality. The few TV channels that were still on air were wrapping up their shows.

I lingered just a little longer to look out once again over Monaco. The mirrored glass of the Mercedes motorhome looked magnificent, but suffered just a little in comparison to the ostentatious Red Bull Energy Station. I wondered if Toto Wolff[14] was content to accept defeat in the battle of the hospitality suites. Somehow I doubted it, but he would certainly have his work cut out to win that one.

The mirrored glass prompted a memory of Lewis Hamilton riding up to the door in 2019 on a bright red, custom-built Agusta Dragster RR motorbike. After just a few seconds cameramen and photographers materialised from nowhere, descending on the photo-op like vultures on a fallen buffalo.

I remembered how Daniel Ricciardo's ever-present smile abruptly vanished in 2016 when his comfortable lead over Lewis Hamilton in this, the most cherished Grand Prix, was squandered when he pulled in for his final stop to change to the supersoft tyres that would guarantee his victory, only to find the pit crew didn't have them ready. But two years later he was again wreathed in the sunniest of smiles when he finally conquered his opponents around the circuit known as the 'Jewel in the Crown of Formula One'.

I recalled my first ever memory of Monaco in 1994 when I managed to cause Michael Schumacher to visibly swell with rage

---

14 Mercedes' team principal.

just a few moments after setting foot in the paddock for the first time.[15] And a few days later, talking on a yacht with a sad Rubens Barrichello about the death of his hero and fellow countryman, Ayrton Senna, who had crashed fatally during the previous race in Imola.[16]

I looked towards La Rascasse, the famous hairpin bend where Schumacher infamously 'crashed' (or, more accurately, parked) his car after securing provisional pole in 2006, so blocking the track and denying his main rival, Fernando Alonso, the chance to claim pole position. The stewards later ruled Michael be sent to the back of the grid, so once again the integrity of the German came under scrutiny with headlines like 'Super Villain' and 'Cheat Storm' circling the globe.

It isn't hard to understand why, apart from perhaps their home Grand Prix, every racing driver who has pulled on a balaclava and a crash helmet and nestled into a high-performance racing car, dreams of winning at Monaco.

I looked around. Most people had now left the terrace, leaving just a few team members to clear up. I still had to send off the footage of the celebrations for the news shows. We had dinner plans at José María 'Pechito' López's[17] apartment and I didn't want to be late. But I wanted one last look at the extraordinary view from the Energy Station.

As views from the office go, this is as good as it gets. I breathed it in, reflecting on my extraordinary good fortune and yet again felt elation mixed with wonder that I really was a TV producer, paid to be in this Formula One fairyland.

'How on earth did I get here?' I mused, as I had done 100 times before.

Now, there's a question. When, 30 years ago, I woke up on a rat-infested rubbish dump on the streets of Hong Kong with

---

15 More on this debacle anon.
16 And this, too.
17 Multiple World Touring Car champion and Le Mans winner.

a raging hangover and the business card of a passing substance-abuse counsellor tucked into my top pocket, I would have been hard pressed to believe I could end up here.

I had, after all, spent the first seven years of my adult life wandering aimlessly around the world living from hand to mouth. I had nothing by way of qualifications or useful work experience to achieve my youthful ambition to work in TV. Every move I made to launch my career (short, of course, of actually doing the necessary study or acquiring any relevant skills) was rebuffed, until a scarcely believable train of events transformed me from hobo to high flyer; at least in the sense of spending a lot of time on jumbo jets.

While some people progress smoothly through life from school, perhaps to further education, a job, home and family, my journey has been more of a mash-up of a roller coaster and a ghost train. I have enjoyed plenty of highs (some natural, most induced), a few lows (some natural, most from over-indulgence), but far more than my fair share of horrific jump-scares. And I have concluded, after much sober self-reflection, that this is because there is something unusual about my brain. I can only describe it like this. I am a concert pianist, but my piano has missing keys. Perhaps a B somewhere in the bass and the D sharp above middle C. So if I'm given the right music to play, I can bring the house down with a sensitive sonata or a bravura boogie-woogie. But when I'm handed the wrong sheet music, I create a cacophony that sets the kittens caterwauling.

So, dear reader, if you are intrigued to know how I went from a rubbish dump to the Red Bull Energy Station in Monaco, let me tell my story. Along the way I will share the funny stories, controversies, disasters, tragedies, scandals and rivalries that makes Formula One the incredible phenomenon it is and I will introduce you to the courageous, combative, fascinating, ambitious, admirable, brilliant, devious and extraordinary characters I have encountered from a unique perspective – up close and personal with the superstars.

Welcome to the frantic, fantastic Flying Circus that is Formula One.

A Clown in the Formula One Circus

SINCE 1994 I have worked at more than 150 Formula One Grand Prix races and there is no doubt the sport is more popular today than it has ever been. Traditionally F1 fans were attracted to the sport because of the glamorous racing locations, fast cars, innovative engineering and the extraordinary skills and bravery of the drivers. But in the last few years F1 has attracted ever-growing support as it has found new ways to help fans get to know the drivers and their supporting teams almost on a personal level.

Between 2014 and 2018 much of my work was in Formula E[18] where the new promotional approach was pioneered. FE provided the press with plentiful access to the drivers, so the viewers got to know them. When Liberty Media acquired the Formula One Group for $4.4 billion in January 2017, they adopted many of those ideas and ever since, F1 has enjoyed its resurgence.

For the preceding 40 years Formula One was developed from a rich boys' hobby into a global brand under the tight control of Bernie Ecclestone. More on Bernie later, but for now let's just say that he ran Formula One with a rod of iron and part of his vision was to maintain an aura of aloof mystique about the sport. Access to the paddock was restricted and the drivers' use of social media (when it became a thing) was tightly controlled.

But if Bernie built the product, Liberty set it free, bringing mass media expertise and opening the engine cover on Formula One. Seeing F1 as an entertainment as much as a sport, Liberty

---

[18] The electric single-seater motorsport World Championship which was started in 2014. More on this later.

introduced a raft of changes that are transforming fan engagement. F1 TV, a subscription streaming service, provides exclusive analysis, original content and detailed coverage of the lead-up to races as well as the main event. Real time data from hundreds of in-car sensors is used to create sophisticated graphics comparing car and driver performance, indispensable information for the true F1 geek. An F1 app puts much of this content on to mobile devices so people can stay connected wherever they are.

Restrictions on the drivers' use of social media were lifted and more celebrities, sponsors and guests were invited to mingle with the stars. To be in tune with the times, if not to universal approbation, glamorous Grid Girls were replaced by Grid Kids, at least until the pandemic enabled that not-so-popular idea to be quietly shelved. New race venues were introduced and old ones revived. In 2020, despite the pandemic, F1 managed to deliver a staggering 17 Grands Prix. By 2023, it was 23 with more planned in the future.

New rules were introduced to make racing more competitive and a spending cap launched to give less well-funded teams a better chance. A further raft of changes in 2022 were designed to make overtaking easier by reducing the turbulence the cars create.

Perhaps most influential of all, the highly successful Netflix series *Drive to Survive* has provided fans with a 'fly-on-the-wall' insight into the personalities under the helmets, as well as the team principals, owners, investors and other personalities in the sport. Guenther Steiner, the team principal of Haas, became an unlikely celebrity, struggling heroically to keep his less affluent team on the grid while effing and blinding affably in English, his third language, and snapping playfully at the heels of the biggest of dogs, Toto Wolff, the team principal of Mercedes, in his native German.[19]

Drive to Survive reveals the drivers as human beings, with soaring ambitions and poignant insecurities and shows the unbridled joy of success and the utter dejection and despair of failure. It explains the

---

19 Guenter was born in South Tyrol, an autonomous, German-speaking province of Italy.

rivalries, politics and pressures that add texture, colour and interest to the always-spectacular track action. It has caused a resurgence of interest from existing fans and brought new followers into the sport in their hundreds of thousands, particularly in the United States. Though facing some criticism for manufacturing storylines, it has, without doubt, been hugely successful in bringing more people into the Formula One fold.

I have seen world champions crowned and rank outsiders win races against all odds. I have waited anxiously outside hospitals for reports on the condition of injured drivers. I was in the Williams garage when leaking fuel exploded, injuring 31 people. I have driven past flaming tyres at anti-government protests on the way to the Bahrain International Circuit and watched billowing smoke from a missile attack aimed at Aramco, an F1 sponsor, just a few kilometres from the Jeddah circuit. And, as well as fearing I would be run over by Lewis Hamilton in the pit lane, on a different occasion I pulled out at a roundabout into the path of the very same Lewis Hamilton on the way to the Monaco circuit on his aforementioned motorbike. This time, I really was in his way, rather than imagining it, but he expertly swerved to avoid me and luckily didn't look back to see who it was. Or perhaps he did, as I now recall he was a little frosty an hour or so later in the interview pen!

I have interviewed 20 Formula One world champions, past and present, including one of the greatest of them all: Michael Schumacher. At his last race in Brazil in 2012, my final question to him was this:

'Michael, I think I speak for everybody here when I say you will be sorely missed by all the paddock reporters and most definitely by me. What do you think you will miss most after leaving Formula One?'

I will never forget how his voice cracked and his eyes welled with tears as he made his halting reply. I was so moved by the emotion, that I'm afraid I didn't listen properly to what he said. Though it's probably safe to say it wasn't, 'Well Kris, most of all, I'll miss you.'

A CLOWN IN THE FORMULA ONE CIRCUS

I have chit-chatted to members of the Monégasque and British royal families, interviewed Hollywood royalty including Will Smith, Michael Douglas, Benedict Cumberbatch, Antonio Banderas and Owen Wilson, film directors George Lucas and Ron Howard, TV legends Matt Le Blanc, Gordon Ramsay and Rowan Atkinson, world famous sports personalities including David Beckham and multi-Grammy award-winning musicians Will.i.am and Katy Perry. Although, to be honest, the latter encounter could hardly be called an interview. Just as she was leaving the grid, Juan pointed and shooed me to go after her, so I sprinted halfway up the pit lane to catch her up. But when I did, I was instantly star-struck and then somehow got lost in her eyes. So, I could only manage:

'Katy, sorry, it must be horrible having to do interviews with the likes of me.' Which isn't even a question, come to think of it. But, dewy-eyed, I put the microphone to her fulsome red lips.

'Oh yeah, horrible, I hate all this attention!' she sweetly replied with a wink and touching self-awareness. But then her rather intimidating minder stepped between us and whisked her away. So, it was scarcely an exclusive scoop.

Formula One is the pursuit of perfection. While the drivers, or to some degree, the team principals, are the public faces of the team, behind the scenes there are dozens of people in the garages, paddock and pits and many hundreds more back at the factories, dedicated to delivering a car at peak performance. The difference between success and failure can come down to one-hundredth and amazingly often, even one-thousandth of a second. Tiny adjustments to the tracking[20] can make the difference between gaining the fraction of a second that secures the coveted pole position, or clipping a guardrail, losing control and hitting the barrier, the car crumpling like a broken marionette.

Formula One is also a $4 billion business employing 50,000 people in more than 30 countries. The Abu Dhabi 2021 finale

---

20 The wheel alignment.

attracted 108 million[21] TV viewers. The US, Mexico and UK events were each attended by over 350,000 fans. Its social media audience grew 40 per cent in 2021 to 50 million and its cumulative broadcast audience was an astonishing 1.55 billion people.

But most of all Formula One is an entertainment, a travelling circus. As in days of old, the troupe swaggers into town with carnival music, glitz, hoopla and fancy caravans. It pitches the Big Top and sets up the funfair, sells tickets on a grand scale, presents the show with audacious chutzpah, pizzazz and razzamatazz; then strikes camp, packs up and moves on, leaving only open fields and empty streets.

So where do I fit in? Sometimes, I feel I am just an observer, part of the crowd, watching in awe as the drivers and their teams perform their particular brand of circus magic. Of course, in a small way I am part of the show, helping to bring the action to the global audience and to showcase the outrageous talents of the star performers. Sometimes I give a little extra insight, perhaps revealing the drivers and members of the teams in moments of triumph, reflection or vulnerability.

But there is no denying that, on occasion, when I catch my reflection in the shiny glass panels of a hospitality motorhome and realise my trousers are too baggy or my nose too red, perhaps from the sun, but more likely from the local hooch, I can't help but consider that perhaps my greatest talent is to play the clown.

What circus would be complete without one?

---

21 Figures from sportspromedia.com.

How (not) to Become a Formula One TV Producer

IF YOU have to work for a living there can be few better ways to do it than as a TV producer in Formula One. Indeed, many people would call it a dream job and I have to say I wouldn't argue.

It's not for everyone, of course. Like any job, there are downsides, which we will come to. But if you would enjoy travelling the world, to work for a few days, but with time between to catch up with family and friends; or if you like to stay in five-star hotels (even if your slumber is often disturbed by Uli's snores, which sound like Alain Prost's 1991 Ferrari 643 V12 exiting Portier and roaring into the tunnel in Monaco); or if your idea of a good time is dining in charming and diverse restaurants; or if you feel you might enjoy hobnobbing at cocktail parties in Formula One teams' hospitality suites; or over-indulging on the champers at wild post-race parties in extravagant venues; or if you think you would like to go to horse riding exhibitions at Michael Schumacher's private stables, motocross with Kimi Räikkönen, play camel polo with Max Verstappen or go-kart racing with Fernando Alonso; or if you just love the glamour and the buzz of the greatest motorsport in the world; well, a Formula One TV producer would be an excellent career choice.

You may well ask, 'But Kris, to work in that field, don't you need an engineering degree, lots of other qualifications and a deep knowledge of Formula One?' Well, I imagine it helps, but I make no such claims. Quite the contrary. I have managed to find a role in the Formula One circus despite having no qualifications and a brain which is clearly missing a critical component or two.

So how did it happen? Well, dear reader, as you have been good enough to give me a little of your attention, I will share my secret. I did it with a pinch of charm, a lot of bluff and a large dollop of blind luck.

Charm should not be confused with good looks, but I trust you will not think me immodest if I recall that a few decades back, my then girlfriend, after a Chardonnay or three in a low-lit bar, observed a supposed resemblance to Mel Gibson (he of the *Mad Max* mullet). But the years have been no kinder to my appearance than Mel's outbursts have to his popularity in New York. I blame my decline from film star good looks on the loss of my once abundant curly locks. And I guess the additional years and pounds haven't helped.

As far as charm goes, if I possess any at all, it's simply because I try to be friendly. I will talk to anyone who will listen and I will listen to anyone who wants to talk. Be they doorman, hotel receptionist, arresting officer, prostate examiner, rogue, rag-and-bone man or royalty, I am always up for a chat. I am interested in people and people usually like people who take a genuine interest in them.

But for any *soupçon* of charm, there has been plenty of bluff and a wagonload of luck, as we shall see. And I have needed Lady Luck's help every step of the way, as I seem to have a knack for getting myself into embarrassing or chaotic situations. I managed to clonk one racing driver on the nose with my microphone, which I can't say went down well (very sorry Paul Di Resta). I grovelled at the feet of Fernando Alonso at a worldwide press conference, scrambling to recover the eight batteries that had just clattered loudly to the floor having slipped out of my cordless microphone. Fernando looked down in disbelief. I got halfway through an interview with *X-Men* and *Mad Max* (remake) star Nicholas Hoult before Uli tapped me on the shoulder to let me know I was holding a compact umbrella instead of the microphone, much to Nicholas's delight. And I forced Sir Frank Williams to wait outside a disabled toilet, to my deep and eternal shame.

It's fair to say my face better suits voice-overs than front-of-camera. I can read a script in a sporty way, so I have voiced a host of sports magazine shows such as *Rally World*. But I do get in front of a camera from time to time, appearing on *Nitro*, the Fox Sports motorsport news show, and I sometimes even do the odd report in Spanish – but only when there is no native speaker within 200 miles. My command of my second language is a little shaky, so those reports can require quite a few takes to get right. So usually I am behind the camera, producing and editing TV programmes, or interviewing drivers and sports personalities for Asian and American audiences.

As well as F1 and Formula E, I have covered three Le Mans 24-hour races, two Macau Grands Prix (the unofficial Formula 3 World Championship) and worked at countless other races in categories ranging from Formula Asia, World Endurance Cars, the World Rally and the World Touring Car Championships.

But there is nothing quite like the world of Formula One: the exquisite car designs,[22] the spotless garages,[23] the excellence of the engineering, the silky aerodynamics, the fabulous venues, the passionate fans, the epic rivalries, the out-of-this-world driving skills, the pressure and purity of the racing and the extraordinary people who risk their lives to race for glory.

---

22 There have been exceptions. Google 'the seven ugliest Formula One cars' if you wish to outrage your aesthetic sensibilities.
23 Spotless garages are just one of the ways Bernie Ecclestone burnished the Formula One brand. He would go bananas if he saw even a spot of oil on the floor.

Searching for a Seat

*Jersey, Channel Islands 1967–86,
the World 1986-92*

MY STORY can only start with a few words about my childhood. My father, known as Bill, was eleven and my mother, Stella, ten when the Second World War broke out, which gave them a certain perspective on life. Mum was born in the small town of Ottery St Mary in Devon in a house made of wattle and daub. For those unfamiliar with the rural English building methods of yesteryear, wattle is a lattice of wooden strips and daub a mixture of soil, clay, sand, straw and animal dung. There were two electric points in the house, one for the cooker and the other for the iron. She took a candle to bed. There was a shared toilet at the bottom of the garden and old newspapers were cut up and used for ... well, you get the idea.

Her father, Harry, was the 13th of 14 children and just young enough to avoid the First World War trenches. He worked in a brickyard which was ironic given he lived in a mud house. My mother's mother, Bessie, was a short, stout, dark, loquacious woman who quoted reams of Shakespeare at any opportunity and had a worrying appetite for Guinness.

My father's father was badly injured fighting in France in 1918 and died aged just 40, leaving Nan, as we called my grandma, to bring up her two young sons alone. In 1944 her house in east London was destroyed by a V1 'doodlebug' flying bomb, which buried her in the air raid shelter in her back garden. She was claustrophobic for the rest of her life.

My father's older brother, Laurence, went ashore in Normandy three weeks after D-Day and fought in his tank all the way to the Rhine. When he went home on leave for a richly deserved week of quiet, rest and relaxation away from gunfire and bomb blast, he visited my Nan. No sooner had he arrived, than the siren sounded and he was just entering the air raid shelter when the doodlebug hit. His clothes were shredded and he coughed up mud for years.

My father was evacuated twice from London, aged 13 in the 1940 Blitz and again when the doodlebugs started to fall. His second evacuation was to Ottery, where he met my mother at an 'excuse me' dance. After a prolonged courtship, they married in 1953 and later moved to Jersey.

'Hitler had a lot to answer for,' as my father loved to say.

So, my point is, that if you grew up in Britain in the seventies, your petty worries or concerns were trivial indeed compared to the traumas and privations our parents and grandparents had just lived through. It was enough to be alive, have a warm bed and something to eat. An optimistic outlook, never mind ambition, could only lead to disappointment.

So, Stella was always a pessimist, particularly concerning the life prospects of her offspring. Aim high and you are bound to be disappointed was her philosophy. My older brother, Ian, won a place at Cambridge University, but Stella still insisted he learn to drive a heavy goods vehicle during his holidays as she didn't think a science degree would help him get a job. Then she made him learn to touch-type, not because she foresaw the rise of the personal computer, but so he could get a job in a typing pool if neither the science nor the lorry driving worked out.

My own prospects, based on her assessment of my school reports, which admittedly did not compare particularly well with my brother's, appeared to her to be even bleaker. She diagnosed me, with zero medical training, as autistic.

Stella also fancied herself qualified to give careers advice. After much research she concluded that the only job I would be able to handle was a bus conductor. Not a driver, nor mechanic and certainly not the head honcho at the bus depot, mind, but specifically the ticket clipper. So, it was something of a catastrophe when she read in the newspaper that bus conductors were being replaced by ticketing machines.

'Did you read this, Bill?' she said to my father, jabbing at the newspaper, her potentially autistic child in earshot. 'They are phasing out bus conductors. What the hell is Kris going to do for a job now?'

Don't get me wrong, I adore my mother. She brought me up well and is still a healthy, popular nonagenarian. We have had many happy times. No, she was only trying to protect me from failure. Expect little and you might be pleasantly surprised.

But I did get the message that I should set my career expectations to 'low' and I can't say I felt brim full of self-confidence. Now that bus conductors were on the way out, I had, like my mother, no idea what else I could do.

Around that time the British TV crime drama *Bergerac* was being made on location in Jersey. It ran for nine series, attracted audiences of up to 15 million and did wonders for the island's tourist industry. To fill minor roles they advertised for local people and my mother, seeing herself in the passenger seat of John Nettles'[24] 1947 Triumph Roadster and, more to the point, fancying the advertised £49 appearance fee, sent in her application with the required photo. She chose a flattering image from a good few years earlier, posing with our spaniel cross, Smudge.

The following year, the phone rang and I picked up. A woman's voice announced she was the *Bergerac* casting director and asked to speak to my mum. Excitement, however, gave way to disappointment, when the lady said it was not my mother they wanted to appear on the show, but the dog. Sad to say the photogenic mutt had long since chewed his last Bonio and was now scattered around the garden.

Still, my mother's application, I guess, must have hung around at the top of the pile, because a few days later they phoned again

---

24 The lead actor who played Jim Bergerac.

and this time she was offered a small part. I convinced my mother to take me along, fantasising that someone would shout, 'Hey, we need someone about 17, with a *Mad Max* Mullet to do half a page of dialogue with John Nettles, and we need him now!'

On the big day my mum was dressed up in a pinny and hair net by the costume department to perform her role as a cleaning lady. She gamely made a few passes with a hoover behind one of Jim Bergerac's sidekicks to indicate that dawn had broken and the young detective had been up all night diligently studying a tricky case.

I sat at the back of the set, wide-eyed. It was a magical whirlwind of activity as scripts were consulted, cameras and lights were adjusted and coffees were sipped. The director and producer chatted with the actor and a make-up artist fussed about, patting the sweat from the star's nose. Even the clapperboard and boom microphone guys seemed like gods to me. Somehow it all made sense. I understood what everyone was doing and I could see how it would translate on to the screen. And, after ten minutes, not only did I think of myself as an expert in television production but I knew exactly what I wanted to do with my life.

But first I had to complete my schooling. To the undisguised astonishment and dismay of my teachers, I decided not to leave school at 16, but to stay on and study for A Levels, the exams English students take aged 18. Top students achieve A grades in three or four subjects. Bs and Cs are respectable and Ds and Es can still be good enough for university entry.

But there are two grades for those who don't, er, make the grade. An O means you only reached the standard expected for a minimum pass in the exams taken by 16-year-olds. Even worse is an F for Fail. An F is as low as you can go. An F is a complete, ignominious bust. The examiners' message is unambiguous. 'F-F-Frankly, it would have been better for everybody if you hadn't shown up.'

At the time our postman was an Irishman who insisted his name was Patrick, but naturally I shortened to Pat. Every time I ran into him on the doorstep, I would wittily sing the theme tune to the kids' programme *Postman Pat*. It now occurs to me that perhaps it wasn't the first time he'd heard the joke and maybe that explains why he never seemed to find it quite so thigh-slappingly hilarious as I did.

But one day in August 1985, I was less cheerful than usual. Today was the day exam results were being distributed to 18-year-olds across the UK. I feared the worst and Pat scented the opportunity for revenge.

'How did you do?' he asked, innocently enough. I opened the small brown envelope and had a tentative look inside.

'OOF!' I groaned, as if a furious Tyson Fury had driven his fist deep into my solar plexus. 'OOF,' I repeated. And 'OOF' it was. Not just my agonised grunt, but the actual result, O for Biology, O for Technical Drawing and F for Physics. In a haze of flustered shame, I showed Pat the paper. He laughed uproariously.

'Now I'm no expert, but that doesn't look good,' he jeered. 'On the bright side, you can always get a job at the Post Office. They couldn't care less who they hire down there.'

'I hope your black and white cat dies horribly,' would have been a decent comeback, but I was too mortified to speak. So, after two years of arduous study, I had failed to improve in two subjects and managed to get measurably worse in the third. That's pretty impressive when you think about it.

So how did that disastrous start prove to be the ideal foundation for a career in Formula One?

That evening my dad showed me an advert in the *Jersey Evening Post* for an intern to work in the local Channel Islands News network, exactly the sort of job I was after. I was reassured to see it made no reference to qualifications. I was also pleased to learn that my father knew the man who had advertised the role. So, everything would be fine after all. I sent in my sparse résumé with a covering letter, knowing my future was secure. The job was in the bag! And it needed to be, as it really was the only suitable position on the island.

'It's not what you know, it's who you know,' I confided to my old man, tapping the side of my nose, winking knowingly and patting him on the back.

'OOF, really?' He fired back. 'How's that even possible? You studied for two years, at great expense, learned nothing and forgot stuff you already knew?'

I was called to attend what I expected to be a rigorous selection process in the Channel Islands News offices. However, the acquaintance of my father asked after my family but little else. The other interviewer was even less interested in my achievements (or perhaps he just couldn't discern any) and spent most of the time talking about an expected cold weather front, gazing out of the window as if he expected it to blow in at any moment. Yes, bad weather was definitely on the way.

A day or two later our petulant postie Pat brought another small brown envelope containing more bad news. No doubt out of consideration for my father, they sugared the pill by saying that I had made it to a shortlist of two, although I am pretty sure only two of us applied. The other candidate, a guy I knew from school, had been interviewed just before me and I saw him skipping out the door as I went in. He aced his A Levels so, not surprisingly, was hired. It turned out his father also knew the employer, which now seemed to me outrageous corruption and nepotism.

I had no option but to take an intensely boring position as a cashier at Barclays Bank while I considered my next move. Dreams can fade quickly when you're working nine to five, but I longed to be free from the world of low finance and the suffocation of island life. As soon as I had banked enough money to buy a round-the-world ticket from Trailfinders, with a little left over to survive for a month or two, my best friend Mark 'Reb' Rebindaine and I went in search of new horizons.

My one-year, round-the-world trip became five as I found I could work my way and pursue a hedonistic lifestyle in Thailand, Indonesia, Australia, New Zealand and Hawaii, ending up in California. I met some lifelong friends, which alone made the trip worthwhile. But none of the jobs I found on the way did anything to build towards my ambition.

'Wanted – TV Producers – Travel the World and Party! No Experience Necessary', was not an advert commonly posted on the bulletin boards of youth hostels. But I needed to work and took any job that would pay my living expenses and top up my entertainment tab. Most had a catering theme. I toiled in bars, restaurants, ice-cream vans and even a food truck that provided a rich and varied menu, providing you wanted a baked potato.

One lowlight was my stint at the Sydney Swans, an Australian Rules football team, when I was hired to be an M&M. They dressed me up in lime green tights, emerald boots and avocado gauntlets. Then they produced (you guessed it) a bright-green M&M-shaped shell with the bright white M&M logo painted large on both sides. It looked unnecessarily bulky and tough. The carapace was heavy, cumbersome and uncomfortable, but gave me an important insight into why tortoises, turtles and terrapins always look so bad-tempered.

At half-time I was shoved on to the pitch. From the moment my lime-coloured boots touched the green, green grass, I started to worry that the shell was not, in fact, nearly tough enough. Half-eaten steak pies and three-quarter full cans of lager rained down upon me. Every direct hit reverberated thunderously inside the capsule. But deafening as that noise was, it was nothing compared to the crowd's roars of approval. I felt like a contestant on one of those weird Japanese game shows where participants are put through endless pain and humiliation for the honour of being crowned king or queen of enduring endless pain and humiliation.

When it dawned on me, after two games, that a career as a chocolate candy offered few prospects of promotion or a pay rise, I moved on to the relatively safe Sydney Public Authorities Superannuation Board. When I realised that the payment of accurate superannuation required levels of diligence and concentration I did not possess, I quit to clean windows. Then I was a dishwasher in a diner and spent a brief spell as a chef, until I was fired and replaced by an actual chef, my friend Lucy, who had studied to become a Cordon Bleu. There were no hard feelings as I was eating or burning more food than I was getting out to the customers. I was more than happy to move back to the bar, where free drinks were in more ready supply.

But there was no sign of lights, cameras or action.

On arriving in California, I at last made a tiny step towards my goal when I scored a job in the mailroom at Capitol Records in Hollywood. I delivered the mail throughout the iconic cylindrical building (perhaps Postman Pat was prescient in predicting my postal prospects?). At last, I felt I was on my way. The music business was at least a little bit like the television industry.

But after five fun-filled, fantastic years of travelling, it was time to get my act together; and an 'act' it would most certainly have to be. Despite my excellent work experience as an M&M and baked potato salesman, I felt I had ground to make up.

So, in 1991 I moved to London and enrolled in a BTEC college course in television production and design. I had no intention of finishing the syllabus. Two years' study, even just two days a week, seemed an eternity to a hummingbird like me.

No, I felt that, based close to the industry action in old London town, I would rapidly get a job at a TV channel or one of the numerous production companies in the UK. In no time I would start earning money and respect.

But all my applications were rejected out of hand. One came in the form of a hand-written letter from a producer at the BBC who was sufficiently unimpressed by my application to pick up his pen and write me a personal note.

'Five years of directionless globetrotting on the lash ...' (how he reached this uncannily accurate conclusion from the evidence of my carefully crafted letter and résumé will ever be a mystery to me) '... did not count as the type of experience the world of television production was looking for.'

He was good enough to elaborate further, observing that 'a part-time BTEC course in TV production and design would do nothing to make me a suitable candidate for the BBC', and then, 'I should perhaps save myself from wasting more time and incurring further expense by considering other career options.'

I have often thought about that letter. At the time I was outraged at his high-handed and arrogant tone. But here was a presumably busy and senior man who took time to take out his pen and tell me some hard truths. Years later, I wonder whether he did it out of pomposity, pity or kindness. Whatever his reason, he certainly made his point. When I had consumed his double-plus-sized helping of tough love, I decided to drop out, leave the hostile London scene and try my luck abroad.

I moved to Hong Kong.

Why We Can't Be Formula One Drivers

Azerbaijan 2022

I AM sitting opposite Esteban Ocon on the terrace of Alpine's hospitality suite in Baku. The lens of Uli's camera is pointing at the Frenchman over my right shoulder. It's late morning on Thursday and the paddock is relatively quiet. Esteban is, as always, chatty, respectful and friendly while answering questions he has doubtless been asked 100 times. But I am intrigued to talk to him about the emotions he felt after his win in the 2021 Hungarian GP at the Hungaroring.

The race started with Lewis Hamilton on pole and his Mercedes team-mate Valtteri Bottas in second, followed by the Red Bulls of Max Verstappen and Sergio Pérez. Esteban had qualified his Alpine in eighth.

There was rain before the race, which may have contributed to the spectacular fiasco at the first corner. Bottas, who dropped three places off the start, went into the first corner behind Lando Norris's McLaren but braked too late and rear-ended Lando's car, shunting him into Max Verstappen's Red Bull. And just in case Valtteri felt he had not made himself sufficiently unpopular with the Red Bull team, he then slid into Max's team-mate Checo. Meanwhile, in a separate incident a few places back, Lance Stroll in his Aston Martin shunted into Charles Leclerc's Ferrari, who in turn forced Daniel Ricciardo to spin into the other McLaren. Bottas and Stroll were both handed a five-place grid penalty for the next Grand Prix.

But Esteban stayed out of trouble and so moved up from eighth to second behind Lewis Hamilton. The race was then red-flagged[25] to remove the debris. When the cars followed the safety car on to the drying track for the restart all the drivers except Lewis Hamilton dived into the pits to change from intermediate to slick tyres. So, the race restarted, rather strangely, with just Lewis Hamilton on the grid and the rest of the field emerging from the pits some distance behind. But it was soon clear that Mercedes had made a mistake, as the field closed in rapidly on Lewis, leaving him with no option but to pit on lap four. Esteban was now in the lead and Lewis last.

Later in the race Esteban came under tremendous pressure from Sebastian Vettel but coolly held him off. His team-mate, Fernando Alonso, did Esteban a huge favour by holding up a resurgent Hamilton for just long enough, something which would surely have given the Spaniard considerable satisfaction given his historic rivalry with Lewis.[26]

So, Esteban went on to win the unlikeliest of victories, becoming just the 111th driver to win a Formula One race. It was his first win in any motor race since the 2015 GP3 series and the first win by a Frenchman with a French team, powered by a French engine since Alain Prost won the 1983 Austrian GP in a Renault.

When he had finished recounting that epic victory, I wanted some contrast in the interview, so I asked Esteban about the lowest moment in his Formula One career. He didn't hesitate.

'Thanks for reminding me,' he smiled. 'Of course, that was when I lost my seat at the end of the 2018 season. It hurt, because I didn't go out because of bad results or lack of speed, so it felt like it was for the wrong reasons.'

Esteban became the fall guy that year after his team, Force India, ran into financial problems under Indian owner Vijay Mallya. A group of investors, led by Canadian billionaire businessman Lawrence Stroll, father of then Williams driver Lance, purchased

---

25 The red flag suspends the session, requiring all drivers to slow down and return immediately to the pit lane.
26 More on this later.

the assets of the Sahara Force India F1 team, and rebranded it as Racing Point F1 in February 2019. The new owner wanted to give one of the driver seats to his son and, as team-mate Checo Pérez had a longer contract, there was no room for Esteban. To make matters worse, it was too late to secure a seat with another team for the 2019 season, so Esteban was left without a drive.

The disappointment was softened slightly when Toto Wolff offered Esteban the role of reserve and development driver at Mercedes, but when he arrived in Australia in 2019 having been promised a big test programme, plans had changed and he learned he would not be driving the car for six months. When leaving Albert Park in Melbourne that day, the Frenchman climbed into his rental car in the parking lot, closed the door and burst into tears. But he never gave up hope.

'You never know in Formula One,' he told me, 'and I kept believing. After 2020 nobody would have thought I would ever get back into an F1 car, never mind win a race. I kept working on my goal and I'm not going to back off.'

Esteban now has a contract with Alpine until at least the end of 2024, one of the longest contracts on the grid.

Yes, Grand Prix winners sometimes cry in parking lots and, believe me, to become a Formula One driver, you have to take a lot of hard knocks. I have spent countless hours talking to racing drivers, often just a few sentences before or after track action, but also in lengthier one-to-one[27] interviews and at other times.

It takes a quite exceptional person to become a driver in Formula One, but there are plenty of hopefuls who want to give it a try. I have met numerous young drivers in the various racing categories from karting, Formula Four 'national' championships and up to Formula Two. I often ask them what their dream is. In the United States, Indy 500 or NASCAR might get a mention, but the great majority will say, 'My dream is to drive in Formula One.'

---

27 One-to-one interviews are exclusive slots occasionally granted by the teams to a TV channel, allowing a more extended dialogue with the driver or team member than is usually possible in the paddock.

But they have a far, far better chance of being struck by lightning than achieving their dream. The deck is just too heavily stacked. It is fiendishly difficult to get to the top of any sport, but while thousands of soccer players can become professionals in dozens of national leagues worldwide, in Formula One there are currently just 20 seats and they are nearly all occupied by immovable incumbents, or bought. To make it into one of those seats is to be the 'crème de la crème de la crème' (and plenty more 'de la crèmes' after that) of motorsport and to hold on to a seat requires an extraordinary range of talents, abilities, skills and character traits. Oh, and iron-clad self-belief, fanatical determination and, most of all, extreme good luck.

Despite the big improvements in driver safety since 1994, motor racing remains a highly dangerous sport. So, courage, or what might be characterised as recklessness, is just one trait an F1 driver must possess in abundance. Most drivers seem oblivious to risk, or just accept it as part and parcel of the life they love to lead. As Checo Pérez succinctly put it, 'Racing drivers are different. We are crazy.'

Drivers must be extremely fit and strong to handle the physical demands of supercharged driving for up to two hours in temperatures that can rise to 50 degrees Celsius. Reclining in a near horizontal position, just centimetres from the ground, their necks must routinely be able to withstand lateral forces of five or six G, which in tight corners makes their heads and helmets alone weigh around half their body weight. If they crash, they can be subjected to G-forces up to ten times higher.

They must be able to concentrate intensely throughout a race when even a moment's lapse can lead to disaster. They must, without taking their eyes off the road ahead, accurately use the many buttons, dials and paddles on the steering wheel, which can be used to tune aspects of the car's power management or performance. They must adapt to changes in the car's handling as the fuel tank empties and the car's weight decreases, or tyres warm up and then deteriorate, or as racetrack conditions change. They must decide in fractions of a second how to keep the car on the racing line, when to brake, how to accelerate and how to avoid being held up by slower cars. They must know how to overtake and avoid being overtaken when their car is slower. They must deal with unforeseeable technical problems that will always occur when driving high technology machines at the bleeding edge of innovation.

Driving a Formula One car fast means pushing the machine to the limit of what the track and weather conditions allow, but without crossing the gossamer thread that divides maximum speed from the mistakes that slow the car down or send it crashing out. Drivers learn these precise skills from countless hours of practice, through trial and error in cars of increasing power and performance as they progress up through the motor racing categories. They develop instincts that allow them to find the fastest lines through corners, the last possible moment to brake and when and how to apply the throttle in the continual search for speed.

And that's just what they need to drive the car. They also need sound engineering knowledge and leadership skills to be able to guide their mechanics and engineers to squeeze every millisecond of performance out of the vehicle. They need good communication skills to work with their teams and to handle the press, who are, for good or ill, an all-important part of the Formula One circus.

If English is not a driver's native tongue, they must learn it, as it is the lingua franca of the sport. Many F1 drivers speak several languages. Charles Leclerc, Pierre Gasly, Fernando Alonso, Carlos Sainz and Sebastian Vettel are all impressive linguists. The 2016 world champion, Nico Rosberg, speaks German, English, Italian, Spanish, French and even some fiendishly difficult Finnish for good measure.

More difficult still is handling the immense pressure that is heaped upon them by their team principals, owners, their engineering team, the media, sponsors, managers, their fellow competitors and in many cases, most intensely of all, by the other driver in their own team. Rivalries between team-mates can become intense to the point of mutual destruction. Losing to a driver in a different type of car is one thing. There are all sorts of reasons why an opponent's car might be faster. But losing to one's own team-mate is another thing entirely, because the two drivers are equipped with essentially the same machinery. So, while car set-ups may differ somewhat (and occasionally drivers complain that their team-mate is getting more attention from the mechanics, or first dibs on upgrades from the factory) the only substantial reason for being second is that the other driver is faster. And the second-best driver is always at risk of losing his[28] seat.

The pressure to win World Championship points is crushing. A single point can be worth literally millions of dollars in Constructors' championship prizes if it means beating a rival. The top teams are, of course, looking for victories or podium finishes, but there are also games within games as lower teams struggle frantically to beat their nearest rivals in the middle or at the back of the grid. They need to be seen to be on an upward trajectory or, from the driver's selfish point of view (and is there any other?), to show their potential to move to a better team. Every point is crucial.

Team principals are only as good as the results their team is delivering and the half-life of gratitude for previous success is short. Support from team owners and sponsors, who are likely to be investing heavily, will last only as long as they believe the team principal is delivering results or can be expected to do so soon. After all, who wants to spend money on, or have their brand associated with, losers?

And when a race is done, for every happy driver who makes the podium, 17 do not. For every driver who earns points, the same number leave empty-handed. And winning only affords a brief respite from the stress, worry and fear of failure because, the summer break aside, the next race is only a week or two away.

In any business, because that is exactly what Formula One teams are, pressure and stress applied to the boss is passed down to the

---

28 Five women have entered Formula One races and two qualified to start the race. Desiré Wilson won at Brands Hatch in 1980 in the short-lived British Aurora F1 Championship in 1980 and now has a grandstand named after her. However, at the time of writing there are no women drivers in Formula One, so we use the pronoun 'he' when referring to people in that group.

team. Most of all it comes down to the driver. Losing generates soul-searching, strategic assessments, performance reviews, tactical plans and tacit ultimatums. Always close to the top of the agenda is the question, 'Is our driver to blame? Did he make a mistake? Is he pushing hard enough? Is he pushing too hard? Is he being reckless? Should we replace him?' Or (perhaps more worrying for the team principal), 'Is he doing so well he might leave us for a better team?'

All this piles tons of pressure on to the driver to deliver better results, which may just not be achievable, because the competition is tougher than a racing car's titanium halo.

So, there aren't too many people in the world who can ever hope to possess or acquire enough of the qualities needed to get within a million miles of the required standard. But even if our aspiring go-kart champ can meet these stringent demands, he or she will still be disappointed. The greatest barrier of all is that to make it, you must start young and then dedicate the rest of your young life to practising and racing, which requires a highly supportive environment and a large amount of money. Max Verstappen was given his first kart by his F1 racing driver father Jos[29] at the age of four-and-a-half.

Only a tiny minority of racing drivers have come from humble beginnings. What makes the Lewis Hamilton story so inspiring is that his family started with so little, but due to the single-mindedness and the selfless dedication of his father and the unwavering support of his family and closest friends, he became the standout exception to the rule. But far more drivers have enjoyed the support of wealthy parents, or generous sponsorship from an organisation, politician, or private individual, that helped and financed them every millimetre, every fraction of a second and every penny along the way.

This level of support is available only to a vanishingly tiny minority, so even the most talented and determined of karting champs is destined never to make the grade.

---

29 Jos Verstappen raced for seven different teams over eight Formula One seasons, achieving two podiums and success in Formula Three and at Le Mans. He then coached and managed Max. More on Jos later.

Useless Business Cards

Hong Kong 1992

DECAMPING TO Hong Kong was an easy decision because my friend, Dean Ayle, an American I lived with in Los Angeles, was already there. He offered me a couch to sleep on, the perfect base as I rebooted my dream to become a television producer.

When I arrived, the Star TV Network had only been broadcasting for two years to the 48 countries in the Middle East and the Asia Pacific region. I felt I had a more realistic goal. Within days, thanks to Dean's connections, I was bartending in the trendy French hotspot Le Jardin in Lan Kwai Fong, the ideal place, I optimistically imagined, to meet people in the TV industry.

Dean had warned me that English-speaking positions in Hong Kong were usually advertised and recruited outside the territory. If you lived there, he explained, your chances of being employed were drastically reduced.

'You, dude, are filth,' he told me, as we sipped Sea Breeze cocktails on the terrace of a restaurant on the Peak a few weeks after my arrival.

'Well if you hadn't hogged the bathroom, I would have had time to shower this morning,' I replied defensively.

'No, dude, I mean F-I-L-T-H.' He spelled it out. 'Failed-In-London-Try-Hong-Kong. It sums up the expat work force.'

'Isn't that FILTHK?' I was about to say, but he continued.

'I'm serious. A-holes you wouldn't trust to fill out a betting slip in a London bookie become well-paid stockbrokers in Hong Kong. Illiterate douchebags who didn't finish high school make a comfortable living as journalists. Chicks from Down Under who couldn't get a date in the southern hemisphere come out here and get their picture splashed on the front cover of fashion magazines.'

I looked out over the Hong Kong skyline to the harbour beyond and reflected on Dean's ominous words. But optimism and elation bubbled up inside me. Here was an English colony awash with well-paid incompetents. This was a place I could really fit in. After all, I had failed miserably in London and indeed a lot of other places. I now knew that my chances of getting a job in television in the UK were zero. I had missed my opportunity to start as a 'runner' or assistant and now was too old, inexperienced, ineffective and unqualified to start at a higher level.

'So, with all these "A-holes", as you call them, running around in high-paid jobs,' I asked Dean, 'surely I could get my first break in TV here?'

'Dude, the only chance you have to get a job in television, with your douchebag credentials, is to find a cool person working in the industry who is influential enough to help you out.'

'Okay, great, easy, so that's what I'll do,' I replied, with the naïvety of a Swedish backpacker asking for hiking directions in South Central, Los Angeles.

'Don't be an A-hole. The point is,' Dean continued pessimistically, 'there are no cool people in Hong Kong willing to help you, or anyone else, out. They're either too smug and arrogant to talk to lowly bartenders like us, or petrified you will expose their incompetence and take their job.'

I took his cynical words with a pinch of salt. Literally, because we had just switched to Tequila shots.

There were five channels transmitting on the Star TV Network: MTV, the Movie Channel, Prime Sports, the Kids Channel and the Chinese Channel. I loved music, movies and sport and could even tolerate kids, in small doses. I could barely pronounce the Cantonese street name where I lived, so I didn't waste a stamp applying to the Chinese Channel, but I sent off four résumés that stretched my working experience shamelessly and attached a covering letter that sold me as a hard-working, charming and experienced young man. At least I could still pass myself off as reasonably young without too much debate.

I waited impatiently for a response, but in vain. They never phoned; they never faxed (though I wasn't sure the fax machine for the bar that I listed was even plugged in); they never wrote. I scanned the 'situations vacant' but suitable opportunities were infrequent and my applications were ignored. After six months I had failed to get to know anyone remotely connected to the TV industry and exhausted all possible means of getting an interview at Star TV. I began to suspect that Dean's pessimism was justified.

Then, one evening, a familiar face came up to the bar. It belonged to Danny McGill and I recognised him because he was an MTV presenter at Star TV. He ordered a drink and we had a minute or two of affable conversation. I told him I loved his show and mentioned that I was in the process of applying to Star TV. I added that I didn't have the office address.

He responded in the way all Hong Kong expats did by reaching for his wallet. Not in search of a high-value banknote to leave as a tip, mind, but to take out his business card. It was part of the culture in Hong Kong at that time to hand out a business card to anyone you met. Everyone did it, usually to brag about their impressive job, but never, in my previous experience, to offer the recipient any favours. In fact, it was hard to go anywhere without complete strangers thrusting their personal details into your hand. I once asked someone in a restaurant for directions to the toilets and ended up holding his business card.

'Call me if you need any further directions,' the geek in the corduroy jacket told me. 'Incidentally, I am the marketing director of an advertising agency. See just there, that's my name in gold.'

'Thanks, I'll be sure to flush that when I'm done.'

However, Danny had no need to brag and did leave a generous tip. I didn't have a business card of my own. 'Kris Henley, Barman, Le Jardin' didn't seem like information worth sharing, but Danny did pocket the piece of paper I optimistically

USELESS BUSINESS CARDS

scrawled my name and phone number on. He wished me luck and disappeared into the crowd, sipping his Margarita. I saw him a few more times, but beautiful people were always surrounding him and monopolising his attention, so I didn't have a chance to restart the conversation.

In no time I had collected over 100 Hong Kong business cards from random strangers and both Dean and Wanda, a friend of ours from Los Angeles who had recently moved in, had accumulated a similar number.

To pass the time, we often sat with our piles of cards and somehow the game of 'Useless Business Cards' was invented. The rules, such as they were, required you to pair and discard cards that had similar information, for example, two marketing directors, two people called Wang, two people working for the same company, or with offices in the same district.

The objective was to avoid holding the last unmatched card. The penalty for losing was to pick up the telephone and, in front of the other delighted players, make a call to whoever it was on the card and ask to meet them for a drink. The game served as a kind of pre-internet version of Tinder combined with the once popular card game Old Maid. The game was designed principally to get Wanda into embarrassing situations and highly effective it was. She tended to lose, because Dean and I would evilly conspire, disputing her card matches but supporting each other's. On at least two occasions I saw guys whose business cards had been somewhere in the stack sneaking out of the flat in the early hours.

One afternoon, after a few drinks, we decided to play, but this time, I was the one left holding the last card. I looked down and was mortified to see the name of Danny McGill. I had forgotten I even had his card. I couldn't call this superstar video jockey. It would be like asking Lewis Hamilton to go out to a movie and dinner for two after bothering him for an autograph. But my flatmates were waiting expectantly, laughing demonically and rubbing their hands. There was no getting out of it. I reluctantly pressed the buttons on the phone.

The phone rang once and a young woman answered. 'MTV Asia, Danny's phone, can I help you?' the warm voice said.

'Oh yeah, umm, yeah, er, hi, is Mr McGill there, please? I mean Danny McGill, is Danny available?'

'Hold on I'll find him, who's speaking?' Good question. Who was speaking? Should I give a false name or say I was a friend?

'Um, tell him it's Kris from Le Jardin,' I said, cringing inwardly. I could hear Dean insulting me in the background so I stuck my finger into my other ear to block out the distraction.

'Bear with me,' she said, putting down the phone. 'Danny! It's Kris from Le Jardin on the phone for you,' I heard her call out at the top of her voice. Then came the inevitable response: 'Who?'

She repeated herself and I seriously doubted if Danny was even going to come to the phone. But after an endless minute, he picked up.

'Hi, this is Danny McGill, what's up?' He spoke in a deep, husky voice. What's up? Good question. Everything's up, my heartbeat, my blood pressure, my sweat production.

'Oh, hi Mr McGill,' I said without thinking.

'What a douche,' Dean said, cackling in the background.

'Mr McGill? Please, call me Danny.'

'Of course, Danny, sorry, you probably don't remember me. I'm Kris, the barman at Le Jardin.'

'Sure I remember you, man, you make the killer Margaritas. I gave you my card, you still looking for work?' I couldn't believe he remembered me.

'Thanks, the secret is to use Cointreau, not Triple Sec.' Really, I should get to the point. He didn't need to know how to mix a Margarita. He paid guys like me to do it for him.

'Anyway, I came across your card the other day and I was wondering if, well, I could buy you a beer, or a Margarita and have a quick chat. Maybe you could point me in the right direction. It shouldn't take long. Ten minutes tops.' I felt like a teenage reserve cheerleader asking the star quarterback for a date. I was expecting him to hang up the phone.

'Sure man, listen, I'll be in Le Jardin around seven. Are you working there tonight?'

'It's my night off, but I could still meet you there. Don't worry if you're running late, I'll wait.' Wow, that sounded a bit desperate.

'Okay, seven o'clock then, we can have that chat.'

'Perfect, okay. Yeah, right then, great, so, well, I'll see you tonight then. Thanks, Danny.'

'Yeah man, see ya.' I hung up the phone and looked at my flatmates.

'I've got a date with Danny McGill!' I started singing as I danced around the living room like the demonic child-catcher in *Chitty Chitty Bang Bang*.

'He's never gonna show up, dude,' Dean predicted, no doubt disappointed that my humiliation was milder than he'd hoped.

But Dean was right. Danny didn't show up.

Diamond Geezer at Silverstone

Silverstone 2022

ULI AND I jump off the golf cart driven by our old friend Charlotte Sefton, head of communications at the W Series,[30] who I know from her time working at McLaren. We hug. I thank her for the ride and for the invite to the previous evening's cocktail party in the W Series paddock. Microphone in hand and camera at the ready, Uli and I walk over the bridge to the Fanzone.

Before qualifying begins on Saturday, I often seek out the local fans, waving flags, singing songs, blowing kisses, drinking and celebrating, to shoot some footage. If I'm on my own, I use a small handheld camera or my phone. If Uli is available I can properly interview the fans. Apart from GPs in the Middle East, which has yet to establish a local F1 fan base, there are growing throngs every year.

Fans in Japan are extra special. They are certainly the politest and the most creative, sporting extraordinary costumes and accessories. The Italian *Tifosi* are perhaps the most passionate in their support for Ferrari and the Orange Army in the Netherlands are the most boisterous.

But the British fans are also wonderful. Silverstone was the first venue to host an official World Championship Formula One race in 1950.[31] Although it hasn't hosted every single British GP – Brands Hatch or Aintree were sometimes used in the early years – only

---

30 The all-women single-seater racing championship that ran in 2019, 2021 and 2022.
31 Some races were held under Formula One rules before this date.

Monaco and Monza have hosted more. The fans turn up, year in, year out, rain or shine. They are the deepest-rooted fans of the sport and are happy just to glimpse their favourite driver.

I stopped a friendly looking man in his mid-50s with faded tattoos on his forearms, clearly etched into his skin long before it was trendy to do so. Beside him his wife wore a neon Mercedes bucket hat and was draped in a Union Jack.

'Hi, what are your names?'

''Ello, I'm Dave. This is me wife, Pauline.'

'Are you having fun?' I asked.

'Oh yeah,' Dave answered. 'This is incredible! Look around! I've never seen so many fans here. Amazing.'

'So, it's not your first time at Silverstone? I hear this is one of the most expensive races to attend on the calendar. Do you mind me asking what you paid for your tickets for the race weekend and has it been worth it?'

'Definitely worth it. Not sure what we paid, though.' Dave looked over at his wife. 'What did we pay for this, love?'

'Well,' Pauline began, 'we've slummed it in the past and stayed at the campsite, but this year, as it's our 30th wedding anniversary we went all-out.'

'Oh, congratulations!'

'Thanks! Yeah, so we're staying in a nice hotel in Whittlebury and watching from the grandstand at Beckets. We got a good package deal. With food, drink, tickets, accommodation and everything, not much change out of two grand.'

'How much?!' Dave shouted, turning dramatically to his wife. After what I thought was a tense moment, they fell about laughing and Uli and I laughed along with them.

'Seriously, though,' Dave told me, 'it's worth every penny and we still have qualifying coming up and the race to look forward to tomorrow! And if Lewis wins, or George or Lando, well, we'll be made up! Honestly, every time we come to Silverstone, it's fantastic.'

'Last question, Dave, what is your fondest memory from the British Grand Prix?'

'Always good to see Lewis win, I've seen him do it a few times over the years. I wasn't here when Damon Hill and Johnny Herbert won, but my best memory was when me old man brought me here for the first time in 1992 and Nigel Mansell won. After the race, I went on to the circuit with me Dad and I touched the car as it went by. I'll never forget that. Yeah, that's the moment that will always stay with me. That was something special, that was.' Pauline grabbed her husband's arm and squeezed it affectionately.

'And Sebastian Vettel will be doing exhibition laps in the very same car tomorrow!' I said. 'It's coming back full circle, Dave. We'll be interviewing Nigel and Sebastian in the morning after the run.'

'Wow, I wish I had your job!'

'You're joking, aren't you? Perhaps we could swap. I certainly couldn't afford to drop two grand on a race weekend!'

I thanked the happy couple and moved on, but Dave's memories made me think about my own. Producing programmes about Formula One has meant spending hundreds of hours looking at footage of races, qualifying laps, podium ceremonies, interviews and other material from various archives. On the internet today there is plenty to see, right back to the first Silverstone race, the original images captured in black and white film, but now often 'colourised' and 'upscaled' using artificial intelligence. Motorsport fans can see the greats of the sport in competition, combat, confrontation, clashes and crashes. Channels that hold the rights to the material use it to create title sequences, highlights packages and 'bumpers'[32] that are shown all over the world.

Every F1 fan has a favourite moment. I think immediately of the onboard camera recordings of Ayrton Senna driving some of his finest, blisteringly fast laps at Monte Carlo in 1988. Although the footage breaks up and the video is grainy, I feel I am in that car. I am Senna as I watch the barriers and gantries flash past, his rapid,

---

32 The short video clips with music that separate the programme from commercial breaks.

fluent hand movements on the steering wheel and the noise of the engine like a giant, angry mosquito.

Although it was not on one of those recorded laps, he described his mental state when driving that circuit.

'I realised that day that I was no longer driving consciously. I was in a different dimension. The circuit for me was a tunnel and I was going, going, going. And I realised I was driving well beyond my conscious understanding.'

Sports psychologists now describe the state of mind which elite athletes occasionally achieve at moments of peak performance as 'flow' or 'in the zone', but when you watch those laps at Monte Carlo you can see why Senna preferred the term 'the tunnel'.

At the start of the film *Schumacher*, released by Netflix in 2021, there is a sequence showing Michael driving the same circuit. His voice-over says:

'You have to become one with the car. You should know exactly how much stress you can give to the car, because there is a limit, always. And you should be careful, like with everything in life you like; you have to have that feeling not to go over the top or under it and if you do that, then both of us will be satisfied. The car and I.'

Two of the greatest drivers of all time, each a poet in their own characteristic way, describing their feeling when performing at their absolute peak at the most iconic Formula One circuit of them all.

There are hundreds of thousands of recorded hours of wheel-to-wheel racing, overtaking manoeuvres, spins, shunts, exploding tyres and the always entertaining spectacle when a driver, or his strategist, is tempted to try to eke out one more lap on slick tyres before rain starts to fall. When they get it wrong and the rain comes down, the beautifully engineered piece of machinery is instantly transformed from a snarling cheetah to a giraffe on ice.

Every incident builds into the season's story which unfolds corner after corner, lap after lap, race after race into its own epic saga, sometimes a majestic procession and sometimes a tense fight to the finish. For every triumph there is a disaster and for every winner there are losers whose dreams are shattered. There are outbursts, sulks, furious tantrums, angry exchanges and from time to time pushing, shoving and even punches thrown as drivers confront their own failures, or rivals that they deem responsible for slowing them down or crashing them out.

There is the tension on the faces of anguished families who watch their loved ones from the pits, one moment all hope and excitement, the next anguish and fear. The twin imposters, Triumph and Disaster, visited the Massa family in less than a minute in Brazil in 2008, when they watched their beloved Felipe win his home Grand Prix for the second time in front of his adoring fans. The win meant that Felipe would claim the World Championship providing Lewis Hamilton came no higher than fifth in the race, and Lewis was sixth and so far behind the Toyota driver Timo Glock, that there seemed no possibility whatsoever of him catching the German.

The Massas began to celebrate, Brazilian style, hugging each other, tears of joy welling in their eyes, relief and elation all at once. After years of chasing the dream, Felipe Massa was world champion!

Or was he? Glock, who had not changed his tyres when showers threatened, lost grip as the rain came down. Agonisingly for Massa, Hamilton passed him on the penultimate corner of the final lap, finishing fifth and claiming the four championship points needed to earn his first drivers' title. Glory was snatched from the devastated Massa by a single point in the cruellest of circumstances. The news came in from a Ferrari mechanic who head-butted the garage wall. The poor Massa family were shell-shocked and heartbroken. It finally sunk in when they saw confirmation on the monitors in the garage. Formula One is a brutal sport.

Extraordinary moments abound through the decades of Formula One coverage and many of them featured the peerless Ayrton Senna. But one man to stand up to him, both on and off the circuit, was the Englishman Nigel Mansell, with his trademark moustache and Brummie[33] monotone.

---

33 A person from Birmingham in England.

During the 1987 Belgian GP, following an attempted overtaking manoeuvre by the Brit in a Williams-Honda on the Brazilian in his Lotus-Honda, the cars collided, ending the race for both. Mansell blamed Senna for purposely taking him off the track. 'I was,' he said, 'then like a great big bull in a ring and everything I saw was red. Then I thought, *Well I'm going to go and see my friend Ayrton.*'

The Brit caught up with the Brazilian in his garage and angrily confronted him, grabbing him by the collar of his overalls, pushing him up against the wall and shouting in his face. The incident prompted one of Senna's many classic quotes:

'When a man holds you round the throat, I do not think that he has come to apologise.'

So, there was no love lost between them before the inaugural Barcelona Grand Prix in 1991. On this occasion Mansell, driving a Williams FW14 Renault, managed to tuck in impossibly close to the rear wing of Senna's MP4/6 Honda and then whip out of the slipstream to pull alongside. The two titans went wheel-to-wheel down the main straight at 185mph, even appearing to eyeball one another, neither yielding a centimetre.

Vapour trails spiralled away from their rear wings and sparks cascaded from underneath the cars as the titanium skid blocks touched the asphalt, the downforce pushing the cars tight to the ground. On this occasion it was Mansell who braked or lifted (or both) latest, taking the corner in front of Senna, from where he would go on to win the race. That moment, when those two Formula One luminaries were racing side by side at maximum speed, will forever be etched in the memories of millions of fans all over the world.

Despite the rivalry, there was a touching moment later that year after Mansell won the British Grand Prix at Silverstone for the third time. On his lap of honour, he came across a stranded Senna, whose McLaren-Honda had run out of fuel attempting to catch Mansell on the last lap. Mansell stopped his car and invited Senna to hop on, giving the world another unforgettable Formula One image:

Ayrton Senna perched precariously on the side-pod of the Williams as Mansell drove him gingerly back to the pits.

It warmed the hearts of motorsports fans, showing as much humanity in that moment as the overtaking move in Barcelona had shown their courage and commitment at the controls of the fastest cars on the planet.

Paddock Survival Skills

THE FORMULA ONE paddock is not a place for faint hearts. While the competition on the track is fierce, there is just as much in the paddock. You might well overhear the clashing of antlers as team principals engage in a little 'friendly banter', as the alpha stags try to keep rivals in their place. But the main competition for the TV producer comes from other television crews, all eager to get their scoops ahead of you.

For European races, the teams' motorhomes are driven into the paddock and provide the catering, offices and the drivers' quarters. They have become more and more salubrious over the years. For the so-called 'flyaway' races outside Europe, the teams must fit into the facilities on offer and some of these hospitality areas can be as simple as a couple of tents, although the teams are also increasingly sending out 'pop-up' facilities by ship in a vast logistical operation that is planned months before the season begins.

The paddock is where the FIA and FOM offices and the media centre for the world's written press and photographers are usually found. The TV compound, where the technical crews are located and from where race footage is sent off by satellite, is usually a brisk walk away.

Once the event starts, traditionally on a Thursday at most venues, the regular TV crews with the odd newbie or local outfit, huddle up in the paddock at the back of the garages or in front of sponsorship boards outside the team's hospitality suites waiting for the drivers to appear. Before the interviews begin, the paddock is a friendly place full of high fives and idle chat. But it can turn into a bear pit as the tension builds and race day approaches.

We prepare questions about the week's hot topics, the previous race, or expectations for this one. There is a similar set-up in the paddock on Friday after the practice sessions, when you find out how the cars are performing, but on Saturday after qualifying[34] and on Sunday after the race, the drivers come to the interview pen, which is usually, but not always, a more civilised set-up.

The journalists from the written press get their turn in a different time slot from the TV crews. Drivers under pressure can be asked deliberately provocative and aggressive questions by the more outspoken of the tabloid press, such as 'Why are you so slow compared to [your team-mate]?' or, 'Given your poor results, do you really expect to be driving for the team next season?' hoping to provoke a reaction that might make for a cheap headline of the 'driver loses his cool' variety.

In the world of TV, cameramen and interviewers often 'piggyback' other reporters' questions, meaning they record answers given to another reporter, sticking their microphone in front of the driver. It's all footage that may prove useful and the practice is accepted.

I spent the 2012 season 'piggybacking' the questions of the highly respected broadcast journalist and presenter Lee McKenzie, then working for the BBC. The drivers would willingly come and talk to Lee and she would usually ask all the questions that needed to be asked, so when it came to my turn, the only remaining question I could think of was 'how's your mum?' which really didn't seem the way to go. So, I rarely asked anything. Broadcast material often has the questions edited out unless it's the channel's own reporter talking, so it doesn't matter who asks them.

Whether you should ask a question yourself depends on the situation but there is plenty of peer pressure not to ask something stupid. The effectiveness of a question is measured by the length of the answer that the driver gives. A one-word answer followed by a

---

34 When the drivers determine their positions on the grid with timed laps against the clock.

walk off is what every interviewer dreads, because now no one gets any material and whoever asked the question is immediately highly unpopular. Lewis Hamilton has done this to me a couple of times to help me understand that some of my questions fall short of his exemplary standards. I got the point and upped my game to save further humiliation!

Once the race has started and I have watched the first lap or two, there's no time to kick back and watch the rest of the race. Juan, an expert in Formula One, is monitoring and commentating live on the whole race, so he covers that side of things.

I spend my time editing the material we have already recorded to get it ready for the magazine highlights shows. I could wait until after the race, but then I would have to deal with an impatient Juan or Uli asking how long I will keep them hanging around before we can all leave the circuit, as it makes sense to use the reliable high-speed internet in the media centre to send material, rather than risk sending it from a dodgy hotel connection.

I have an hour or so before the chequered flag to get everything together, so I will just need to add the post-race interviews and the team celebrations, record Juan's reports for our various news and highlights shows, and edit and send them off. I answer WhatsApp messages from the team in Buenos Aires, run to the pen to interview any driver who abandons the race and ensure everything else runs smoothly. I don't have time to keep up with race developments, apart from glancing up at the monitors in the media centre occasionally.

Next time you are seated comfortably in front of your TV watching the absorbing action, bear in mind that what you see is being selected for your pleasure from over 100 camera feeds by a knowledgeable director and a team of producers. They tell you the story of the race. The cameras are located on board the cars, beside the track, attached to helicopters or drones, on gantries and jibs, moulded into kerbs, on zip lines above the pit lanes and on the shoulders of strategically placed ENG (Electronic News Gathering) operators.

You also benefit from knowledgeable commentators, analysts and experts who explain what is going on. During the pandemic, when I was able to sit back and listen to the F1 World Feed, I became quite the armchair expert thanks to the Sky UK commentary and analysis. But when I'm working at the circuit, I rarely know what happened during the race or even where anyone finished. So, before I start the post-race interviews when Juan is otherwise engaged, I take a photo of the final results graphic from the monitors by the pen and refer to it repeatedly. Then I have to bluff.

It's not unusual to find myself with a driver walking towards me – looking me in the eye to signal he is ready to talk, with the world's press all around – having to ask a question with no idea how the session went. After guessing wrongly a few times and receiving a tacit rebuke, I have learned to ask neutral questions.

'Thoughts?' is a good one. Or even better, and one at which I have become quite expert even if I do say so myself, 'Well,' then pause for effect, breathing out through the nose, while making an expression that simultaneously covers all scenarios from 'what a nightmare for you' to 'that was absolutely brilliant', followed by, 'can you talk us through your practice/qualifying session/race, please?'

If I finish editing, I can watch the last laps of the race on the monitors by the interview pen with the rest of the press, who mill around like angry bees when their hive is attacked. I try to make sense of what's happening, as I have learned from hard experience that it's best not to advertise my ignorance with wide-eyed observations such as:

'Hold on a second. Max was miles ahead a few minutes ago. Why's he no longer in the top ten?' Such professed naïvety will earn me only the exaggerated eye-rolling and incredulous shakes of the head that those-in-the-know keep for anyone less-well-informed.

Much better to keep quiet and let paddock experts explain. Then I can put on my knowing 'yeah, that's exactly what I was thinking' face, supplemented with a thoughtful nod of the head and possibly even a Sherlock Holmes-style stroke of the chin. Then, when the next virgin to the paddock flounces by, perhaps a bored freelance cameraman or a local blogger trying to make friends, and asks a foolish question, I simply repeat what I was just told with the benevolent air of a kindly clergyman ministering to his flock.

That's how I have survived in this cut-throat business but, let's face it, that's how most people get through life. A few people know what they're talking about, at least some of the time, but most of us just repeat what we have read or heard. The good news is that I work with people who are genuinely knowledgeable; but the bad news is they're usually speaking Spanish, so I don't always fully understand what they're saying.

However, do you need video editing? I can do that. We need a cameraman! I'm your guy (if you're willing to risk the credibility of your channel). We forgot our microphone cable. Give me a minute, I'll talk to someone I know. Visa papers not in order? I know a man in the embassy. Glass of water, Juan? Massage? Shirt ironed?

Actually, I did once iron one of Juan's shirts. He enquired in some detail about my competence to handle the job and I was, frankly, a little disgruntled at the implication that such a simple task might be beyond me. However, once I got to work, I was briefly distracted by whatever it was on my hotel room's TV and managed to scorch a triangular-shaped burn into the immaculate white cotton, just below the Fox logo. Had he noticed the ugly discolouration before going on air, I'm confident he would have enjoyed seeing the output considerably more than he seemed to. But I digress.

To survive in the paddock, there are just two things you need to do.

Number one: schmooze three groups of people. The most important, by far, are the press officers responsible for organising the all-important one-to-one interviews with members of their team, particularly the drivers and team principals.

The glittering prize is a 10- or 15-minute slot where you have the full attention of the driver or team principal and can ask them anything you like (providing, with more 'sensitive' teams like Ferrari, the questions have been signed off in advance!).

Good relations with these paddock gods are absolutely essential, take years to cultivate and can be destroyed in a moment. Mess with them at your peril. If you turn up late, or worse still, don't show up at all to a pre-arranged interview with, let's say, Lewis Hamilton, unless there's been a death in the family (and in-laws, ancient aunts, cousins and much-loved pets won't cut it) don't expect ever to talk to him again.

But once you're in, providing you maintain their respect, you're laughing. I wouldn't say self-organisation is my strong point. Far from it. But, having experienced their wrath in the past, I take great care not to upset the press officers, because I know they really count. If you have no access to the top drivers, it doesn't matter how good your questions are, because you won't have anything to report.

The second group to foster is your paddock peers in general and the cameramen in particular. It is safe to assume, in my case with a high degree of confidence, that they will be far better organised than you are. So, if you forget to bring, say, a lapel microphone for your interview with Sebastian Vettel when he is sat in the cockpit of his car, uncomfortable and impatient, you must be able to borrow one, fast. You build these relationships when you are standing around waiting for an interview. Always be respectful of what they need and never let your microphone intrude into their shot, or heaven forbid, walk between the camera and the live reporter. Socialising away from the circuit helps too. A good friend in the paddock is invaluable, as you have someone who will help you out of your latest Formula One bungle.

The third group to keep on the right side of is the caterers, who oversee team hospitality. Now, perhaps this is not quite such a vital group, but it is essential to keep your energy at peak level with lunch, snacks, water and coffee.

Number two (remember I said there were two things): you need to be ready to handle the constant stream of trials and tribulations that rain down upon you, or, more simply put, solve problems. I spend most of my time fixing difficulties that someone else has caused and, without generalising about national traits, as I work almost exclusively with Argentinians, they are usually the source of my frustrations.

The people I refer to will call my mobile and start by asking after my health, which immediately makes me suspicious.

'*Que haces, Kris? Todo bien?*'

A little small talk will follow. Perhaps a polite enquiry after my wife or family. Their conversation will then gather pace, perhaps shifting to the latest gossip. Among all this, cunningly disguised as a throwaway remark, will be the tiniest, the merest whiff of a hint that something, which could be anything from a tiny mishap to a full-blown disaster, has occurred. But then they rapidly veer away to some other topic.

This is the moment of extreme danger, because if I don't get to the bottom of whatever it is, my caller will likely escape, believing I have been properly informed. Or at least believing they are entitled so to claim. So, I dig a little deeper and, after a while, the real problem will bubble up. The next thing I will hear is that my caller is in no way to blame, but the fault lies with an anonymous '*chabon*' (bloke) back in Buenos Aires, who can never be reached to explain himself. So now the problem is mine.

Yet, with a bit of common sense, the gift of the gab and a few allies strategically positioned in key areas in the paddock, you can occasionally be a star when you resolve a showstopper. More often, though, it's a thankless task.

So, profession wise, what could be easier? Well, not much, really, even though I manage surprisingly frequently to make a right balls-up of many seemingly simple situations. But more on that a little later.

Track Slide Camera

Abu Dhabi 2021, Race Day

MEANWHILE, BACK in Abu Dhabi, I was lifting the tripod with the camera perched on top and it was a good half a metre above my head. The camera was mounted on a metal attachment plate, which slid neatly into a housing on top of the tripod. I would not need the weighty, cumbersome tripod again until the post-race interviews, so I planned to switch to an improvised lightweight monopod that I would fasten to my belt clip to stabilise the camera. But to do this conveniently, I had decided to attach the plate to the tripod the wrong way round. Which was fine, providing the camera was carefully secured in place with the black nylon wing screw.

But as I looked up at the camera, now high above my head, my stomach executed a triple-back somersault with an agonising twist. I had forgotten, in a moment of crass carelessness, to lock the nut, and the camera was now sliding forwards out of the housing. As my hands were occupied holding the rearmost legs of the tripod, a reaction catch was utterly impossible.

In a moment the camera would be in mid-air and spectacularly rich in high-tech features though the Sony camera is, an airbag is not included. In a panicked moment I saw my future unfold before me.

The first part of the camera to hit the ground would be the spherical plastic protective cover around the lens, which would instantly be obliterated. The wide-angled lens, lovingly fitted in Buenos Aires to enhance the visual spectrum for our cherished viewers, would shatter into a thousand shards.

Back in the studios in Buenos Aires and Mexico City the directors, instead of the feed from our exclusive camera revealing enthralling behind-the-scenes action, would see only shadows and blurred daggers of light on their monitor. There would be no carefully scheduled last-minute grid interview with Checo Pérez beside his gleaming Red Bull, just moments before he roared off on his warm-up lap. And there would certainly be no scooped one-liners from Lewis or Max.

The main camera lens, where the wide angle was attached, would then snap off from the main body of the camera, turning off the lights completely. The luxury viewing experience offered to millions of fans from Patagonia to the Texas border and Spanish speakers across the Caribbean and the USA, would black out. Rich bachelors sipping cocktails on their sofas watching giant flatscreens in luxury penthouses, impoverished slum dwellers huddled around an old PC streaming from illegally acquired cable, and indeed everyone else, would instantly be deprived of the fabulous viewing experience that cost ESPN Fox LatAm a large amount of money to procure.

I would doubtless be on all fours scrambling around the broken pieces of the camera. A few of my closest friends from the paddock might rush to my side, mutter condolences and forlornly try to help. Some would, unsuccessfully, fight the urge to laugh out loud. Most would just give me a cursory glance and perhaps a shake of the head, incredulous at my blundering, but too preoccupied to pay much more attention.

It would then be time for Max Verstappen and Lewis Hamilton to cross the paddock and perhaps even spare a microsecond to register my meltdown. They would be deep in their zones of intense concentration, as their epic season-long battle went to the wire. But they would be unable to ignore the crazy Englishman, face stained with tears of self-pity and frustration, scrabbling on the floor among the lens shards, trying hopelessly to put Humpty the camera back together again.

As the camera teetered in mid-air, Juan, oblivious to our impending doom, was awaiting my arrival at the pit lane entrance, while my 30-year TV career plunged to its catastrophic conclusion.

It was not as if I had no experience with a camera. I had done the odd shoot for our magazine programme and was once a last-minute replacement for a professional cameraman for a live motorsport event. The renowned hypochondriac, Santi Álvarez, had diagnosed himself with appendicitis, so I was flown out to Berlin. It turned out Santi was suffering from nothing more serious than intestinal gas caused by a supposed 'detox diet' of fruit juice and legumes. But even after he was cleared of a more serious condition, the bloated neurotic remained unwilling to leave the comfort of his home and, more importantly, the proximity of his bathroom; so, I stood in.

But otherwise, my cinematographic résumé consisted of countless slow-motion phone shots of my daughter twirling a hula-hoop or doing cartwheels in the garden and a few half-hearted attempts to record my son trying to breakdance, using an old Panasonic camcorder that someone left at my house after a drunken evening when we decided it would be a great idea to improvise a sketch show. It wasn't.

I would like to be able to say that apart from this incident, my work as a cameraman had demonstrated nothing but calm competence and professionalism. Regrettably, that was not so. 'Mistakes were made,' as the politicians say. For example, if you were, tomorrow, asked to be a cameraman, operating power-hungry electrical equipment well away from the mains power supply for long periods, what would be your first thought? No doubt, you would already be checking your stock of batteries to make sure they were fully charged and readily available. Anyone would. It's only common sense.

To be fair, I usually managed to remember to charge up my batteries, but turning the camera off when not in use was beyond me. So, I often needed the spares; but they were never to hand when I needed them. I had a lot of kit to manage: a tripod; microphones; camera stands; cables; lights; battery chargers; GoPros;[35] a monopod;

---

35 Mini cameras.

and sundry other stuff. So, some items got left behind. One such occurrence was during a live one-to-one interview with Fernando Alonso who, to his great credit, remained unfazed and continued to answer Juan's questions while the crazed cameraman tore his rucksack to pieces looking for a spare. As I mentioned, it wasn't the first time I had scrambled for batteries around the feet of the Spaniard.

And believe it or not, this wasn't close to the top of my list of embarrassing forgotten battery incidents. One evening outside our hotel in Saudi Arabia, just ten minutes before we were scheduled to stream a live news piece for a show in Chile, the warning light on the cordless microphone began to flash, telling me the battery was running low. Worried it would conk out, I made the flustered decision to sprint back to my room to collect a spare. Juan was in the parking lot looking for the tripod I had left in the car and there was no one else around, so I had to take the camera and the LiveU video transmission pack with me on my back. I reckoned I could make it back before Juan knew I had gone.

At times of stress, I do find it helps to talk to myself. We Brits used to believe that a 'stiff upper lip' was a virtue. Never show your weakness. Least said, soonest mended and all that. But now we know better. Now we know that bottling up one's frustrations with life in general and oneself in particular, can lead to mental health issues. So much better to vent those little frustrations and get them out of your system. Vocalising can also help to clarify important decisions about measures one might take to improve one's lifestyle.

So, as I made the panicked dash, I expressed myself out loud, forgetting that the video and audio were being transmitted. The increasingly enthusiastic news crew back in Santiago could see the interior of the hotel bouncing around wildly and they could clearly hear my commentary.

'What the *fuck* is your problem, Kris? You can't remember to bring a back-up battery with you? Are you insane? How many times are you going to make the same mistake? You must stop drinking. It's seriously affecting your brain.

'Where the hell's the lift? I don't believe it; didn't I press the button? Are you kidding? Wait, are there two lifts? I just missed it! Nooo! Oh thank God, it's coming. It's taking forever, what the fuck?'

Back in Santiago the news crew saw the lift doors open and, a second later, my finger feverishly jabbing at the lift button for the seventh floor. Picture and audio crackled off as the doors closed, pausing the marvellous entertainment. Was I done?

Hell no! The doors opened and the signal resumed.

'Shit, which way is it to my room? Christ, I've gone the wrong way up the corridor. Can't you read the fucking room numbers? How can I be lost in a hotel I've stayed at for five days? Who gets lost in a hotel? What is wrong with you? I hate myself. Tomorrow, I start a detox. Just fruit juice and legumes.'

Juan arrived back in the car park well before I did and was screaming my name when I found my way back seconds before we went live. And of course, I had the microphone back-up battery in my pocket the whole time.

My lapses from exemplary professionalism did not stop there. I managed to record free practice one[36] in Abu Dhabi with something greasy smeared across the wide-angled lens, so I had to re-shoot in free practice two. I also misunderstood 'white balance', a basic concept in photography, but still beyond me and so I recorded a stream of orange images on one occasion and blue on another.

While attempting to clean the viewfinder lens, I succeeded in dislodging it completely. This meant an entire afternoon was wasted recording out-of-focus images of the Old Town in Saudi Arabia. I thought the automatic focus would compensate but I had set the camera to 'manual'. My dramatic pans and zooms (extremely creative ideas, if I do say so myself) were lost in a blurred haze. To my mortification, Juan fixed the problem of the displaced lens in less than 20 seconds by opening a compartment in the viewfinder housing that I didn't know existed. Juan had been a cameraman himself earlier in his career and knew exactly how they worked.

---

36 The first session when the drivers get to drive the circuit.

I once watched him fix a problem by dismantling a camera into hundreds of screws and dozens of parts, before speedily rebuilding it in perfect working order.

To be frank, I had struggled with focus throughout the two weeks. I mislaid my eyeglasses two days into the trip and was too busy running around to find the time to buy a new pair. In the Old Town, as I recorded the beautiful surroundings, the images appeared doubly blurred, once for the misaligned viewfinder and once for my myopic eyes. And no, they didn't cancel each other out.

As my camera fell towards the Abu Dhabi tarmac, at least I could take comfort from the fact that I was certain to become a social media celebrity. When you work in the Formula One paddock, you can be confident that there are enough live cameras around to ensure nothing goes unrecorded, especially at a time like this. So, it was a racing certainty that at least one of my fellow cameramen would capture my butterfingered buffoonery as I extinguished the exclusive Grand Prix experience for millions of Spanish speakers.

I could also be sure, as there is strictly no honour among reporters, that these images would rapidly be distributed to news channels, Facebook, TikTok, Instagram, Reddit and the like, starting a multitude of new memes, with gleeful commentaries in every major world language, every crash, smash, tinkle and wail audibly enhanced.

I had always fancied 'going viral' but I had in mind something heroic, like catching Bernie Ecclestone if he were to fall from the second floor of a team's hospitality suite. He looks light enough, so I reckon I could at least break his fall. Or perhaps rescuing a drowning calf from a fast-flowing river, all rugged and manly with my shirt plastered to my chest. But for this performance I would get more 'likes' than 'Gangnam Style' and 'Charlie Bit My Finger'.

My anguished face would probably make it to *The Oprah Winfrey Show*. I could hear her opening monologue:

'You ever have a bad day at the office? Well, we all have, right? But this guy, well, he takes it to a different level!

'You know the biggest story in Formula One, history, right? Yes, Lewis Hamilton versus Max Verstappen, last race of the season, all to play for. Well, this was in Abu Dhabi, before the race, moments before this cameraman was going live to the whole of Spanish-speaking America! Yes, live. I'm going to play the tape for you now, but don't worry, if you look under your chair, there's a copy of the incident on a memory stick for you all to enjoy at home later and to show your family and friends. Oh, and if you lose it, just check out oprah.com/crazy-british-guy-smashes-camera-into-tarmac. You ready?' Cue: Cheers from a delighted crowd.

'Oh, and by the way, we did invite him to appear on the show today, but he hasn't replied to our attempts to contact him. And who can blame him?' Raised eyebrow and knowing smile to camera.

'Let's take a look.'

I had dabbled with cosmetic surgery in my youth to improve the angle of my protruding ears, which had earned me the nickname of 'Wingnut' among the less supportive of my family and friends. But this was going to require something substantially more radical if I was ever to venture out in public again.

They say that as you approach the moment of your death, time slows and your life replays before your eyes. The plummeting camera certainly sharpened my mind and I was already formulating the opening statement for my defence.

'I was not supposed to be the cameraman for this defining moment in history, your honour. It was insanity, members of the jury, that one such as I was put in charge of such a crucial piece of equipment, without so much as a minute's instruction. Especially considering the importance of the occasion, m'lud. I'm just a half-wit from Jersey! I can't handle this kind of pressure!'

Yes, that would be the angle I would take. But though it took only a fraction of a second to formulate this case for the defence, I already knew that nobody would listen. When the dust of the glass lens settled, I would just be the guy that ruined a sumptuous viewing experience for millions and they would be sure to blame me. My workmates and everyone else in the paddock. The fans, my friends, my wife, my mother, my children and my sausage dog (which was only to be expected; she has never shown me any respect), but even my supernaturally loving, forgiving and loyal golden retriever would be unable to hide her disgust. I could already see her expression of mournful but uncompromising reproach.

No, there would be no trial, no judge and no jury. No special pleadings or background reports. There would only be a baying lynch mob and a savage, sudden and brutal execution.

Joker in the Hole

MANY READERS will be familiar with Texas Hold 'Em, a popular form of poker, which has cost me a fair few pay cheques over the years. At the start of every hand, each player is dealt two 'hole cards' face down. Players bet by putting money into the pot depending on how promising their hole cards are.[37]

It seems to me that Hold 'Em provides many metaphors for life. A skilful player who works hard, studies the game and accurately calculates the odds has a big advantage and will usually win. Then there are the eternal losers who delight in telling you about their 'bad beats' when they lost because the fates conspired against them. But poker is a great game because you can also win by bluff, by betting big on useless cards, so that you persuade (or intimidate) your opponent to throw their better cards away.

But the most satisfying way to win is with blind luck. Not even Canadian poker champion Daniel Negreanu, for all his six World Series of Poker bracelets, can beat a palooka who consistently fills his inside straights or is dealt the fourth-of-a-kind on the river.

By now you may well be asking how all this is relevant to my route into TV and then on to Formula One? Well, I have come to believe there are things either written in the stars or in my genes over which I have no control. Let me explain.

Have you ever considered which two hole cards the fates dealt you at the happy moment of your birth? It would be extraordinary if

---

[37] Then three community cards are dealt face up (the flop), a fourth (the turn) and finally the river card. There are rounds of betting at each stage, when players evaluate their chances to make the best five-card poker hand by combining their hole cards with those on view. All the money in the pot goes to the winner.

you had, but I have spent many hours musing upon this important philosophical question, usually after smoking some home-grown flowers, it must be said.

After much solemn contemplation I reached a conclusion. My first card was certainly an ace. I was, after all, born on the affluent and peaceful island of Jersey in the late sixties with many advantages. I have never been hungry. I am healthy. My parents were kind, happily married and modestly successful. Four generations of Henleys before me were obliged to put on a uniform and fight in wars, but I was spared that misfortune. And I have enjoyed, from time to time, as we shall see, stellar good luck. Yes, few had a better start in life than me.

The second card, however, was always more of a mystery.

I toyed with the idea that perhaps it was a king, which would give me AK, known in poker circles as the Anna Kournikova, famous for looking better than it plays. That would be nice, but no, that is far too big a card. What about an eight, which would give me half of the dead man's hand, aces and eights, which Wild Bill Hickok was supposedly holding when he was shot dead by Jack McCall? No, way too dramatic and far too serious.

Perhaps it was an off-suit three which, while certainly a poor card, could occasionally be used to make a sneaky pair, flush or run? Possibly, but it didn't quite explain my comedic passage through life. After many years of solemn reflection, it came to me. I had been looking in the wrong place. My second card in the hole had to be the joker, a card that is usually wild and so valuable in many card games. But not one that you find in a Hold 'Em deck.

That joker, the prankster, the gremlin, would gleefully wipe my memory clean of everything I diligently learned the moment I sat down to an exam, or turn innocently meant compliments into gauche-sounding remarks. The joker makes me speak when I would better be served by staying silent. And when the moment does come to say something intelligent to impress an important person, the joker inserts irrelevant gibberish instead of the knowledgeable commentary I had intended.

I sometimes wonder if I am the unknowing star of a hidden camera TV show like *Impractical Jokers* or *Candid Camera*, where the evil producer has carefully manipulated situations designed to expose my incompetence.

Cue: cheesy Hammond organ chords. A guy with a wide smile, sharp suit and confident, excitable demeanour walks centre stage. He picks up the microphone, beaming, teeth impossibly white, gleaming and perfect.

'Welcome, Formula One fans, to *How Will Kris, Deal With This?!* Coming up on this week's episode, Kris is the cameraman for the most important Formula One race in sports history. Yes, that's right, the Max Verstappen versus Lewis Hamilton showdown in Abu Dhabi. But the catch is … let's hear it?'

'He has no F1 idea what he is doing!' the audience joyously shrieks.

'That's right, folks, not a clue. But before we see how he got on this week, let's look ahead. In next week's show we have two delicious disasters! First, we push Kris on to a helicopter to fly from São Paulo to Pirelli's test Circuit Panamericano to interview the chief executive of the Formula One Group Stefano Domenicali and the head of Formula One and car racing for Pirelli, Mario Isola.

'But … let's hear it?'

'He's no F1 idea what he is doing!'

'Yes, you guessed it. His internet connection didn't work [cut to evil producer grinning conspiratorially and waving a disconnected plug in the air] so he hasn't got a clue who these guys are. So, what questions will he ask? You'll just have to wait and see, but one thing's for sure:'

'He's no F1 idea what he is doing!'

'Then we'll see how Kris, after a routine visit to the TV compound to send some material back to Argentina, gets completely lost on his way back to the paddock and ends up on a tour of Abu Dhabi, because …'

'He's no F1 idea what he is doing!'

'That's all to look forward to, but for now, let's see how his stint as a cameraman works out. Roll tape!'

So, yes, that would certainly explain it. I am lucky, but I am jinxed. I am blessed, but cursed. My ace in the hole has made me many winning hands, but the second card, the joker, the jolly jester, the harlequin-in-motley, the gremlin, the fool, is ever-present, making me often a lucky winner, sometimes an unlucky loser, but always the clown.

Money, Money, Money!

Saudi Arabia 2022

IN MARCH 2022 I was in Saudi Arabia for its second ever F1 race. Wandering out of the media centre during free practice one on Friday, I looked up and noticed dark smoke trails in the sky. I spotted Edd Straw, an experienced journalist and broadcaster and the kind of guy who knows what is going on. I asked him what he thought it was.

'A missile attack on the Aramco Oil Refinery,' he told me.

'Seriously?'

'Must be. It's coming from the area the Yemen Houthi rebels targeted last week.'

'Well, that's not good. How far away is it?'

'Ten, maybe twelve miles.'

'Yikes. So what does that mean? Will they cancel the race?'

'That depends,' Edd replied.

I looked back at the smoke and wondered what would happen next. Ten miles might seem a long way, but Max Verstappen radioed his team while on the circuit saying, 'I can smell burning, is it my car?' 'We are happy it's not your car,' was the reply from his engineer, who elaborated no further.

The next day a meeting took place to decide the fate of the Grand Prix. The world's press waited outside the F1 offices for over four hours as various groups came and went, including F1 officials, drivers, team bosses, the FIA and local authorities. Rumours circulated that there were drivers who would not race in the threatening conditions.

'If Sebastian Vettel was here,[38] he definitely wouldn't race!' opined someone.

'I hear Lewis and Charles won't either,' speculated another.

I turned to Carlos Sainz's cousin and manager Carlos Oñoro and asked him if he thought the race might be called off.

'You're joking, aren't you?' he said, looking at me as if I had just fallen off the Christmas tree. 'There is *no chance whatsoever* they will not race. Think of the money that would be lost if the race was cancelled! And if any driver doesn't want to race, believe me, there are plenty of Formula Two drivers standing by, ready to take their seat.'

Of course, Carlos was right. Mohammed Bin Sulayem, the FIA president, and Stefano Domenicali, Formula One president and CEO finally came out to meet the press, who pounced on them like hungry wolves. I blindly stretched out my arm holding a microphone through the throng of bodies hoping to capture a soundbite. Someone grabbed my hand and pushed it away as Uli bustled to get our camera shot, doubtless contributing to the chaos. The two men asked the mob to move back before confirming that all the teams and drivers were now in agreement. Surprise! The event, that Saudi Arabia had paid $55 million to host (just saying) would go ahead as planned.

The fact is that Formula One is fuelled by money and almost everything that may seem odd or unusual about the sport can be explained if you follow the cash. Consider the race schedule. At the beginning of every season, motorsport fans study it and savour the prospect of the upcoming racing, picturing themselves sipping their favourite beverage and munching salsa-dipped nachos. But those of us working in Formula One look at the calendar differently. The first question Is, 'How many back-to-back races are there?'[39] And then, 'Is there a dreaded triple-header?'[40]

---

38 He wasn't. He had Covid and was replaced by Nico Hülkenberg.
39 On consecutive weekends.
40 Three race weekends in a row.

Races on consecutive weekends are tough, leaving an awkward couple of days to travel to the next race. It's particularly exhausting for the team's staff who have to arrive earlier and leave later than the drivers and also for the mechanics, who work long hours over any race weekend, particularly if they are forced to 'break curfew', that is, work through the night to change an engine, put in a new gearbox, or rebuild the car after a driver has smashed it to smithereens.

So, when I first looked at the official calendar for the 2022 Formula One Grand Prix season I was stunned. And not in a good way.

'That's just ... ridiculous,' I said, even though nobody was listening. There were 23 races[41] scheduled over 36 weeks with seven double-headers and two triple-headers. So, you can imagine the furore in the media centre when Formula One CEO Stefano Domenicali hinted at the possibility of increasing that number to 30 races in the future. While mechanics have the greatest cause to complain, they don't have cameras, microphones, blogs or newspaper columns, so it's the press that get to voice their outrage. But the protests fell on deaf ears and 23 races were again scheduled in 2023 and 24 in 2024.

I'm afraid that complaining about increasing numbers of races is like the captain of a ship railing against the sea. More races mean more money and there are plenty of countries keen to host Grands Prix. Every race brings in millions of dollars in airport taxes, accommodation fees, restaurant bills, shopping, taxi fares, circuit admissions and much, much more. There are also soft benefits in terms of prestige and publicity, which in turn encourage more tourism and other commercial activity. Circuits are chosen primarily because they pay handsomely for the privilege.

Sure, it might be tough for those working in the circus and there will be plenty of complaints and concerns expressed about 'burnout' and wellbeing. But, hey, it's not as if those who don't like it can't be replaced.

---

41 Russia was later cancelled. Pre-Covid, 20 or 21 races in a season was usual.

It's expensive to travel to races. Plenty of regulars in the media centre – bloggers, journalists and photographers – don't have a television network or a widely circulated publication to meet their expenses, so need to economise. One way to save money is to book flights and accommodation months in advance. Another is to eat lunch in one of the team's hospitality suites. Every press party where free food and drink is on offer will attract hungry reporters anxious to save the cost of dinner. But although some race venues offer free food, others don't. Shared accommodation is common practice. Some journalists have been known to sleep in their cars and use the shower in the circuit facilities each morning.

At the other end of the scale, let's suppose you want to get into the F1 racing business and create a new team. Be prepared to spend about $140m[42] on the people, systems, components and facilities you will need to design, build, test and improve your racing car. If that sounds a lot, take comfort from the fact that it's less than it used to be, because the authorities introduced a budget cap on car-performance-related spending in 2021.

Then you will need to stump up for your three senior managers who won't be cheap, your drivers (Lewis Hamilton and Max Verstappen each cost around $40m in 2022), your hospitality suites and for your team to travel to pre-season testing and to the Grands Prix themselves. Oh, and don't forget the consumables: fuel, oil and tyres. Your cars won't go far without them. If you manage your costs tightly, you might come in under $200m.

So, unless you are fabulously wealthy and wish rapidly to become less so, you will need to find some sources of income to cover these eye-watering costs. After a few years of competition, you should become eligible for an annual payment from Formula One Management (FOM) of $35m. FOM brings money into the sport by selling TV and content distribution rights, race hosting fees and sponsorship deals. You can also expect prize money of between

---

42 2022 figures. Source: onestopracing.com.

$17m and $66m[43] depending on how well you do. Your competitors receive substantial further payments from FOM because of their track record. Ferrari, Mercedes, Red Bull and McLaren each get an annual payment of $35m and Ferrari get a further cool $68m for being a 'long-standing team'. Yes, just for hanging in there for so long![44] There are other payments that go to Mercedes, Red Bull, Ferrari and Williams for various historical reasons. But, as a newcomer, I'm afraid you won't get any of that.

Manufacturers (of cars or energy drinks, for example) might see a benefit in investing in your team to get their company logo visible to millions of fans in the glamorous world of Formula One. The publicity and feel-good factor generated for their brand helps them to sell more cars or energy drinks. The amount invested varies. Daimler (the parent company of Mercedes) support their team to the tune of $80m. Aston Martin pay their team, formerly Racing Point, $25m.

In 2018 Red Bull invested $82.9m.[45] To recover that sort of money they need to shift a colossal volume of drink, but that's exactly what they do, selling over seven billion cans a year, about one for each person on the planet. And people are prepared to pay premium prices for their Red Bull energy drinks, so the margins are substantial.

Without such investment, you will need to find sponsors. Formula One teams sell sponsorship deals to commercial companies who receive a package of benefits which may include the right to put their logo on the racing cars, or on the drivers' helmets or suits and/or allowing the sponsor and their own clients to come to the Grands Prix and be entertained in the hospitality suites.

It helps to sell sponsorship if your drivers are marketable in their own right. You may have noticed there aren't too many unattractive Formula One drivers. After all, what sponsor wants

---

43 2021 payments.

44 This may seem odd, but as Toto Wolff said, 'Formula One needs Ferrari much more than Ferrari needs Formula One.'

45 Source: Watsonpost.com.

Joe Ugly associated with their product when they could have the ravishingly handsome Carlos Sainz, the boyish charm of Charles Leclerc or George Russell, the Teutonic good looks of Sebastian Vettel, or the effortlessly charming Daniel Ricciardo? Which is not to say you are not a great looker too, Dan! And apologies to the rest of the fabulous-looking drivers. I ran out of superlatives.

Family connections help to attract sponsors. There have been 13 drivers[46] who have followed their father into Formula One. Among the most successful were the Brits Graham and Damon Hill who won two and one World Championships respectively, Finns Nico and Keke Rosberg, one each, and Canadians Gilles and Jacques Villeneuve. Gilles came second in 1979 before dying in a crash at the age of 32. His son Jacques, who was just 11 at the time of his father's death, followed him into the sport, becoming world champion in 1997. Mick Schumacher is the son of seven-time winner Michael. Bruno Senna, who was active in Formula One from 2010 to 2012, is Ayrton Senna's nephew and of course Max Verstappen, already F1's most successful son, followed his father Jos.

Doubtless the success of the second generation is mostly because they grow up immersed in the car-racing culture and have the means and encouragement to compete from an early age. But their inherited names open doors and are certainly attractive to sponsors, even if they are no guarantee of success.

Sponsors flock around the top teams and famous-name drivers. The big teams have all the advantages in generating revenue to cover their costs and indeed they sometimes make a nice profit. But for the less established teams it's a perpetual battle to get enough revenue to keep solvent, never mind be competitive.

Which brings us to another topic which may seem strange to those new to Formula One, that of 'pay drivers', who appear to be able to jump the queue and race ahead of drivers who might seem more talented.

---

46 Source: F1experiences.com.

But let's be clear. Every driver who races in Formula One is highly qualified to do so. They all possess an FIA super licence which is earned by, among other things, winning 40 points in the ferociously competitive qualifying series. They must take a theory test and complete at least 80 per cent of two seasons in one of the approved single-seater championships. They must drive a recent Formula One car at over 300 kilometres an hour. So, without question, all drivers in Formula One are extremely skilled. But a pay driver, instead of being paid a fee by their team, brings money into the team in exchange for their race seat. Their own remuneration comes directly from a sponsor, a friend or a family member.

So, when a team further down the financial grid has a choice, the extent of the driver's personal sponsorship makes the team's decision for them. This is hard for the aspiring and talented but impoverished driver to understand, but I can help him. Follow the money. In Formula One money speaks louder than the roar of the engines.

It's even better for your racing prospects if your dad is a billionaire and is prepared to contribute directly or even buy the team. As mentioned, Aston Martin driver Lance Stroll's father, Lawrence, owns the team and supports it financially. Russian billionaire Dmitry Mazepin bankrolled his son, Nikita, into the Haas team alongside Michael Schumacher's son Mick in 2021, which enabled the team to stay on the grid. That arrangement, however, was just one of the countless things destroyed by the Russian invasion of Ukraine. Though judging from the Mazepins' behaviour shown on *Drive to Survive*, I shouldn't think too many of the Haas team were sorry to see them go.

While some pay drivers may not be quite as good as the top drivers, it certainly doesn't mean they don't have enormous talent and all the necessary attributes to race and win in F1. Many fantastic drivers have been sponsored during their careers.

Checo Pérez got his start in F1 in 2011 through a partnership deal between his sponsor Telmex, the Mexican telecoms company, and team Sauber. He has since driven for McLaren, Force India (later Racing Point) and now Red Bull and claimed over 30 podiums. Perhaps his most remarkable performance was when he won the Sakhir Grand Prix in Bahrain in 2020 when his place in Formula One was under threat and, after spinning off in an accident that caused the race to be restarted with him at the back of the field, Checo fought his way from last to first. At the end of the season, he was recruited by Red Bull, where he commanded a salary of $8m.

Three-time world champion Niki Lauda also paid for his first drives in the March team and then the more competitive British Racing Motors team, BRM. Lauda borrowed money against his life insurance to get his foot in the door, but was later reimbursed after he demonstrated his commitment, engineering smarts and driving talent.

Juan Manuel Fangio, who claimed the world title five times in the fifties, was sponsored by the President of Argentina, Juan Peron. Even seven-time world champion Michael Schumacher had backing from the German manufacturer Mercedes to secure his seat in a Jordan halfway through the season in 1991, before he defected to Benetton. He would go on to achieve his first two consecutive World Championships in 1994 and 1995 with the Italian team.

And we certainly won't forget Pastor Maldonado. But he gets a chapter of his own a little later.

Creative Writing Crash Course

Hong Kong 1992

I ARRIVED at Le Jardin to meet Danny McGill, for once, in good time. But as seven o'clock passed and the minutes ticked by, my feeling of elation gave way to concern, then doubt, worry, anguish and finally despair. I drank first to pass the time and then to drown my sorrows. By the time I gave up waiting, I was completely inebriated and staggered out of the bar and up the steps towards my apartment in the Mid-Levels feeling extremely sorry for myself. I thought fortune had at long last smiled upon me, but it was just another cruel bust.

Halfway home, the upward path and steps were crossed by Staunton Street and on my right was a wide pavement square where an old bed and mattress had been dumped. That was most convenient as, I must say, I did feel a little tired and rather woozy, so I decided to sit down for a moment's rest.

It was 8am when I woke up, face down in the dirty foam next to a pile of rancid rubbish on the side of the busy pedestrian walkway. I groaned. The sun was bright in my eyes and my head was splitting. I was parched. I shudder to think how many rats had run across my sprawling limbs during the night. Hundreds of people must have passed me by on their way to work. I prayed that Danny McGill was not one of them.

An elderly Chinese man walked by and perfunctorily dumped four leaking black rubbish bags next to my head, so it seemed a good time to climb shakily to my feet and survey my surroundings. I could now see that I had spent the night in an area used for dumping garbage. Coincidentally, Dean had pointed it out a few weeks earlier, as he had found an Olivetti typewriter there. But today there was no office equipment, only my bed and two dozen stinking bags of trash. Apart from two young Chinese girls who were giggling shyly, the rest of the onlookers didn't seem at all surprised to see a drunken 'gweilo' (a white ghost) waking up on the side of the road.

My frontal and temporal lobes ached furiously as I dusted myself down unsteadily and continued my journey home. It was then that I noticed the tip of a piece of white card sticking out of my shirt pocket. I pulled it out and tried to focus. I couldn't believe it. It was another gratuitous business card. On it was written 'Doctor William Chau, Substance Abuse Counsellor and Mental Therapist'. You couldn't even pass out in a coma on the streets in Hong Kong without someone seeing it as a networking opportunity.

When I arrived back at the flat, Dean was sat at the table.

'Dude,' he said, 'so how'd the meeting go with the big shot video jock?'

I wasn't really in the mood to be ribbed by Dean. I went straight to the kitchen tap and sluiced down about a gallon of water, followed by three paracetamol tablets. That done, I sat down on the couch that doubled as my more usual bed and squeezed my temples to try to reduce the pain.

'He no-showed, right? Just like I said he would?'

I shook my head in confirmation, not denial.

'So, like a douchebag you went on a bender and spent the night on the streets? I know you didn't get lucky, that's a given.'

'I did share a bed last night ...' I struggled to speak. Good God, I was still thirsty. 'But with a colony of rats.'

'Course you did. Well, dude, I have some surprising news that might cheer you up. Danny's assistant called to say sorry he stood you up. Something about a change to his schedule and they couldn't get through to the bar. But he's organised for you to see one of the bosses at MTV production, someone called, ah, Cheryl Coleman at 2pm today. And she said, bring your résumé.'

I looked suspiciously at Dean. If he was messing with me there were going to be grave consequences.

'You serious?'

'I called you last night at the bar. The bartender, Joe, told me you had just staggered out, hammered out of your mind.'

'You're bullshitting?'

'No, that's what he said.'

'No, not about Joe, I mean about the interview.'

'Here's the number, dude, you need to confirm.'

I dialled warily but soon heard the voice I recognised from two days before, which turned out to be Danny's assistant, who picked up and confirmed that, yes, Cheryl was expecting me and would see me at 14.00 if that was convenient.

I could hardly believe it. The fates were smiling after all. But I also knew I was at the last-chance saloon and, instead of being sharp, I was bleary eyed and dehydrated with my head strumming and my liver pickled in tequila.

As well as the horrible hangover, something else bothered me. My résumé, even stretched as it was to the limits of credibility, was still horribly threadbare. The fact was, in this grand poker game of life, I held no cards. So, I did what a poker player must do when he desperately needs a win, but knows he has a losing hand. I raised the stakes and bluffed.

What I needed was a new, improved version of my résumé. I took out Dean's Olivetti typewriter, the one that he found in the rubbish tip where I had just slept. I typed 'the quick brown fox jumped over the lazy dog' to test all the letter keys. To my amazement the old machine, although in sore need of a good clean, worked perfectly. No time for cleaning. I located a copy of my old résumé for reference, put a new piece of paper in the typewriter and set to work retyping the introductory information.

First, I considered my time at Capitol Records in Los Angeles which was currently mentioned in the 'Miscellaneous' section. That surely had more potential, so I moved it up the charts to become the main entry under 'Work Experience'. With a few taps on the sticky keys

I went from 'mail boy' to 'production assistant' in the video department. Well, most job titles are overblown, so what was the harm?

I did have one bare smidgeon of experience related to television; a job at a small video duplication company in Elephant and Castle in London where I worked part-time while doing my BTEC course. I loaded VHS videos into dozens of identical video recorders, pressed 'play' on the Betacam master deck and then 'record' on the slave machines, producing hundreds of copies of videos of the Scottish Highlands. As a child of six could have performed the task, it didn't merit a job title, so I didn't think anyone would mind if I made one up. 'Head of production' seemed inspired as it was true, in a way, if blatantly disingenuous.

But the credentials still seemed pathetically sparse. Now, I must confess that there does come a point where the truth can be stretched no further and something a little more morally dubious is required. Whether you call it economies with the truth, inaccurate memories, terminological inexactitudes or fairy tales, the final update to my résumé, I'm ashamed to say, did cross a certain line. I am not proud of it, but I held no cards. And once you have decided to bluff, there is no point in raising the stakes by so small an amount that your opponent can easily afford to call.

So, I went all-in and added that I had worked for an entirely fictitious special effects company in London called 'FXU' for six months. The only remote element of truth in this claim was that I had once visited a movie set to help a guy I met in a bar set up a sprinkler system to simulate the 'special effect' of rain. My contribution was to carry the bases, stands, hosepipe and showerheads from the truck to the set the night before the shoot, nothing more. Which reminded me. What I really needed right now was a shower.

Rat droppings and the Hong Kong grime went down the plug hole and I dressed as coolly as my wardrobe permitted. Blue jeans and Dr Martin boots, a 'Misfits' T-shirt and a paisley shirt worn like a jacket. Dean kindly bolstered my confidence by commenting that I looked like a douchebag (his go-to word for me) but it was too late to change. I left the apartment in the Mid-Levels just after midday.

Finding the Fun in Formula One

OVER THE years, some members of the press have forged strong and genuine friendships with drivers and their families. My affable colleague, the renowned technical journalist Giorgio Piola, famed for his beautiful hand-drawn technical artwork, has attended over 800 Grands Prix, more than any other member of the press, and has many stories about time he spent with some of the great F1 drivers including Nelson Piquet and Riccardo Patrese. He was particularly close to Elio de Angelis before Elio died in 1986 from injuries sustained in a crash at the Paul Ricard circuit in France when he was just 28. It affected Giorgio so much he became wary of forming such close relationships again.

Some reporters socialise, play sport or perhaps go for a meal with drivers, but strong bonds are less common than they used to be. James Hunt's wild parties after racing (and before racing come to that) are a thing of the past. The tabloid newspapers and social media put paid to all that.

I don't claim to have any F1 drivers on my speed dial, but I was invited to Sergio Pérez's wedding, even though I rarely get much more than a nod from him when Juan is interviewing him in Spanish. As Juan and Uli had been given nice formal invitations some weeks before I did feel the verbal invitation from Pérez's assistant might be something of an afterthought, so I let Juan carry the flag for our channel. I hope Checo and his bride didn't spend too much of their special day fretting over my whereabouts!

But we certainly spend a lot of time with the drivers, interviewing them in moments of triumph and, perhaps more revealingly, disaster, which means we get to know aspects of their personalities.

One thing is for sure. Although the list of attributes required to become a Formula One driver is long and exacting, those that rise to the very top don't seem to me to conform to any identifiable stereotype. Consider the reserved, laconic Kimi Räikkönen; the combative but generous Michael Schumacher; the charismatic, charming but ruthless Ayrton Senna; the shy and cerebral Alain Prost; the bubbly and quick-witted Sebastian Vettel; the brave and fussy Nigel Mansell; the unflappable and cordial Mika Häkkinen; the outrageous, bohemian James Hunt; the candid and calculating Jackie Stewart; the stoic and level-headed Damon Hill; the uncompromising Max Verstappen; and the cool, ultra-professional fashion icon, Lewis Hamilton. You would be hard pushed to identify any particular personality trait that they share, apart from, of course, their love for racing. While all the drivers on the grid are highly professional, it is great when they are prepared to let their playful side show. It brightens my day and makes for great TV.

Lando Norris has a surreal and cheeky sense of humour. After the 2022 Abu Dhabi GP, I asked him what his plans were for the Christmas holiday. He told me he was planning to play golf and lose weight.

'Yes, you look like you could lose a few pounds,' I told the superbly slim and fit-looking McLaren driver. He knew I had my tongue in my cheek but was quick to respond by raising his eyebrows sky high and pointing at the area protruding embarrassingly over my trouser belt.

Whenever I ask Lando a technical question, I always get the feeling he is well aware I have no idea what I'm talking about but plays along, with only a slightly raised eyebrow, to let me know that he knows. Despite being one of the youngsters on the grid, he is full of confidence and not afraid to gently ridicule his more experienced fellow drivers, with subtle facial expressions or succinct put-downs.

Yuki Tsunoda, the pocket-sized Japanese prodigy, is just 159cm (5ft 2in) tall and so holds the record for being the shortest ever F1 driver. He requires a substantial adjustment to the height of the microphone stand when he comes into the pen. But his small stature is more than made up for by his colossal personality, backed up with a surprisingly foul mouth. Yuki is not afraid to say what he means with passionate, potty-mouthed outbursts over the radio during a race, for which he subsequently apologises with disarming humility and deep regret. I have heard many drivers calling the Japanese driver a legend since he started in F1.

Yuki is the lowest-paid driver on the grid with a yearly salary of 'just' €650,000.[47] After Sebastian Vettel's last race in 2022 the drivers all went out to a restaurant in Abu Dhabi to say farewell. The next day Yuki confided, 'Lucky Lewis Hamilton paid the bill, or I'd be broke.'

Valtteri Bottas is a driver who likes to have fun in the paddock, growing comical moustaches in November and dressing up in silly hats or flamboyant Hawaiian shirts when he talks to the press. After his seventh position in the Miami Grand Prix, he posted a photo of himself cooling off by skinny-dipping in a stream in Aspen, Colorado, with his rear end on show above the crystal-clear water. It caused quite a sensation, so Valtteri saw an opportunity to raise money for charity, selling 5,000 prints in 24 hours and making €50,000 in a day.

I told Valtteri I was most impressed with the bottom line of his money-making scheme. He laughed heartily.

But no driver does more to give the press something entertaining and funny (as well as informative) to report than Daniel Ricciardo. He will always find a considerate way to answer even my daftest questions. I once asked him what was in his water bottle when I observed a green slush in the plastic container he was sipping from and he spent a couple of minutes explaining the mix, but threw in a few clearly made-up ingredients like kale with snail and an extra helping of Viagra.

The ever-affable Australian, who was always a paddock favourite because of the happy way he handles the press, then became a fan favourite through his appearances on *Drive to Survive*. He is always

---

47 2022 figure.

game for a laugh, either spin-passing an American football to his mechanic, or playing 'keepie-uppie' with a football. He used to launch his water bottle high into the air and then catch it just before it landed on some innocent fan's head, although I haven't seen him do it for a while. Perhaps he was told off by the FIA.

Daniel is the man who managed to turn the 'shoey', the practice of drinking champagne out of his sweaty driving footwear, into a trademark which was registered by F1's branding department, Formula One Licensing, in 2017. He was not the first person to perform the ceremony, which he credits to the Aussie surfing/fishing/comedy group the Mad Hueys. Nor was he even the first person to perform the shoey on a motorsport podium. That honour goes to Daniel's fellow Australian Moto GP rider Jack Miller, who did it after his maiden win at the 2016 MotoGP Dutch TT.

But it was Daniel who made the shoey famous when it became a part of his podium celebration ritual. Daniel's charisma is never more powerfully demonstrated than when he persuades others to sip the champers from his sweaty shoe. Fellow countryman Mark Webber was the first at the Belgian GP in 2016. Others who have since supped include Max Verstappen, Nico Rosberg (who immediately regretted it), Lance Stroll, Christian Horner, Zak Brown and even film stars Gerard Butler and Sir Patrick Stewart, *Star Trek*'s Captain Jean-Luc Picard. (Yes, Sir Patrick, we know you have done a few other minor parts like Hamlet and Macbeth but come on.)

The most surprising person to partake was Lewis Hamilton, because he had previously and quite understandably said, 'I stand firm on the toe jam stuff. The juice from the foot is not something I wish to drink.' But after the Imola GP in 2020, which Lewis won with Daniel in third, mellowed by his victory, he relented. He said afterwards that 'it definitely didn't taste great', but added endearingly that 'Daniel's mum thinks I was a good sport, so I'm grateful for that.'

Lewis can also show a gentle sense of humour when he's in the mood.

The Australian clearly has a knack of getting people to do unlikely things. He won bets with both McLaren boss Zak Brown and his former boss at Renault, Cyril Abiteboul, with both agreeing to get a tattoo if he got a podium result for them. He delivered and eventually the team principals honoured their commitments. Zak chose the outline of the Monza track where Dan achieved McLaren's first victory for nine years, his first win since his brilliant victory for Red Bull in Monaco in 2018.

Many of us were sorry to hear Daniel had lost his seat at McLaren for 2023 and it is great to see him back.

Cowboy Meets Cowgirl

Hong Kong 1992

ON THE ferry ride to my interview at Star Television in Hung Hom on mainland Kowloon, I considered how I would describe my musical taste. I decided not to mention my love for popular artists like Phil Collins, Elton John or Rod Stewart, but go for hipper bands like Galliano and Massive Attack. It was a hot, clammy day. The walk from the ferry to the Star TV building left me dripping with sweat and feeling somewhat nauseous from the lingering hangover. I earnestly hoped that it was last night's tequila exiting through my pores. I wished I had left the paisley shirt at home. Now I looked at it more closely, I wished I had left it in the shop where I purchased it.

On arrival, I proudly told the pretty Chinese lady at the front desk that I had an appointment with Cheryl Coleman. She seemed surprised, but dialled the extension. I sat on a sofa in reception to wait.

All Star TV channels were displayed on five large monitors in the reception area. I turned my attention to the one showing MTV, hoping to see something I could use to break the ice in the interview. As the channel's promos ended, someone called Richard Marx began singing. You could tell it was a gooey power ballad, even though the sound was turned down.

I began feeling nervous and the nausea welled up again. At least the air conditioning was drying up the sweat and booze. As Dick continued crooning in silence, a tall lady, who was the spitting image of the country and western singer Bonnie Raitt, appeared at the door of the reception area. I jumped to my feet as she offered me her hand.

'Cheryl Coleman,' she said sternly with a soft yet forceful southern state accent. 'Would you come with me please?' It was more of an order than a question.

'Hi, I …' I was about to make a comment about Richard Marx's big hair to break the ice, but she was already five paces up the corridor. Lucky I didn't, because once she sat at the desk, I realised that she had exactly the same hairdo. I held out the résumé I had typed that morning which she snatched and began studying.

'So, Kris, you're from Jersey,' she began without looking up or giving me a chance to confirm or deny. 'You've travelled around a fair bit I see. Oh, how interesting, you worked for Capitol Records. I used to work in their offices on Hollywood and Vine too. Now there's a coincidence.'

I felt my stomach tighten and more odoriferous sweat started to leak from my skin. Oh shit! She would surely know that there wasn't a video department in Capitol Records. 'I was there a bit before your time,' she continued. 'I worked in the country and western department with Mick Osman, d'you remember him?'

I relaxed a little. I did remember Mick Osman. Delivering mail meant I knew, or at least had seen, almost everyone in the building. Normally I would forget the names of old work colleagues, if I could call him that, but when you see someone's name written on a package or envelope, day after day, they do tend to stick.

Mick Osman was a big man who always dressed in a Stetson hat and cowboy boots. He reminded me of Johnny Cash.

'Yeah, good old Mick,' I said confidently. 'We used to call him Johnny Cash in the mail …' I caught myself, '… in the video department. I often delivered video tapes to him,' which at least was a true statement. There were hundreds of video tapes from hopeful bands circulating around that building. Then I added, to fill the silence and hoping to ingratiate myself, 'Very nice guy.' She was looking straight at me.

'Small world, isn't it?' I added cheerfully, trying to match her gaze, but failing.

'It sure is.' She looked back down at my résumé. I relaxed a little, having proved there was at least some truth amid the misrepresentation. But I wanted her to quit probing and tried to draw her attention away from the freshly typed A4 paper, so I said, 'Heard anything from Mick lately? Do you know how he's doing?' I was speaking to the top of her head.

'I neither know, nor care,' she said deadpan. Shit. I was getting the definite impression she didn't like him. Or me much either.

I could imagine the joker in the hole starting to cackle. Why did I have to go and say he was a 'nice guy'? I didn't know him any better than I knew the real Johnny Cash. All I did was drop off packages to his secretary and occasionally see him in his office speaking on the phone with his black cowboy boots up on the desk. He could have been a horrible bastard for all I knew, up to who-knew-what skulduggery. So, as I was deep in my own burial pit, it seemed only right to keep on digging.

'I guess there's not a lot to like about those country and western types with their cowboy boots,' I said, then instantly realised my mistake. She had just told me she worked in the country and western department at Capitol, so of course she was a fan. I glanced down in embarrassment and fuck me if I didn't see the toe and heel of a black and white snakeskin cowboy boot poking out from below her desk. Another dozen shovels-full of earth piled up beside my grave.

'I'm not saying all cowboy boots are naff,' I added lamely, awkwardly pointing down with my index finger and thumb cocked. 'I love snakeskin boots for example. They are …' I had to peel my tongue away from the top of my mouth '… really, very cool indeed.' I felt my buttocks clench. Six more shovels. The joker was loving it.

She was staring at me again with her head cocked and her eyebrows raised.

'It's nothing to do with his taste in music or his dress sense. I'm just not interested in what he's doing.'

I was getting the strong impression that she wasn't going to be interested in what I was doing either in a few moments. She looked back down at the paper in front of her.

'I see you worked for a special effects company in London. Funny,' she paused, 'I worked in London for MTV Europe for several years, with lots of special effects companies and I've never heard of FXU. Are they new?'

What the hell? Had she worked everywhere I'd been? I felt my not-so-carefully constructed bluff start to unravel.

'Fairly new, yeah, three years old.'

'So, looking at the dates here, you worked with the company before it existed?'

'Exactly,' I said. Which at least was a quick reply, although I had no idea where I was going next. I was all-in with a bust and the other player pushing in her stack.

'I was more involved before they began operating. I helped to test the equipment. Made sure the water sprinklers worked, that sort of thing.'

'The water sprinklers?' She raised her arched eyebrows high into her frizzy hairline.

'Yes, rainmakers as we called them.' Remarkably, at that moment, I recalled a fact from the conversation I had with the bloke who hired me while we drove to the film set.

'Even if it is actually raining on the day a rainy scene is shot, normal precipitation is too small to show up on the screen so you need to make the raindrops bigger. Hence the rainmakers.' I was genuinely delighted with myself for recalling this interesting fact and amazed I had remembered the word 'precipitation'.

'Yes, thank you, I understand the theory of a rain rig,' she said cuttingly.

'What I don't understand is why would they need someone like you to test one a year before the company was formed?'

'Cutbacks,' was all I had to offer.

'Cutbacks?' Disbelief was writ large on her face. But instead of delving into that ludicrous statement, she switched her angle of attack.

'Okay. Let's move on. Who owns FXU?'

Oh dear God, why was she asking that? She smelled a rat and was not going to let it go. The 100 per cent proof perspiration was now beading on my face. I could still taste the salty tequila around my lips. I desperately tried to remember the guy from the pub who had paid me 30 quid to lend a hand. Dave? Steve? No, it was Phil, for sure it was Phil.

'The owner's name? Well, it was set up by a guy called Phil …' I faked a sneeze to get some time to think, but what with my dry mouth and the absence of any real sneeze, it sounded so obviously bogus, I was positively ashamed. I was in a terrible state of panic. Cheryl was waiting for a surname and I was racking my brains to think of one. Any family name in the world would do. Except this one.

'… Collins,' I said brightly. A moment's relief, but then the sphincter-cramping realisation. Of the 30 million family names in the world I could have chosen at an MTV interview, I had chosen Collins to match with Phil. Not something commonplace like Phil Jones or Phil Smith. Nor something a little more unusual like Phil Hatzakiriakidis or Phil Bellagamba. But Phil Collins. The joker snorted with glee.

'Phil Collins?' she repeated, eyes wide with disbelief.

'Not *the* Phil Collins, obviously,' I added, just to clear up any possible confusion about whether the former Genesis drummer and solo sensation had started a special effects company on the side. Perhaps he had a mother like mine who encouraged him to have a back-up career just in case the pop superstardom stalled?

'Another Phil Collins,' I confirmed. 'In fact, funny story, he hated having the same name as a middle-of-the-road pop icon. Made his blood boil.'

'Never heard of him, but I do love Phil Collins, the artist,' she said, flinging my obviously phoney résumé to one side.

She knew. I knew she knew. And she knew I knew she knew.

Now seemed like an excellent time for Cheryl to kick me out, so I could crawl back to the stifling heat and save us both from further excruciating torture. But no, she was far from finished. She said she wanted to ask me some quick-fire questions, which she called a 'TV Pop Quiz'. It sounded friendly enough, but it was more like an interrogation by the Gestapo.

She fired a volley of questions at me, starting with the basic, 'Who would you expect to find working on the studio floor of a TV station?' I managed the presenter and camera crew, but after struggling for others, I thought I should mention the cleaners. That triggered a roll of her eyes.

Then she asked: 'What's timecode?' I didn't have the faintest idea so I shrugged. More rapid-fire questions followed, to all of which I had to say, 'I don't know.' Then she asked, what the difference was between a long shot and a medium shot. I was too humiliated to say 'I don't know' yet again, so I guessed that the long shot was an image that the cameraman didn't have much chance of getting, like a sprinting hare in the distance, but the medium shot was a little more achievable, like a fast-walking tortoise. This at least made her laugh and she wrote something in her notebook.

Then she moved on to more technical areas, inquiring, 'What lighting arrangement would one need to shoot two people sitting around a table in a studio?' Aah. I vaguely remembered something about this from the BTEC course, so this was my chance to shine. I asked for a pen and sheet of paper from her notebook and sketched out a somewhat confusing bird's eye diagram with lights that looked like human eyes.

'Not even close,' was her appraisal when I handed her my work.

I couldn't focus. My brain has erased the rest of the mortifying experience. It must be some sort of psychological defence mechanism to protect me from post-traumatic stress, but I don't think it worked.

I can, however, remember that I started most earnestly to hope she would reach into her desk, get out some bull-nose pliers and a chunky mole wrench and get to work on my fingernails. It would certainly be far less painful.

My fundamental problem was that I knew nothing about TV production. I demonstrated a complete lack of even the most basic relevant knowledge and a proclivity for exaggeration and falsehood. What started out as small chinks in my armour became, as she probed away, gaping holes, exposing vast tracts of soft underbelly and other far more sensitive areas. Which I guess is the point of a well-executed job interview. My mind began undulating, tuning in and out, just like you feel when you realise you drank five tequila shots too many.

Eventually Cheryl put out her hand to signal the end of my suffering and I shook it limply with my clammy paw. I smiled like an imbecile as she thanked me for coming in. I was about to slink away when she snatched the phone from her desk and pushed four buttons. No doubt she was going to tell the security guards to give me a damn good kicking on the way out.

'Wait a moment, Kris,' she told me sternly. Then in a cheerful, friendly tone that seemed quite out of character, she spoke:

'Hi Vince Freidman, how are you doing? It's me. Are you busy?' She tapped her Bic pen on her front teeth and looked at me vacantly. Whatever it was that Vince said, it appeared to please her. 'Well, I suppose that's true if you like sports, but it's not really my scene.' I was amazed to hear her giggle.

'Listen, I have a freelancer by the name of Kris Henley here in my office. He's not *quite* …' she emphasised the word '… what we're looking for at MTV, but I think he would do well in Sports. I know you have a lot of work on right now. Do you have anything for freelancers?'

She looked up at me and to my utter astonishment, winked. I would have been far less surprised had she reached under her desk, taken off one of her snakeskin cowboy boots and used it to beat me around the head.

'Okay then, fine, I'll send him through. Thanks, Vincent.' She hung up the phone and looked at me. 'He hates it when I call him Vincent. Play your cards right and you could be lucky over in Prime Sports.'

I was gobsmacked.

'Listen, Kris. Don't worry if you haven't got any real experience in television, you don't need it. Not in Sports, anyway. Just relax and try to be yourself. And here,' she handed me a tissue, 'wipe your forehead, you're dripping on my desk.'

'And one other thing, Kris. If you are going to falsify your résumé, best to check you didn't send one in beforehand with completely different information.'

From her in-tray she plucked the original résumé I had sent to MTV when I first applied and she held up both for me to see. My hole cards were face up and both were jokers.

I stared at her in silence with my head jerking spasmodically and my mouth opening and closing, but no sound emerged. Which was a good thing, because nothing that had passed out of my mouth so far had advanced my case in any way whatsoever.

'Take this one,' she said, delicately handing me the original version, then crumpled the second into a ball, tossed it in the air and volleyed it towards the rubbish bin in the corner of her office with one of her big cowboy boots. The crumpled paper ball missed the bin and settled on the floor beside several other similar balls. 'It has a sportier slant.'

She gave me directions to Vince Freidman's office. As I turned to leave, she said something that I didn't catch.

'Sorry?' I said, leaning my head back into her office.

'I said, send Phil Collins my regards if you see him.'

The Engineering Edge

Bahrain 2022

IN 2022, Bahrain hosted the season opener for the second year in a row. On race day, under the floodlights, I found myself back on the grid with a microphone in my hand. Uli, thank the stars, was by my side with the camera, even though the parsimonious budget did not include a live RF feed. For the pre-race build-up, Juan would do the opening link from his phone (if the internet connection was good enough) and then switch to the LUCI app to commentate live with the other commentators back in the studio. Meanwhile, I would record pre-race interviews for our *GP1* show.[48]

Beside Lando Norris's McLaren, I spotted a tall, slim man wearing sunglasses with grey, swept-back hair and a salt and pepper moustache. He looked like the archetypal British Army brigadier. I recognised him from interviews on YouTube.

'I think that's Gordon Murray!' I said to Uli. A quick peek at Gordon's pass confirmed my suspicion. This was too good an opportunity to miss.

While Gordon's name might be less familiar to some F1 fans than those of race winners, without him many famous names would not be known at all. For all the attention paid to the swashbuckling and charismatic F1 drivers, the fact is that the real competition in Formula One is between the boffins: the car designers, engineers and mechanics who strive to build the fastest and most reliable car.

---

48 *GP1*, short for Grand Prix obviously, is the magazine programme we produce for South American F1 fans often showing race highlights, but also other interest pieces.

Gordon Murray is one of the most successful and innovative of them all. In the seventies and eighties he designed, or was associated with, many of the most successful Formula One cars built by Brabham and McLaren.

'Hi Gordon, have you got a moment?' I asked. He smiled broadly and nodded enthusiastically.

I asked him about his thoughts on the changes to the rules[49] introduced in 2022 to promote fairer racing. He seemed genuinely excited, saying he was looking forward to more competitive racing. I asked him what he missed most about his time with Brabham and McLaren.

'Formula One was more like a family back then, but now it's more commercial. The thing I remember most is being able to innovate. You could have an idea in the bath, get into work the next morning, make the bits and take a second and a half off the lap time. I used to love that.' He paused before adding, 'And Bernie did too.'

An improbable image of Bernie and Gordon sat together at opposite ends of a bathtub surrounded by rubber ducks and bubbles flitted across my mind. I'd bet Bernie got the end without the taps.

Perhaps Gordon's most famous innovation was the Brabham BT46B 'fan car'. In 1968 wings[50] were added to racing cars to enable faster cornering by improving the grip of the wheels on the track. But useful though they are for improving grip, wings also increase aerodynamic drag and reduce straight line speed.

But there is another way to create downforce. The so-called 'ground effect' works by creating an area of low pressure under the car which 'sucks' the car on to the track. In 1978 Gordon designed the Brabham BT46B which sported a large fan on the back of the

---

49 The Formula One Technical Regulations run to 178 pages covering every aspect of the car's design, starting with the requirement for four wheels (the 1976 Tyrrell P34 had six), car height and width, minimum mass; fuel, oil, coolant, transmission and electrical systems; suspension, safety features and much, much more. They also ban most 'driver assist' technologies such as anti-lock braking systems and traction control.

50 Wings (actually upside-down wings to generate downforce instead of lift) are now ubiquitous on the rear of racing cars and indeed on many 'go faster' road cars.

car which ran at up to 8,000 revs per minute. Brabham claimed it was there primarily to cool the engine. That it also evacuated air from under the car, increasing grip and enabling faster cornering speeds was, supposedly, incidental.

In 1978 at the Swedish Grand Prix at Anderstorp, Niki Lauda qualified the 'fan car' in pole position but concealed just how fast the car was by driving on a full tank of fuel. When the race was over there was an outcry from the other teams. Lotus-Ford team principal Colin Chapman said the car was illegal and the drivers complained that the fan was shooting dust and stones at them like some kind of baseball pitching machine, although Mario Andretti, the competing Lotus driver, permitted himself a little smile when recalling that allegation. As he said, when you are being blasted, you need to find a way to fight back. But, in fact, all they did see was dust, as Lauda won the race by 34 seconds.

Under pressure from Lotus and Tyrrell and after an intervention from the FIA, the Brabham team principal, one Bernie Ecclestone, whose first priority was always to keep the F1 show on the road generating cash, withdrew the BT46B from racing, much to Gordon's disgust. But the car still has the unique distinction of a 100 per cent record in Formula One racing.

The pursuit of that sort of engineering edge has always been, and will continue to be, at the heart of Formula One. FIA technical regulations change every year and sometimes even during the year, to keep up with technological innovation, respond to environmental concerns, improve safety or make for more competitive racing. If such rules did not exist, it is entertaining to imagine what grotesque menagerie of machinery would be brought out to race. For sure they would be super-fast but also, no doubt, highly dangerous for everyone involved. A Grand Prix would be more like a Robot Wars Gladiator Fight than the sleek spectacle it is today. Each new specification is assessed by the car designers and engineers and turned into a concept, a design and then a car that will, they hope, be fastest. Oh, and keep going for the whole race and the rest of the season.

Designers push the boundaries with innovations that deliver extra speed. So, it is scarcely surprising that, however detailed the rules are, interpretations differ and disputes arise. Rarely does a season pass without controversy. Teams and drivers watch their rivals' cars like hawks and will readily copy ideas or make accusations of foul play if they think they are losing out.

The ground effect remained the focus for innovation in Formula One car design in the late seventies and early eighties. Engineers discovered that they could generate downforce by shaping the underside of the car in such a way that the flow of air created an area of low pressure which had the magic effect of pressing the car down on its tyres. (Actually, to quote Toto Wolff years later, 'It's physics, not mystics.')

But to make it work, the car had to ride low and stay consistently close to the track, which meant that the suspension had to be hard-sprung, making the driver so uncomfortable that his performance was compromised. In 1981 Colin Chapman (who founded Lotus cars) introduced the Lotus 88 which got round the problem of the uncomfortable ride by building two chassis. The external one was shaped to create the ground effect and was stiffly sprung to hold the car tightly to the road. But the inner chassis, which housed the driver, was softly sprung to make the driver's ride tolerable. The design caused another uproar and although the car appeared fast in testing, it never raced.

In 1983 the FIA banned ground effect cars because of concerns over the faster cornering speeds, or rather, concerns about what would happen if the ground effect was compromised while a car was cornering at high speed. The rules were changed to require the underside of the cars to incorporate a one-centimetre flat wooden plank and a minimum height from the plank to the ground was defined. Wear on the plank was limited to one millimetre. Teams worked around that restriction as well, but that is another story.

The ground effect made its return in 2022. A problem with the aerodynamic design of Formula One cars beforehand was that they left turbulent or 'dirty' air behind them, which disrupted the downforce on the chasing car, making it hard to handle when attempting to pass a slower car, particularly when cornering. Given the much-improved safety measures now in place, the FIA decided to reintroduce ground effect cars to make racing more exciting. A defining story of 2022 was how Mercedes' new car design 'porpoised'[51] alarmingly, a fault it took most of the season to bring under control.

Back in 1982, Ferrari and Renault gained a legal advantage over their rivals by switching to turbocharged engines, using a turbine driven by the car's exhaust gases to force more air into the engine's combustion chamber. It gave them more power than rivals who were still using the older, normally aspirated Cosworth engines. Now, as you know, my knowledge of physics was summed up by the examiners as an F for fail, but I do vaguely remember another 'F', something about Newton's second law, $F=ma$, which says, for our purposes, that if your competitor's car generates more force from its engine and you don't want to be left far, far behind, your only option is to reduce the mass of yours.

But there's the problem. The rules clearly stated that the mass of the car had to be a minimum of 580kg and that it would be weighed both before and after the race. But the rules also said that cooling fluids could be replaced before the car was reweighed. So, the devious concept of the water-cooled brake was born, which was essentially a large water tank which sprayed water in the general direction of the brakes, not so much to cool them, as to shed weight during the race, cancelling out the advantage of the turbocharged cars. At the end of the race the water tank could legally be topped up again. A nice idea, debatably within the letter of the law, but certainly not its spirit.

After Nelson Piquet in a Brabham and Keke Rosberg in a Williams finished first and second in the Brazilian Grand Prix

---

51 'Porpoising', or more simply put, bouncing up and down, happened because cars were sucked so close to the track by the ground effect that the air flow underneath them stalled, removing the suction. The car then bounced up as the suspension decompressed, before kicking in again once the car was clear of the surface. It affected some cars more than others and Mercedes worst of all.

there was a protest and the stewards held the cars to be underweight and disqualified them. The loophole was abruptly closed.

Another example of innovative engineering genius occurred in the winter of 1996. McLaren chief engineer Steve Nichols was thinking about the perennial question of how to make the car go faster. If you wanted to get your car around a corner more quickly, he reasoned, how about braking on just one side of the car? In much the same way as a toboggan can be steered by grounding a foot, the effect in a racing car would be to reduce understeer[52] and so get round the corner faster.

This lightbulb moment became the 'brake-steer' (later and rather pejoratively called the 'fiddle-brake' by Ferrari technical director Ross Brawn), a second brake pedal in the car which allowed the driver to brake on just one side of the car. Mika Häkkinen tested the prototype, which was assembled with just £50-worth of spare parts available in the workshop. He was able to take a sensational half a second off his lap time at his first attempt.

And why was the brake-steer only implemented on one side of the car? Well, that was all they had to start with. Most Formula One races are on a clockwise circuit so more corners tend to be right-handers. But the pedal could be connected to either side and in practice the team chose which side to put the brake after analysing the track layout and deciding where they most needed reduced understeer.

It was midway through the 1997 season, after the Austrian Grand Prix, that my friend Darren Heath, an eagle-eyed *F1 Racing* magazine photographer, developed his photographs and noticed that the brakes were glowing when the McLaren cars were under acceleration in the corners. He began to suspect why and went to his editor Matt Bishop (who would later work with McLaren). They decided to get to the bottom of the mystery.

To back up his theory, Darren needed pictures from inside the cockpit of the McLarens, but that was no easy task as the cars were

---

52 The tendency of a car to keep going straight on when the front wheels turn.

usually closely supervised. But Darren realised that there was a time when they were left unattended; on the racetrack if a car was retired from a race. At the following Luxembourg Grand Prix, Matt was set up to watch the race on TV at home and tip Darren off on his mobile if a car was retired and give him its position on the track. As luck would have it, both McLarens did indeed retire from the race when in front, but the incidents happened during commercial breaks, so Matt was no help. But Darren located the cars anyway. He could not get a photograph of the inside of the cockpit of David Coulthard's car as the steering wheel was still in place so he couldn't fit his camera in. But Mika Häkkinen had removed his steering wheel and so Darren was able to take the photographs he needed to reveal the extra pedal. They were published in the November 1997 issue of *F1 Racing*, earning Darren a sensational scoop.

By 1997 McLaren had developed an improved version of the brake-steer allowing the driver to select the side he wanted to apply the brake by toggling a switch. But the cat was out of the bag and even though other teams were starting to introduce their own versions, the design was banned on the grounds it was four-wheel steering, which was not allowed. McLaren tried to argue it was a brake, not a steering device, but because they themselves had called it the brake-steer, they struggled to get their argument taken seriously!

Prime Time

Hong Kong 1992

I CLOSED Cheryl's door and winced with the humiliation. I had to pull myself together. Amazingly I was still in the game and now had 30 seconds before my interview with this other guy. Now, what was his name again? I had totally forgotten. Vick, was it? Vick Freid-something? Fried egg? Oh, bollocks. I couldn't possibly go back to ask Cheryl. I decided to look for his office and hope he would introduce himself.

Thankfully, the name of my next interviewer, 'Vince Freidman', was printed boldly on his office door below a red, white and blue 'Prime Sports' sticker. I could see he was talking on the telephone through the open blinds of the glass-fronted office, so I waited politely outside. When he noticed me, he waved me in. I opened the door, stepped in and gave it a good push to close it. It swung more freely than I expected and, fearing it would slam, I turned quickly to slow it down, but a mini basketball hoop, stuck on the back of the door, struck me painfully on the bridge of my nose. I fought the urge to cry out and sat down abruptly on a leather swivel chair in front of his desk. Fortunately, Vince was leaning back in his chair with his phone pressed to his ear, his eyes fixed on the ceiling.

He was a clean-cut, stocky man in his mid-30s with thick, straight, reddish-brown hair parted sharply to one side and with silver-rimmed glasses perched on his nose. He was squeezing a foam rubber American-football shaped stress ball in his right hand, but it was the absurdly large gold fraternity ring on the middle finger of his left hand that hypnotised me. It made his chunky wedding band look insignificant.

His office walls were covered with posters of the New York Knicks, signed by the basketball stars. Behind him, a black metal cabinet was stacked high with VHS, U-matic and Betacam tapes. Files spilled from the open drawers. On his desk was a muddle of trinkets and promotional sporting items all emblazoned with the 'Prime Sports' logo.

'Yeah George, I know that man,' he was saying in an educated New York accent. 'Thing is, we need the up-link open for the Formula One that's coming down at 22:00 on Sunday. Phil needs two crews for the Chinese soccer and I want John doing an opening link for the motorbikes on-site in Shenzhen. If Phil's gonna be live with the soccer at 18:00 from studio one, let's get dubbing to record John's feed before we start live from Shenzhen.'

He may as well have been speaking Mandarin for all I understood, but I instantly loved the sound of this patois. Vince Freidman was clearly the man that made things happen at Prime Sports. When he finished, he hung up the phone with a bang and gave me the kind of handshake you'd expect from someone in Sports.

'I've forgotten your name,' he said while jotting down his 'to-do' list on a Prime Sports notepad.

'Kris Henley,' I told him. 'With a K.'

'Right, Kris, nice to meet you, I'm ...'

'Vincent Freidman,' I told him proudly. Things were looking up. Even my memory was improving.

'No, it's Vince. Only my mother calls me Vincent and only when she's pissed.'

'Oh, does she like a tipple?' I said fatuously.

'What d'you mean?' he snarled in that way only New Yorkers can.

'Er, you said "when she was pissed."'

He barked a laugh. 'Not pissed drunk, man, pissed mad. Believe me, my mother doesn't need drink to get nasty.' Unbelievable. Another hole blown in my foot. I really needed to learn to shut my mouth. But that resolution lasted two seconds and I opened it anyway to apologise. Luckily, he cut me off.

'So, Kris, as you can see, we are snowed under here right now.' He gestured towards the cabinet behind him. This was a fabulous development. He was talking rather than asking me questions.

'A lot of people are away right now and there's a bunch of stuff to be done. What I need is for you to get me out of a jam. My boss is telling me that we need a marketing video and we need it yesterday. It's a pain in my ass and he couldn't have asked for it at a worse moment. There's nobody free to do it, so that's where you come in. You wanna take it on?'

He paused and looked at me. I had no idea what he was asking me to do, but I nodded thoughtfully and folded my résumé in half. I certainly didn't want that nasty piece of paper resurfacing.

'Great, that's a big weight off. Look, I don't know what you're used to billing, but the daily rate we pay for freelance producers is $150 a day, US. That's not negotiable.' I made a second fold in the dangerous piece of A4 and slid it deep into the darkest depths of my pocket. I swallowed.

'That sounds, um, perfectly fine,' I mumbled. $150 a day! It took a month to earn that at the bar.

'Let's see,' he went on. 'You'll need a week to log tapes, a few days to write the script, maybe four edit sessions, audio, graphics. We're talking 12 or 13 days here, three weeks tops.' My jaw fell open, which he must have taken as negotiation. 'Okay, okay, maybe that's pushing it, we'll see how things go.' I began doing the maths. Although my mind was racing, I continued to nod nonchalantly. For the money he was offering, I would have taken the job of bedpan runner on a dysentery ward.

'Look Kris, I have a million things to do, so I'm going to hook you up with my colleague; he will bring you up to speed with what we need, okay?' I nodded again. 'His name is Bill Browning, he's another Aussie and has just started here too, so you should get on great.'

Proud Brit though I am, my new career in Prime Sports was going far too well to start arguing about my nationality. I was going to collect over $2,000! I felt giddy as Vince dialled Bill Browning's internal number. After a short conversation, he put down the phone and asked if I was free the following day. I furrowed my eyebrows as I pretended to visualise a busy schedule.

'No worries,' I said, attempting an Australian accent. 'I can move some stuff around and start tomorrow.' As the sentence progressed, I drifted back to my own voice, but Vince didn't seem to notice.

'I like that attitude, good stuff, mate.' He also attempted to say the word 'mate' in an Australian accent. But for once I managed to hold my tongue and not tell him that he sounded more like a Jamaican than an Aussie.

'Bill is editing right now, so if you come in at 10am tomorrow, he can explain the nuts and bolts of the project and book the edit time you'll need. You'll have to log[53] a lot of tapes, so you'd better get started tomorrow, sound good?' I nodded. 'Great, thanks, appreciate it,' he concluded.

As I left Vince's office, he was back on the telephone already issuing instructions for other projects. It occurred to me that I had barely spoken but got the job. Keeping one's mouth shut seemed to be the secret to getting ahead at Star TV. I really must remember that.

Before I left the building, I went back to Cheryl Coleman's office to thank her for the opportunity. I knocked on her door.

'Come in,' she shouted, and I popped my head inside her office.

'Hi, Cheryl,' I said as she looked up from her computer. 'Sorry to interrupt, I just wanted to say thank you for, well, talking to Vince like that.' She was looking at me as if she had never seen me before. 'You know,' I continued, 'for what you did. It was really … well, kind of you.'

'Thank Danny McGill,' she said, looking back at her computer. 'I owed him a big favour but now, believe me, we're even.'

'Oh, I will, definitely. Okay then, thanks, goodbye.' I backed out of her office bowing as I went. I had taken 20 seconds to forget about keeping my mouth shut.

---

53 The process of recording where on a videotape the required material is.

It made some sort of sense. Danny was honourable enough to arrange the meeting with Cheryl to make up for no-showing at Le Jardin. As a favour to Danny, Cheryl agreed to see me, but when she realised I was an inexperienced fraud, palmed me off on to Vince, who she knew was so snowed under with work he wasn't choosy who he hired.

But I was elated. The great iron padlock to the gates of Star Television had finally clunked open. Vince was my Willy Wonka and I was a hungry Charlie Bucket, smelling of tequila and cabbage, but holding the golden ticket.

I would be working in television after all!

Charlie and Walter

Abu Dhabi 2019

I WAS breathing heavily as I rounded turn seven on my first lap of the Yas Marina circuit. Sadly, I was not achieving my ambition in the cockpit of a Formula One car. My mode of transport was a racing bike and I was pedalling as fast as I could.

The bittersweet occasion was the 2019 Charlie Whiting Memorial Bike Ride to raise funds for the Grand Prix Trust. Teams of five riders entered, each completing two laps of the circuit in a relay. My Star-Fox team consisted of Fox's Colombian co-presenter Diego Mejia, two members of the Spanish channel Movistar and my friend Chris Medland, who was appearing on *Drive to Survive* at the time. He kindly stepped in as we were one short. I went off on the third leg and we looked set fair for a respectable finish, providing I didn't lose a handful of positions.

Another rider, who I recognised as one of the Williams mechanics, caught me up and then overtook, winking as he went by. My aching quads wanted to let him go, but I remembered something from watching the Tour de France. If I 'drafted' in his slipstream, perhaps I could save myself some energy, which sounded like a most attractive idea as I was running out fast. I used my final reserves to catch up and once I had closed the gap, I immediately felt the difference. I tucked in behind and found I could keep up with much less effort.

It was my second bike race around the 5.3km circuit. The previous year, 19 teams had turned up for the event, but when it was held in Charlie Whiting's memory, 43 participated.

Charlie was one of those people who somehow managed to command universal respect even when working in positions that would normally attract only controversy and criticism. Born in Sevenoaks, close to Brands Hatch, he saw his first Grand Prix in 1964 when, just 12 years old, he climbed over the racetrack fence. Later he earned qualifications in mechanical engineering and worked on rally cars before joining Bernie Ecclestone's Brabham team. He worked there for ten years and was the chief mechanic when Nelson Piquet won the Drivers' World Championship in 1981 and 1983.

He then became technical director and safety delegate of the FIA, responsible for promoting safety improvements. He introduced the HANS[54] device and the safety halo which had been credited with saving Charles Leclerc, Romain Grosjean and Lewis Hamilton from serious injury or death. As if that wasn't enough to keep him busy, he also took on the roles of permanent starter, head of the F1 technical department and the crucial role of race director.

With the benefit of the draft from my fellow cyclist, I completed the first lap with just enough energy to wave cheerily to my four team-mates as they clapped their encouragement. But just in case my Williams buddy and I had any illusions about how fast we were going, the race leaders tore up from nowhere to lap us as we headed into the circuit's first corner for the second time. I recognised my Italian friend Enrico Scudo of the TV Tigers team (Sky UK and Italy) who I knew as a sweet, funny, unassuming guy who worked as a member of the technical crew. But I could now see that he was also a serious athlete, powering along ahead of competitors from the Red Bulls and a local outfit, Team Yas. The three riders disappeared around turn one. By the time we turned the corner they were 20 metres ahead.

I was thinking about Charlie as I pedalled along, but I was distracted from my thoughts as the Williams mechanic looked back at me with an irritable expression.

---

54 Head and Neck Support.

'Oi, I think it's your turn now, mate!' he said, panting and waving me in front. Aah, I had forgotten about the etiquette of cycle racing. It was time for me to take my turn at the front of our two-man peloton.

'Sure,' I said, standing up on the pedals and pumping my thighs as rhythmically and smoothly as I could. But I was now back in the wind and instead of gliding effortlessly along, I felt like I was climbing a steep gravel-strewn hill.

After no more than a kilometre I was exhausted. My legs ached and my breathing was ragged. It was clear that I was not leadership material. The Williams mechanic passed me again, staring me down and shaking his head in disapproval. I considered letting him go off on his own this time, but I had tasted the good life in the slipstream, so tucked right back into the cosy pocket of air and was sucked along like a migrating turtle in the ocean's underwater current. I breathed deeply to recuperate from my kilometre of hard graft.

Now where was I? Oh, Charlie Whiting. When he died suddenly in 2019 from a pulmonary embolism the tributes poured in. Toto Wolff, Mercedes' team principal, described him as the 'pillar of our Formula One community' and Mattia Binotto, the Ferrari boss, called him a 'tireless and enlightened motorsport expert [who] helped make F1 safer and better'. Yes, Charlie was a leader and a go-getter and definitely not the sort of person to sit in someone else's slipstream.

At last I saw the finish line. I had started to get my breath back and it crossed my mind that I might be able to take on the Williams mechanic down the final straight. But that really didn't seem fair, given he had done all the work. So, I followed him into the changeover lane before handing over the GPS tracking device to Chris Medland. I thanked the Williams mechanic for the draft he had unwillingly given me and sat down to recover from my exertions.

As I did so , I recalled the time I managed to annoy Charlie at the Hockenheim Grand Prix in 2018. I had interviewed him from time to time in the paddock about this or that controversy and always found him considerate and helpful, giving me his full attention and explaining decisions made by the FIA clearly and concisely. But our paths had never crossed away from the interview pen.

It was July and we were closing in on the summer break with only the German and Hungarian GPs to complete. But that left a gap in the TV schedule, so I was on the lookout for additional features to fill our magazine show.

We thought it would be interesting for our viewers to hear from Walter Koster, the veteran German F1 reporter, who had become something of a sensation among F1 fans when he asked what became known as 'the longest question in Formula One history' at a press conference in Abu Dhabi in 2014. I was in the room at the time. Six drivers were on the panel seated in two rows of three. In front on the left was Sebastian Vettel. In the middle beside him was Fernando Alonso, with Jenson Button on the right. Behind them were Lewis Hamilton, Nico Hülkenberg and Nico Rosberg.

English is, by a substantial margin, Walter's second language, so he speaks haltingly with a strong German accent.

'Gentlemen, a short view, back to the past,' Walter began, reading from his notepad. 'Thirty years ago, Niki Lauda told us, "Take a monkey, place him into the cockpit and he is able to drive the car."'

The drivers smiled and exchanged glances. Walter continued:

'Thirty years later, Sebastian told us, "I had to start my car like a computer, it's very complicated." And Nico Rosberg said … err … he pressed during the race, I don't remember what race, he pressed the wrong button on the wheel.'

By now the drivers were smiling broadly but Walter soldiered on.

'Question for you two both. Is Formula One driving today too complicated with 20 and more buttons on the wheel?'

By now Sebastian and Fernando were failing to suppress their laughter and Lewis decided this was a good time to look at the floor to cover his smiling face behind his cap visor. But Walter had more.

'Are you too much under effort, under pressure?'

For good measure, Walter then added:

'What are your wishes for the future concerning the technical program, erm, during the race? Less buttons … more?'

Finally, he concluded:

'Or less and more communication with your engineers?' Walter looked up and waited expectantly.

'Can I ask you who that question is to?' the host James Allen enquired.

Sebastian Vettel intervened.

'He said, it's to Nico and myself. You didn't listen …'

And now he had the attention of the room Sebastian paused, before saying, with immaculate comedic timing:

'Can you repeat the question?'

The room exploded into laughter and within days the video had gone viral, immortalising Walter for Formula One fans.

Four years later at Hockenheim I was in the media centre listening to the drivers' press conference that was being transmitted on the monitors. I looked up when I heard Walter's distinctive voice to see Sebastian Vettel grinning on the screens above me. Walter had launched into another colossal question. I stopped what I was doing to listen, already smiling in expectation.

'During the last race at Silverstone, your team-mate Kimi asked for more power, but his engineer refused his wish.' After a pause Walter went on.

'Kimi answered indignantly, "It's not permitted for me to think for myself?" Question. To what extent can you make your own decisions on track and how much is decided remotely on your behalf by the team?'

Walter's tone then became more challenging as he continued:

'I can tell you all, that I know a lot of people who don't watch F1 because the technology is too complicated and they feel the races are manipulated. Formula One seems more removed from the fans than before. Do you agree with this?'

And just in case Sebastian had lost the plot, Walter added:

'And please remember my first question.'

Although Walter's delivery is always idiosyncratic, there was no doubt it was a question from the heart. Sebastian considered making a similar joke to the one four years earlier, but thought better of it and instead gave a respectful and thoughtful reply.

On Walter's return to the media centre, I congratulated him on his question and we shook hands. Then I asked if I could interview him for our magazine show. Once Walter understood what I wanted, he agreed with a vigorous nod of the head.

'So, when for conversational exchange?' he asked, slightly puzzlingly.

'The interview? Well, no time like the present, Walter,' I said, patting him on the shoulder.

He looked at me dumbfounded for several seconds, so I rephrased.

'How about now?' I said.

'Today?'

'Yes, are you busy?'

'At precise moment?'

'Well, I need to find our cameraman. That sometimes takes a while.'

'Repeat please?'

'Are you free now?'

'Minimum preparation time allocation,' he laughed.

'You'll be fine! I'll edit out any mistakes.'

'Wonderful undertakings,' Walter said enthusiastically. This utterance perplexed me briefly, but I decided to assume it meant 'yes'.

I wasn't worried about Walter's occasional lapses from perfect English. I knew his endearing personality would be more than interesting enough for our viewers and any language issues could be smoothed over, as he would have subtitles in Spanish.

I thought the best place to do the interview would be in the press conference room where Walter asks his epic questions. As there had been no track activity for over an hour I was pretty sure it wasn't being used, so Walter, Dario the cameraman and I went up in the lift to the second floor of the Baden-Württemberg Centre.

The door to the press conference room was closed so, not having permission to use the area, I opened it with trepidation. Two cameras were set up facing the long desk and sponsor board where drivers and team principals sit to be interviewed. But there was no one there. Dario set up the tripod and camera.

I asked Walter to sit down, plugged in the microphone and put a spare seat beside the camera to sit on. Dario gave me the thumbs-up and I leaned in with the microphone and asked my standard opening question for features on 'Personalities of the Paddock'.

'For our viewers who don't know you, what is your name, where are you from and what do you do in Formula One?'

'My name is Walter Koster, coming from Germany and now I am retired, but I'm a freelance and, um, it's very great pleasure for me to work for Formula One.'

We were off.

Despite the slight language barrier and occasionally meandering responses, Walter was engaging and entertaining. He told me that his first Grand Prix was in Monaco in 1971 when Roman Polanski shadowed and filmed Jackie Stewart to make the documentary film *Weekend of a Champion*. It featured appearances by Juan Manuel Fangio, Graham Hill, Helen Stewart, Ken Tyrrell and Graham Hill as well as cameos by full-on celebrities including Grace Kelly, Joan Collins and Ringo Starr. And, of course, Jackie gave Roman the conclusion he needed by winning the race.

'Since then,' Walter confided with a wide smile, 'I have been a "prisoner" of Formula One.'

Walter talked about how the sport had changed. The questions he asked in Abu Dhabi and Hockenheim both made a serious point. Walter was worried about the direction of Formula One. He spoke earnestly when he remembered drivers like James Hunt, Jackie Stewart, Emerson Fittipaldi, Mario Andretti, Alan Jones, Carlos Reutemann, Nelson Piquet and Nigel Mansell, describing these men as 'oak trees'.

He remembered partying in the motorhome of his favourite driver, James Hunt, after his victory in Zandvoort in 1976 when the

Englishman celebrated both his win and his 29th birthday partying with friends and the press.

'If I compare this time, with the guys today,' he said, 'young drivers, they are unapproachable. You must implore for an interview. They are screened by their press officers. No fun to meet these young guys,' he concluded.

I was enjoying my chat with Walter, but before we finished, I wanted to ask him about the question that made his name.

'So, Walter, you became an internet sensation when you asked Sebastian Vettel a question in 2014. What do you remember about it?'

It was at this moment Charlie Whiting came into the press conference room, followed by a group of important-looking people obviously waiting to use the area for an FIA meeting. But Walter was pondering and looking up at the ceiling. As he had his back to the door, he had no idea anyone was behind him. Also, perhaps because Walter does not hang out much online, the incident that made him famous was not that fresh in his mind. So, he had to rack his brains to recall. There was a long pause. I started to sweat.

'Aah, the longest question, I don't …' Walter paused again. I could see Charlie trying to catch my eye. Then Walter remembered. 'Oh yes, I think it was in Abu Dhabi. What I ask him? Um, ah, I think it was the question about how many, ah, ah.' But he couldn't find the word.

I looked over at Charlie, who looked back calmly, but his expression made it clear he needed the room immediately and, incidentally, why the hell was I using the room without permission?

'Buttons!' Walter finally said with great satisfaction.

Charlie appeared impatient. I nodded at Walter, but he was far from done.

'How do you say?' He drew circles in the air. 'The *Lenkrad*?' Despite knowing very little German I did know the word he was looking for was 'steering wheel' but I was trying to communicate to Charlie that we were almost done. Walter gave up trying to remember the translation for *Lenkrad*.

'... he had to push many buttons during the race.'

Charlie's eyes were now wide open with reproach and he was snapping his index and middle finger like a pair of scissors to indicate he wanted me to cut immediately. But I couldn't interrupt Walter now, as the interview was nearly over and setting up elsewhere would mean a different background. It couldn't be too long, surely, before Walter concluded.

'I think he [Sebastian] did a joke,' Walter said after a long pause. There was something so innocent and endearing about this man who had to struggle to remember the incident that made him famous. Then it came to him.

'*Ja*, he asked "can I repeat the question". But [really] he remembered.' At this point Walter fell about laughing and I couldn't help but join in.

'The colleagues laughed,' he said. They certainly did.

'Thank you so much, Walter,' I said. 'Thank you for your time.' I then jumped up and went towards Charlie, fully expecting a reprimand and to have my F1 pass confiscated.

'I'm really sorry Charlie,' I said. 'He was on a roll and I didn't have the heart to interrupt.'

But Charlie just smiled and said, confidingly, 'Well, he does go on a bit, doesn't he?'

Dario grabbed the camera and tripod, put back my chair and we left Charlie to run his meeting in his usual calm and collected way.

Black-Flagged

Hong Kong 1992–93

EVEN IF I say so myself, the Prime Sports marketing tape was a resounding success. Both Vince and his boss were very happy with the result. I even completed the task a day earlier than Vince first calculated. This meant a little less money, but I didn't care. The praise and recognition were worth far more to me.

Of course, I needed a tremendous amount of help to get up and running and to see the project through. But Bill Browning was an experienced graphic designer and producer and a man of infinite patience. He was also new to the channel and wanted a successful project under his belt, so he carefully explained the task, sorted out access passes to key areas of the building, walked me through the channel's procedures and told me who I needed to get to know.

Today, some 85 per cent of the world's population own a smartphone,[55] usually equipped with a high-definition video camera and sound recording. An internet connection provides access to a basic edit suite, hundreds of millions of graphics, video clips and all the music in the world, subject to copyright restrictions. You can send off edited video files in seconds. With a laptop and a little training, you can cut a television programme while sitting on a camel in the Sahara Desert.

None of this amazing digital technology, however, existed when I started out and making programmes was a lot more time-consuming, complicated, problematic and costly. Filming was done

---

55 Source: Oberlo.co.uk

with bulky cameras and so camera operators and sound assistants were an essential part of the crew. Post-production was much trickier, requiring precise working methods, more people and a lot more technical skills than are needed today.

Videotape was used to record and store material so, to produce a programme using historical footage, you needed access to a tape library. The precious video tapes were watched over by a tape librarian. Armed with a list of tapes that Bill said might be a good place to start, I set off. At the library two people were waiting ahead of me, so I joined the queue and consulted my list.

Bill did mention something about the tape librarian not being all that friendly but, as I said, charm is something I pride myself on and I was confident I could make a friend.

'Hello!' I said to the unusually tall woman behind a counter, trying to convey my delight at meeting her. 'I'm Kris, a producer for Prime Sports. I need a few tapes.'

'I don't know you,' she said icily in an Antipodean accent. Perhaps Bill was right. She did seem a touch unfriendly but, undaunted, I gave her what I imagined was a winning smile.

'Ah, well, that's because I'm new and I haven't been here before.' I gave her another blast of my irresistible smile, but if it was indeed winning her over, it was not obvious.

'How do I know you didn't just walk in off the street? I can't just hand tapes out to any Tom, Dick or Harry, you know.' My smile faltered, ever so slightly.

'I'm working for Bill Browning.'

She looked at me sceptically, put on a pair of absurd winged glasses and peered at a list pinned on the wall. Then she picked up a telephone and punched four buttons. I heard her say Bill's name. She stared at me with the receiver glued to her ear, looking me up and down. Bill must have cleared me as a bona fide employee, but it changed her attitude not at all.

'So, what tapes do you want?' she asked. My smiles didn't seem to be thawing her, so I thought I would try a little small talk.

'What part of Australia are you from?' I asked.

'I'm not from any part of Australia,' she said, aggressively, elaborating no further.

'Oh, I'm sorry, you're a Kiwi. Well, that's a relief, ha ha! What part?' I battled on.

'Invercargill if you must know.' Maybe that explained her attitude. I had hitch-hiked to Invercargill a few years before, expecting to spend a few nights there. But it was so wet, cold and miserable we left the following morning.

'Invercargill!' I exclaimed, faking delight. 'I've been there! I spent a couple of days there in a wonderful bed and breakfast.'

'Bully for you,' she said.

I decided to stop wasting my charm on her. She was uncharmable, by me at any rate. I handed her the notepad that Bill Browning had given me. She glanced down at it, then thrust it back at me as if I had handed her a tray of tarantulas.

'Where's the tape numbers?' she asked, with an expression of extreme incredulity, as one might expect from a sniffy maître d' in a Michelin-starred restaurant had I ordered a deep-fried Mars bar and mushy peas.

'There's about 60, I'd say.'

'I can see how many there are. Not how many tapes, the tape numbers. No tape numbers, no tapes. I'm far too busy to look up your tape numbers for you.' And just to show how busy she was, she sat down and took a long drink from her oversized Garfield mug.

'Sorry, where would I find these numbers?' I asked. She huffed. 'On the computer system.' She puffed. 'Where else would they be?' Then she blew my house down.

'Didn't Bill tell you anything about the procedure? You new *producers*,' she sneered the word to make it clear she considered me no such thing. Which in my case was perfectly fair, but I don't see how she can possibly have known that.

'Where I come from you had to go to college for three years and work your way up before they would call you even an assistant producer. You come to Hong Kong, walk in off the street and think you own the place.'

This all seemed surpassingly unfair, but by this time there were several people behind me waiting for assistance, all of whom were obviously more important than me. Their body language seemed to indicate that they were inclined to side with the librarian and not the new kid, so I decided to go and find Bill Browning.

'Aah, yes, the new procedure,' Bill said as he began searching for the tape numbers on his computer. 'Rosie is really improving the efficiency of that library,' he observed, deadpan, but commented no further.

When I returned, there was no queue and the 'efficient' Rosie was again sat down, now scoffing a jam doughnut and again sipping from her refilled Garfield mug. She let me stand at the counter for some time before reluctantly getting to her feet with another huff as crumbs cascaded all around her. She wiped her mouth with the back of her hand as I gave her the list, now complete with tape numbers.

'Come back in an hour. I'm on my afternoon break,' she said, resuming her seat.

I went to the reception area and watched the second half of a Chinese football match on the TV monitor until it was time to go back to the library.

'These are the tapes that are here, but most of them are signed out,' she said with vast satisfaction that she could not be more helpful.

'Signed out? Signed out to whom?' I asked.

'Dah! Look in that log and it will tell you.' She pointed at an A4-sized book on the counter.

I'm afraid to say I was beginning to dislike this woman, but I consulted the log and left with the half a dozen 60-minute tapes and the names of the people who had checked the rest out. I couldn't face chasing them down that day so decided to log the tapes I had, noting the timecodes[56] of any clips I might need.

Five of the six viewing rooms in Prime Sports were occupied, so I slipped into the last available booth and closed the door behind me. The door opened several times while I was there and each time

---

56 The position of the required clip on the tape.

an irritable person, laden down with tapes, would groan and sigh loudly, before slamming the door shut.

However, after this most unpromising start, everyone else at Prime Sports was much more helpful. I met the people in the graphics and voice-over departments and then the two most essential people, Mancunian Jim Jackson from the promos department and Fionn Murphy from Dublin, the editor assigned to my marketing tape.

The normal process for such an assignment is to edit the images, mix the ambient sound, apply the graphics and then add a voice-over at the end. But I didn't know that.

I knew more about writing than I did about television production. I had written a few speculative film scripts while living in Hollywood and my first shot at a novel on my travels, so it seemed natural to write the script first. I took my first draft, typed up on Dean's Olivetti, to Vince for his approval. He was slightly confused by my backwards approach, but I caught him at a good moment and he gave the script a thorough going over, adding lines and crossing out text until it was to his liking.

The purpose of the marketing tape was to engage potential sponsors. It was split into eight sections for each of the main sports. Vince particularly liked my idea to finish each segment with an audio line that matched an exciting shot. For example:

'...our Formula One coverage on Prime Sports leaves the competition miles behind!' INSERT: AYRTON SENNA IN A MCLAREN SPEEDING INTO THE DISTANCE, CELEBRATING HIS 1991 WORLD CHAMPIONSHIP.

'...and we deliver the knockout punch with our boxing analysis.' INSERT: MIKE TYSON DELIVERING A COMBINATION AND THE KNOCKOUT PUNCH.

'...when it comes to basketball, we fly high above the competition.' INSERT: MICHAEL JORDAN SLAM-DUNKING.

Once the script was finalised and the channel's regular voice-over artists had recorded it, all I needed to find was the right action shots. I arranged to meet Jim Jackson in the promos department on the second floor. As I approached his cubicle, I saw it was covered in photos and memorabilia of the Manchester United football team.

I think I mentioned that I am not famous for my excellent memory, which may or may not be related to my fondness for a tipple and the odd 'Moroccan Woodbine'. But there was one thing I did retain from my brief spell as a football fan and that was the 1977 Manchester United FA Cup-winning side. So I looked Jim in the eye and recited:

'Stepney, Nicholl, Albiston, McIlroy, Brian Greenhoff, Buchan, Coppell, Jimmy Greenhoff, Pearson, Macari, Hill.' I then introduced myself.

This impressed Jim no end and thereafter he couldn't do enough for me. After a few days he handed over a folder organised into sections for each sport, with dozens of A5 pages, each listing tape numbers and timecodes, with a detailed description of the action that each clip showed. The best shots were highlighted in yellow and told me exactly which of the many signed-out tapes I needed to track down, saving me weeks of work trawling through them all. 'Jacko', as he liked to be called, told me the file had taken two years to compile. But it came with a warning.

'Guard this with your fookin' life! Only 'cos you're a Man U supporter would I even dream of lending yer this. It's the fookin' holy grail. No photocopies a'loowd, that's non-negotiable and get the file back to me by end of the week or I'm comin' down to production to kick some aaarse!'

Now all I had to do was note down the tape numbers on the top of the log sheets and track them down. Then I was ready to enter an edit suite for the first time.

In 1992 the edit suites in Star TV used Betacam or Beta SP videocassette formats with monitors mounted on the wall to view the output. Audio mixers, designed to blend ambient sound, voice-overs and music to the correct levels were set up on the main desktop, close to the edit control keyboard. Specialised generators for adding graphics were positioned between the editor and producer and were used by both.

The editor sat on a chair on wheels and shuttled impressively around the suite, from the edit-control keyboard to the graphics generator to the audio mixing desk, like an octopus propelling itself between its three favourite rocks. The producer would then tell the editor to enter the start and stop points on the edit control keyboard and the required clip was then recorded on to the master tape, adding graphics where needed and mixing the sound.

My editor, Fionn, took the project from there. When the video images were edited in, Fionn added visual transitions and graphics that I left entirely to him. The finished product looked fantastic. It was the easiest money I have ever earned. Best of all, there was no further discussion of my previous experience in TV and the slam-dunk video led to eight more months of work at Star TV, one task leading to another.

First, I worked on repackaging events that were shown live into one-hour or 30-minute shows with commercial breaks. Football, rugby, cricket, basketball, motor racing, golf, you name it, I repackaged it. Then I produced the *Best Of...* series, a compilation of the year's highlights from each of the sports we covered, scheduled to run when everyone was away on Christmas holidays.

I spent the rest of 1992 and the first months of 1993 in edit suites in Hung Hom on night shifts in a dark viewing room watching tapes of sporting events and logging the key moments before taking them to an editor who cut them down into master tapes.

I was working as a contractor, rather than a full member of the Prime Sports team. The regulars were mostly expats from the UK, Ireland, the US, India, Australia or New Zealand, but they worked in daylight hours, so our paths rarely crossed. But the money was great and the tasks didn't require much more than common sense and a general love of sports.

I was very happy with the way things were going but then, out of the blue, I was fired.

Racing's In My Blood

Abu Dhabi 2021, before the race

ON THURSDAY before the 2021 Abu Dhabi season finale, selected members of the press were invited to a karting event where, as well as a qualifying session and a race, there was a track demonstration by test driver Daniil Kvyat, Esteban Ocon and double world champion, Fernando Alonso. They showed everyone how karting should be done as they raced around in circuit karts, outmanoeuvring one another at alarming speed.

Then, Alonso jumped into his own 125cc FA go-kart, developed with Italian Dino Chiesa, the most respected name in the world of karting, and showed us his extraordinary driving expertise, performing high speed 'donuts' with both his hands and one leg in the air, brushing the barriers as he drove at breakneck speed around the track and even throwing in a 'wheelie', something I would have thought impossible in the two-metre-long go-kart with its tiny wheels and engine smaller than a motorised lawnmower.

Then we got to the go-kart race for the press. I'm not saying the racing was more keenly anticipated than the 'greatest ever showdown this sport has ever seen', scheduled for Sunday, but it was a close-run thing. There is no shortage of wannabe drivers among the press and many have spent a fair amount of time in karts and more powerful racing cars. The event provided them with the opportunity to show off their skills and secure bragging rights for weeks to come.

As you can imagine, there was much excited strutting and posturing as the racers put on their driving overalls, fitted their crash helmets, revved up their karts and went out for their qualifying laps.

I decided to play it cool. Frankly, I was feeling confident. After all, my previous karting race against old friends a decade earlier had been a resounding success and I had finished on top of the podium. Without any doubt, I was a natural racer.

I also had a job to do, filming Juan taking part in the event for our *GP1* show. But I knew that as soon as I pulled on my racing lid, I was going to surprise a few people. Most of all I was looking forward to beating Juan.

I have spent plenty of time listening to experts explaining how to drive fast, so I know a little about how one should follow the racing line, when to brake, how to control speed and correct over- or under-steer. During the qualifying lap, however, I did feel a bit rusty and my performance wasn't quite what I hoped. I struggled to maintain the fluency I recalled from my earlier racing and finished the session near the back of the grid. But no matter, I told myself. Qualifying was one thing, but the race was something else. Towards the end of my qualifying lap, I had felt the old magic returning and motorsport has a rich history of talented drivers fighting their way up through the field.

I roared away cleanly when the green light went on, powered by my little motor and a surge of adrenaline. I had heard countless times how the best drivers brake late, but so far that approach had just seemed to send my kart sliding sideways. So, should I brake late to squeeze out that extra split second, or brake early, hoping to get the power on sooner and accelerate away faster? I was considering the relative merits of these approaches as a bunch of us entered the first corner when I rammed, hard, into the back of the FIA business development director, Tom Wood.

Tom's head jolted backwards and his kart cannoned forwards, precipitating a multiple shunt. He told me later that he was also sideswiped by two other karts, adding side whiplash to the back whiplash my contact had caused him. But as yellow flags waved all around the circuit, I found I had benefitted nicely. By sheer luck, I had slowed down just enough to take the corner at the perfect speed and avoid the mayhem. Chortling to myself that the stewards would surely see my incompetence as 'a racing incident', I found I was even closing down the pack in front of me.

Yes, yes, yes! In that moment, I was transported. I heard in my ears the calm, soothing voice of Ayrton Senna as he said, 'Racing, competing, it's in my blood. It's part of me, it's part of my life …' The kart's engine began to hum and it was as if my eyes had opened from a lifetime of slumber. My senses were heightened. Everything was clear. I had found it! My natural gift! I could now see that I had been endowed by fate, by some higher power, by some auspicious combination of my genes, with a supreme and matchless talent. Whoever could have guessed it? Who could predict that, having worked in motorsport for so long, I should only now discover that I had a God-given genius to race motor cars?

I was a resplendent butterfly emerging from its cocoon and soaring away from its caterpillar life. I was in flight! This I could do better than anyone else. This was the elusive thing I had been searching for since childhood, where I was just luckier, better, more skilful and faster than the rest! I was elated. Where could I find the backing to pursue my motorsport career all the way to the podium? I already spoke two languages, sort of. I still had a few of my film-star looks (in my mother's eyes, that is) and I could always cover my bald spot with a cap, balaclava or helmet. After this performance, surely, wealthy sponsors would be queuing up.

I was in the zone, in Ayrton Senna's tunnel. Like Michael Schumacher, I became one with the car.

The fantastical reverie lasted a good ten seconds before I noticed that I was no longer closing on the cars in front and, as I took the hairpin, I saw, with astonishment, that the innocent victims of the pile-up I had caused were catching up fast. The first driver shot past me and, possibly identifying me as the cause of the shunt, showed me, I'm sorry to say, his middle finger as he pulled away. The next driver was also able to spare one of his hands from the steering wheel to shake his fist while out-braking me as I slid sideways. I pushed harder, hurtling into the corners with wild abandon but losing ground at every turn. Soon, even Tom Wood, who must have been untangling himself for a good 30 seconds, effortlessly passed me by. Luckily, he was too busy rolling his painful neck to give me another well-deserved gesture.

Now I was dead last and was being lapped by the front-runners. To complete my humiliation, I span off completely and wedged my front bumper under a metal barrier from where I ignominiously watched my crash victims pass me for the second time. After being helped back on to the track by a marshal, I took the chequered flag in last place, two laps down. A little dejected, I got out of the kart and went to find my camera to resume the other task I didn't excel at.

In 2022, rather to my surprise considering the carnage I caused the previous year, I was invited back. This year I would not be filming, so I had high hopes of an improvement. On my way to the go-kart track, I decided to pop into the Mercedes year-end party. I was running a little late but thought I would treat myself to some nourishment and a quick drink to calm my nerves. As I was striding up the stairs, I saw George Russell and said 'hello' as I passed. On the top terrace I dispatched a few canapés and washed them down with a beer while checking out the wonderful view of night-time Abu Dhabi. In less than ten minutes I was bounding back down the stairs when I ran into George again.

'That was quick, where are you going in such a hurry?' he asked.

'To the go-kart track for a press event,' I told him proudly.

'There's a go-kart track here at the circuit? I didn't know.'

'Yeah, at the entrance.' I guess you don't register the little kart tracks when you are here to race on the big one. 'Oh, by the way, George, fantastic victories in Brazil!' I hadn't spoken to him since his incredible double-win in both the sprint race and the Grand Prix.

'Thank you,' he said, well-mannered as always.

I left the Mercedes hospitality suite and started jogging back up the paddock to pick up my stuff, reflecting on what a decent, sincere gentleman George is. He looks like he could be the next James Bond and I'm surprised he didn't acquire Kimi Räikkönen's number seven when the Finn left F1 and put two zeros in front. He is always extremely polite and informative when answering questions. He showed tremendous character and team spirit while he was driving for Williams, whose cars were not, at the time, competitive, but he became known as 'Mr Saturday' for his consistently excellent performances in qualifying, outpacing his Williams team-mate on almost every occasion and beating many notable drivers in faster cars. When a Mercedes team seat became available at the end of Valtteri Bottas's contract, Russell had impressed Toto Wolff enough to take his place alongside Lewis Hamilton.

George first met his future team-mate Lewis in 2009 when he was 11 years old and racing in the Super 1 National Comer Cadet Championship. Lewis, recently crowned as world champion, paid a surprise visit and George decided then and there that he wanted to follow in Lewis's footsteps.

When he signed for Mercedes for the 2022 season, he must have thought he would have a great chance to win frequently, but the new Mercedes suffered from technical problems throughout the season. But he still managed to accumulate enough points to come fourth and to secure his wins in Brazil.

Sadly, my second attempt at the Alpine Press Go-Karting was not as successful as I had hoped. When I was handed the two-page print-out of the results, I scanned down the first page full of hope. My heart sank. I flipped to the second. Where had my name gone? Perhaps they had recorded it wrong?

But no, there it was, at the bottom of page two. Dead last again.

F!

Hong Kong 1993

AFTER SPENDING a little of my newly acquired riches on a long weekend in the beautiful island of Boracay in the Philippines, I called Vince Freidman to enquire about my work schedule for the following week. I had really enjoyed my days off and was feeling chilled. That mood, however, was abruptly dispelled when, instead of the usual business-like discussion, he told me, with some heat, that my contract at Prime Sports was terminated. In a quick-fire dressing-down he told me why.

First: In an All-Star Baseball show I had produced and sent by satellite to the US just before I went away, I had misspelled the word 'fifth'. It was my job to make sure graphics, statistics and logos were added correctly. But sadly, on every graphic that said 'top (or bottom) of the fifth' (inning), I had missed out the middle letter, so it spelt 'fith' instead. Better than 'filth', I guess, but still no good.

So, the tape had to be re-edited, no small undertaking in those days. There was no such thing back then as 'cut and paste', so the whole editing process had to be repeated. To add to Vince's frustration, I was away when the problem came to light, so he had to give up his weekend to fix the problem himself and then shell out for another satellite uplink. I can understand why that would make him cross.

Second: Vince had told me that he was looking for an opportunity to bring me in as a permanent member of staff, but said that the timing had to be right. One night, when I was logging tapes in the empty offices, the head of the Prime Sports channel, Rick Conway, also an American and Vince's boss, introduced himself.

He asked me how I was enjoying working as a freelancer and we had a brief but friendly conversation. Whatever it was I said, and no doubt I was insensitive to the politics, Rick must have interpreted me as angling for a full-time position and he reported the conversation back to Vince. Having let me know all about my transgressions, Vince ended with, 'And you have the balls to talk to Conway behind my back to try to get a permanent job? After all I've done for you?'

He hung up before I had any chance to respond and, just like that, the iron gates at Star TV slammed in my face, bolts slid into place and padlocks snapped shut. The joker cackled. At first, I was shocked, then rather depressed. It seemed so unfair.

So, with a heavy heart, I resumed my duties at Le Jardin, where they were good enough to take me back. Now I really had to search my soul. Sure, I now had some experience that might prove useful, but the chances of working in TV again in Hong Kong seemed remote.

I was still pondering my plight three months later, when my good old ace shuffled back to the top of the deck. As I was about to leave the apartment for a shift at Le Jardin the phone rang and I picked up.

'Can I speak to Kris Henley?' a sweet female English voice said down the line.

'Speaking,' I replied.

'Hi, my name is Samantha Hague, Prime Sports. I have been brought in to replace Vince Freidman who has moved on to set up a channel in Europe and I'm just getting up to speed.

'Anyway, Vince was kind enough to leave me his Rolodex with all his contacts. I saw your name and number under freelancers with "F1" written beside it, so I guess you're the expert to talk to about Formula One. We will be looking for a producer for the show next year, so I was wondering if you would like to come in for a chat?'

Expert in Formula One? I wondered if I could name five drivers if my life depended on it.

I turned up again at the now familiar Star TV offices and was shown into Vince's old office, where I met the lovely, capable, softly spoken Samantha Hague from Hampshire in the south of England.

I studied her while she was conversing with the people who frequently popped in to ask her advice. She gave clear, concise and decisive guidance. Her cheeks were rosy, her short wavy brown hair was uncombed and her eyes twinkled.

The office bore little resemblance to my previous visits. All the sports décor had gone. The only trace of Vince was the Rolodex on the desk. Our conversation flowed easily and we both laughed as we talked about our lives in Hong Kong. She confided that she was still trying to find her feet, having made the bold decision to leave her unchallenging job as a production coordinator in London.

'What happened to all of Vince's sporty knick-knacks?' I asked.

'Oh, I binned them on my first day. Cheeky of him not to clear his office before he left. I kept this though,' she continued, grabbing his American football stress ball from a drawer and squeezing it assertively. 'It helped with the stress of clearing up his mess!' I smiled. I was really liking this woman.

She spun-passed the toy to me with the dexterity of a quarterback, but I fumbled it and it bounced off my thumb and disappeared under the desk. When I came up from hunting around on the floor, she placed a piece of A4 paper in front of me. My stomach lurched. There were still copies of my bogus résumé floating around somewhere in the Star TV buildings and if one of them resurfaced, I could be back in a whole world of pain. But I need not have worried.

'I like to be prepared,' she began. 'So, I had this contract typed up in case I needed it. After speaking to you, I'm happy to say I'm willing to give you a try.' She was smiling. 'If everything makes sense, just sign over your soul here.' She pointed to the bottom of the piece of paper.

The contract was typed on an official Prime Sports, Star TV letterhead and guaranteed up to five days' work a week for six months. The compensation was generous. There was a brief explanation of my duties and at the bottom were two boxes with our names printed and spaces for signatures and date. She had already signed and dated hers, but I paused.

'Sam, this is incredible, really, but I think you should know something before, well, before somebody else mentions it and you change your mind.' I took a deep breath. 'Vince Freidman actually …'

'Fired you, yes, I was told, but don't worry, he's not here anymore. Can you believe he phoned to ask me to mail that Rolodex to Rome?' She pointed at it. 'I thought he had left it to help me out.

'Anyway, thanks for letting me know, but I checked you out and people had good things to say. I think you can do the job. I'm usually a good judge.'

'That's so …' I felt a lump in my throat. I looked down at the American football still in my hand to avoid eye contact. '… very kind of you.'

'Pleasure, just don't mess up and make me look stupid!'

My conscience clear, I signed the contract, laughing, feeling the worries cascade off my shoulders. But I got the message. She was taking a punt on me. It made me determined not to let her down.

'There are some amazing opportunities opening up in this department, Kris,' Sam said seriously, 'particularly in motorsport.'

I adored Samantha Hague.

When she stepped out of the office to make copies of the contract, the Rolodex was still open on her desk at my record. And there it was. My name and contact details and a large hand-written 'F' in red ink. And next to it another mark. I looked closely. But the other letter was not a '1' as Sam had thought. It was actually an exclamation mark, but the dot was vanishingly faint. I guess the F stood for 'Fired', or 'Failed' (not the first such 'F' I had registered) or possibly even 'Fucker'. But whatever it stood for, Vince obviously felt strongly enough to emphasise it with an exclamation mark.

Not F1, but F! Easy to confuse, but the faintness of that dot launched my career in elite motorsport. As I said, charm and bluff won't always cut it. Sometimes you just need a gargantuan dollop of blind luck.

Crash Test Dummy

Sepang International Circuit 1994 and Paul Ricard Circuit 2018

SINCE THE first Formula One race held at Silverstone on Saturday, 13 May 1950, only 775[57] of the billions of people on the planet have ever taken their place on the grid. A few others have test-driven Formula One cars, but the numbers are tiny. The rest of us, even those with access to state-of-the-art F1 simulators, can only dream what it's like.

But I did get the opportunity to drive a single-seater racing car at the Sepang International Circuit in Malaysia back in the nineties. Formula Asia, a class of open wheel racing which ran from 1994 to 2002, was established to help young Asian drivers make the transition from karting to European formulae. I flew to Malaysia before the category's inaugural season to produce a half-hour show designed to introduce the drivers[58] and their teams to Star TV viewers.

After interviewing one of the team in the pits, he unexpectedly said:

'Hey! As you are going to be following the series for Star TV, you should know what it's like to drive the car. You wanna have a go?'

'Seriously!?' I spluttered. 'That would be amazing.'

'Well, let's get you a helmet.'

---

57 At the end of 2023.
58 Indians Narain Karthikeyan and Karun Chandhok, Japanese driver Takuma Sato and Malaysian Alex Yoong all went on to race in Formula One, Karthikeyan becoming the first Indian driver to do so.

It crossed my mind that there might be rules against novices driving a car with a 16-valve Ford Zetec 1,800cc engine around the Sepang circuit, but I certainly wasn't going to ask.

It took a while to get access to the changing rooms and pull on racing overalls and a helmet. When I found my way back to the garage, a lone Malaysian mechanic nodded, rather sullenly I thought, and gestured towards the car. I felt like the Ugly Sister's foot as I squashed myself into the cockpit. When the mechanic had strapped me in, he crouched by the car and explained how to drive it, confining himself to the essentials. He pointed at the pedals and gearstick.

'Foot down, go. Brake, stop. Clutch, left. Five gear.' He made a squiggle in the air showing the five gear positions and then said, 'reverse', finishing his squiggle bottom right.

I caressed the silver ball of the gearstick with my gloved right hand and made a mental note not to shift from fifth into reverse. Adrenaline surged when the engine engaged. I felt a tap on my shoulder and the mechanic pointed the way out. I pushed down on the clutch with my left foot and shifted left and up into first gear. Then I applied what I thought was gentle pressure to the accelerator and slowly lifted the clutch.

The car shot out of the garage, the mechanic nimbly jumping out of the way. I sped down the pit lane before deciding I should test the brakes by touching the pedal. The car slammed almost to a halt and juddered alarmingly. Just before it stalled, I stepped on the accelerator and the car bunny-hopped forward before accelerating again. In the wing mirror I could see the mechanic shaking his head before sauntering resignedly back into the garage.

Well, perhaps it wasn't the most elegant of garage exits, but I had now picked up enough speed to change into second in the pit lane and then up to third as I joined the circuit. I lifted off the throttle as I snaked through the right and left hairpins and then put my foot down again, changing up to fourth as I approached the first flat-out-third corner. What a rush! I changed up to fifth and was flying down the straight. A quick glance at the speedometer showed

110 mph and I was still accelerating as I braked and downshifted for the fourth corner, a 90-degree right hander, but as I put the power back on, the engine first whined and then I heard a bang. The engine immediately started to misfire, plumes of black smoke billowing from the exhaust.

I tried changing gears and applying gentle pressure to the accelerator but the car was unresponsive. All I could do was trundle along at about 25mph, smoke continuing to belch from the exhaust, filling the cockpit and impeding my view of the road ahead. It was making me feel rather groggy. Perhaps there was carbon monoxide among the smoke? I should probably have parked the car and trudged moodily back to the pits with my helmet under my arm, perhaps using my balaclava to mop my brow in the intense midday heat. Instead, I peered through the fog, hoping the problem would fix itself. But it didn't. So there was no further rush of adrenaline, feeling of euphoria and certainly no G-force. All I felt was relief as I limped back into the pits.

The lone mechanic wisely kept his distance as I pulled up to the front of the garage and put the car into neutral, whereupon the engine, like a salmon returning to its spawning ground, shuddered and abruptly died.

The mechanic shrugged and scratched his head. Sadly there was no pit team standing by to swing into action, fix the problem and send me back out, so my single-seater career ended as abruptly as it had begun. Once my seatbelts were unfastened, I climbed out of the car, took off my helmet and staggered around, gratefully inhaling the fresh air well away from the still-smoking vehicle. When I felt slightly less light-headed, I nodded ruefully to the mechanic and plodded off.

But in 2018, after the Monaco Grand Prix, I did get some idea of what it's like to be in a Formula One car. Lotus F1 were looking to promote their 'iRace F1 driving experience', where, over the course of a day (and usually for a considerable fee) the lucky participants build up their racing knowledge and skills and then get the opportunity to drive the 2012 Grand Prix-winning Lotus

E20 F1 car around the Paul Ricard[59] Circuit. A select group of the press were invited, including Juan representing Fox Sports, David Croft for Sky UK and the World Feed, F1 TV presenter and pit reporter Will Buxton, *F1 Racing*'s James Roberts and RTL's Felix Goerner.

As Uli was unable to attend, I stepped in as cameraman to shoot Juan's adventure, which I would later edit into a feature for our magazine show. Lotus brought along one of their drivers, Pastor Maldonado,[60] to offer charisma, support, guidance and more than a little fun.

'Any tips for Juan when he gets into the Lotus, Pastor?' I asked the Venezuelan, one hand stabilising the camera and the other pointing the microphone towards him.

'My advice to Juan,' he said, with his winning smile, 'is to put his foot down to the floor!'

I laughed and went through to the changing rooms to film Juan being fitted out in his racing kit with the other excited trainees. I overheard Crofty doing a link to camera saying he had read the small print in the briefing document with his wife that morning and learned that the Lotus he was about to drive went from 0 to 100mph in under four seconds. Impressive, but somewhat sobering, if you are about to get in it.

The trainees were ushered into a conference room where iRace experience creator Fredrick Garcia and his team briefed them on safety protocol and track etiquette and gave them a driving tutorial. The cost of the cars and the repercussions should any damage be done to them was mentioned more than once. They were also told that a) contrary to Pastor's playful advice, they should most definitely not 'put their foot down to the floor' and b) the Lotus team were not looking for new Formula One drivers, as both seats were already taken. Instead, they were urged to enjoy the experience.

---

59 Paul Ricard was the French industrialist who invented the eponymous anise-flavoured drink and subsequently built the Grand Prix racing circuit at Le Castellet in southern France.

60 Much more on Pastor later.

Fredrick guaranteed they would never look at a Grand Prix race in the same way again.

The next step was a body massage and physical warm-up on the terrace. I filmed Juan as they followed the instructor's workout routine. Next the trainees each got to drive a Formula Renault 2.0 behind a safety car to learn the circuit and get used to driving at speeds of up to 140mph. After a few laps the safety car pulled into the pits and they were on their own.

The next step was to experience a little more speed as a passenger. I filmed Juan as he climbed into the back seat of a two-seater Lotus. The driver was Nicolas Prost, son of four-time champion Alain, who whisked Juan off around the track on a flying lap.

The final step before the main event was a ride in a modified Formula One Infiniti Red Bull Racing car. The driver sat where you would expect, but two passenger seats had been built into the car's side-pods.

Now Juan, as you will already have observed, is a shrewd and practical man with plenty of experience of the dangers of motor racing. He eyed the side-pods with little enthusiasm because it was hard not to notice that there was little, indeed nothing at all, by way of protection for the passengers, should the car lose its grip and slide into the barriers. Having carefully weighed up the risk, Juan decided that this was one he saw no need to take. What he needed, instead, was someone expendable.

Well, as I have already said, the producer's job, in South America anyway, is to do whatever needs to be done. But as it was highly unlikely that I would ever be offered a seat in an F1 car again, I was more than happy to be the 'crash test dummy'. I put down the camera and went to get fitted with a racing suit and helmet.

When I was 'safely' strapped into the car, I gave the thumbs-up to the driver who was giving me the 'okay' sign. Felix, the German presenter in the other side-pod seat, did the same. Of course, a three-seater can't reach the speed of a single-seater Formula One car but it was still more than fast enough for me. The acceleration was intense, exhilarating and like nothing else

I have experienced. At Ferrari World[61] in Abu Dhabi there is a roller coaster designed to give the sensation of an F1 car starting a race, but the exhilaration didn't come close to what I felt in the Red Bull. Nor did a crazy tandem parachute jump I once did in Hong Kong, perhaps because there was no visual reference point, apart from the plane disappearing.

But in the Red Bull, so close to the ground, there were reference points aplenty as the track, barriers, gantries, trees and kerbs whipped past my eyes. And braking was an even bigger shock as the car, approaching a hairpin, went from a top speed of around 200mph to 20 in a couple of seconds. The Red Bull took the rapid changes in velocity in its stride, sticking to the ground through the chicanes and corners as if it were on rails. But my internal organs did not. My stomach turned inside out and my heart bounced around inside my ribcage. But I loved it, although I have to confess, I was quite relieved when we arrived back in the pits and I climbed out. I fist-bumped the driver to thank him and show my respect for his skill and courage.

This was my highlight of the day, but Juan, Will, Crofty and the others later realised their dream when they were all allowed to drive the real F1 car, the Lotus E20 F1 used by Kimi Räikkönen when he finished third in the 2012 World Championship. Kimi achieved seven podiums that year including a victory in Abu Dhabi in the car.

By the end of the day the trainees had done what they had been reporting, writing or talking about all their adult lives. I listened to their reactions as they returned to the pits after their allotted three laps, each in a state of euphoria.

Will Buxton waxed lyrical about how racing was like a drug and that he wanted one more hit. He high-fived his producer, Jason, who was also standing in as cameraman, before he began cursing himself for not stepping later on the brakes.

---

61 Claimed to be the largest indoor theme park in the world. See ferrariworldabudhabi.com.

Crofty stayed in the Lotus when he was finished, joking to camera that he didn't ever want to get out of the car. As for Juan, he was beside himself with joy as he tried to capture in words the emotions he felt, speaking excitedly into the camera I was holding. I had never seen him so happy.

Sure, the Lotus that they drove was set up for beginners, the track was clear and the conditions perfect. But, although they would never experience what it was like to be in a Grand Prix, they had still joined the tiny group of people who have been at the controls of a Formula One car.

As for me, though I thoroughly enjoyed the thrill of sitting in the side-pod of the converted F1 car, I left Paul Ricard that evening seething with jealousy.

Four Steps to Heaven

Hong Kong 1993–94

SAM HAGUE blew through Prime Sports like a hurricane, but instead of devastation she left order and efficiency in her wake. Within a week, I had my own desk and a personal computer to write scripts, check mail and, as if life could get no better, I could order tapes directly from the library. I was even granted access to the edit suites during daylight hours. Before long I was a cog in the Prime Sports machine; a small one perhaps, but undeniably a part of the team. I was hungry to learn everything I could as fast as possible.

Sam designed a four-step programme for me to learn about television. Step one was to familiarise myself with the brand-new Digi Beta editing suites. I produced several 30- or 60-second filler promos for the sports we covered to air in commercial breaks. Music copyright was not a problem at Star TV, so I could cut video to my favourite songs. The promos started to get noticed.

Step two was to assist with live studio productions. The studio floor and production control room were connected with soundproof glass. The presenters sat at a desk in front of large sporting photographs, lit by the lighting director. Three large cameras, mounted on wheeled tripods, provided the shots. The floor manager ran that area and everyone had audio contact with the director, who sat in the control room, telling the crew when to cut to live pictures, when to cut to the studio floor, which studio floor camera to use, what graphics to add and what video inserts to run.

The producer oversaw the journalistic content and might ask the director to cut to live pictures or pass on relevant information to the presenter through their earpiece. There was a camera mixer who switched in whichever shot the director chose, a graphics operator in charge of overlaying graphics such as the names of those on screen, statistical information, maps, charts, graphs or diagrams and perhaps a director's assistant. There was also a sound mixer, wired into the director's instructions, usually located in a separate booth, away from the noisy gallery.

When I first began to assist with live studio broadcasts, I was stationed in the control room in charge of running either pre-edits or replays of the action. Source video decks were stacked on racks. My role was to cue up the required videotape and wait for the director's command to 'roll tape' before pressing 'play' on the machine. Simple enough, you might think, but under the pressure of a live broadcast I managed to balls it up a fair few times, pressing either 'fast-forward', 'rewind' and once even the 'eject' button instead of 'play'. Directors are quick to react and switch away, but they will be screaming and cursing as you desperately try to re-cue the shot.

However, the odd blunder notwithstanding, I became quite proficient at lining up what was required and running it at the director's command.

'Video 1, real time, standby, in three, two, one, run tape and take VT1 and standby Video 3, slow motion, in three, two, one, run tape and take VT3. Stand by Video 2, real time, standby, in three, two, one, run tape and take VT2 and standby studio in one, two, three, take camera 2 and cue Johnny!'

It took 100 per cent of my concentration, but it was a buzz working in that live environment.

I then progressed to step three of Sam's crash course and went to my first onsite broadcasts, covering tennis, golf, motor races and soccer. Back then, an outside broadcast crew consisted of a cameraman, a camera/light assistant, a sound engineer and a producer. I joined the team to learn the ropes, helping as required. I would carry the equipment, hold boom microphones or light reflectors, or fetch lunch. But it wasn't long before I was taking on some of the tasks of the producer, directing the camera crew and interviewing the sports personalities.

For step four, Sam sent me to events with a camera crew and microphone in charge of production. Afterwards I returned to the Prime Sports office, logged my footage, wrote the script and worked with an editor to create the video package. A voice-over artist added the commentary.

I can't imagine a better way to make up for the wasted years. For the first time I felt part of something and I didn't have to bluff. At the end of my six-month contract, Sam offered me a permanent position as assistant producer and I jumped at the chance. At last, I was a bona fide member of the Prime Sports team.

Six months later I was promoted and the word 'assistant' was removed from my title. It was official. I was a TV producer. At the same time, I was given the honour of producing the *Formula One Show*, the programme that drew the channel's highest ratings. I overflowed with joy.

Star TV moved their offices from the grotty area of Hung Hom to a luxury glass building on the waterfront. Star TV were on their way up and so was I. My new position came with a floor-to-ceiling glass-fronted office that looked out over the harbour. I was issued with my own embossed business card with the Prime Sports logo and my name on it, Kris Henley, Producer.

I was so proud I handed them out to everyone I met, even if they only wanted directions to the toilets. I was sure to point out to the bewildered recipient exactly where my name was on the card and, more importantly, my impressive job title.

Snappers

I FIRST noticed Joshua Paul crouched in front of Kimi Räikkönen's Ferrari on the grid at the US Grand Prix in 2014. In fact, it wasn't Josh I noticed. What caught my eye was his black box-like camera with its concertina-style body. It looked 100 years old, not the sort of equipment you normally associate with Formula One.

'Hey buddy!' Josh said, looking up at me as I moved in to take a closer look. 'You like my camera?'

'I do, what is that?'

'It's a 1913 Graflex RB,' he said. Well, my guess was close. The camera was actually 101 years old.

'The old RB, eh? A classic! The Red Bull brand has certainly changed with the times, no?' He understood I was making a feeble joke but enlightened me anyway.

'RB stands for "revolving back", so I can quickly change from vertical to horizontal compositions.' He showed me how the camera's main feature worked.

'Cool!' I said, offering my hand. 'I like your style!'

'I'm Josh from New York. Nice to meet you, man.'

'Kris, from old Jersey. Pleasure's all mine.'

I left him kneeling in front of the Ferrari and followed Juan and Uli in the direction of pole-sitter, Nico Rosberg.

I would later see many of the beautiful and evocative black and white photographs[62] Josh takes with this antique camera. Some he prints in his *Lollipop* magazine and others he sells as fine art. It

---

62 Some of the photographs described in this chapter can be seen in the plates section. The rest can be seen online by googling the photographer's name and subject matter.

was then I realised that although a modern smartphone can take amazing digital photographs, there is far more to photography than framing an image and touching the red button.

Josh and I became good friends. I get on well with the Formula One photographers, perhaps because of the respect I have for what they do. Most are employed by teams or agencies, either as salaried staff or freelancers. Agencies act as middlemen, selling the photographs on to the Formula One teams, the circuits, sponsors or other customers. A few earn money through their web or social media sites.

They go about their business like commandos. Cameras and monopods hang from shoulder harnesses like sidearms. Spare lenses and accessories are strapped to their belts like grenades. They crouch behind cover, their telephoto lenses poking out over Armcos[63] or old-tyre barriers, like snipers. Often, they are stock still for long periods, patiently waiting. But when the critical moment arrives, they move with great speed and purpose towards the action, always looking for a clean shot.

A photographer's never-ending quest is to capture a moment that is somehow unusual, spectacular, beautiful, interesting, intriguing, poignant, shocking, or even horrifying. A great photograph, shot in perfect light, perhaps from an unusual angle, can often tell a far more complex and nuanced story than can ever be achieved with words or moving images.

For the *GP1* show, I occasionally produce a feature called 'My 10 Favourite Photos' where I interview a respected F1 photographer who selects signature photographs from their portfolio which we discuss, telling their stories using footage from the relevant race.

Some F1 photographers have very specific jobs, perhaps to produce photographs that show off a sponsor's logo. Others, such as Vladimir Rys, the Greek photographer we met in chapter two, who has been a part of the Red Bull team since 2007, have complete artistic freedom.

---

63 Named after the American Rolling Mill Company, Armcos are the ubiquitous metal crash barriers seen on motorways (expressways in the US) as well as racetracks.

'The Red Bull brand looks for something different,' he told me sitting on the long sofa in the Red Bull Energy Station. 'As I am a creative person, this means everything to me. I can do a portrait or an action shot. Or I can be "arty". This you can do in Formula One, whereas in other sports you can only wait and shoot what is happening in front of you. In Formula One you can go and find the pictures. You can transmit your personality through your work; how you see things; your life, philosophy, sensitivity. You put everything into your pictures.'

Some photographers would give their eye teeth for such a brief, but Vlad admitted it took him three years to become fully accepted by the Red Bull mechanics and engineers. There's not much space in the garage and there are a lot of people doing high-pressure jobs. So having an arty photographer look for perfect light while a mechanic is trying to fix an urgent issue can cause conflict.

'I look around all the time to be aware. Now they have got used to me, they help me, but it wasn't always the case.'

F1 photographers come from all over the world, but many are English because most of the teams who hire photographers are based in England or have their HQ there.

Steven Tee, the MD and chief photographer of LAT and Motorsport Images, has attended over 500 Grands Prix since 1984 and told me that luck is sometimes needed to capture an iconic image.

Steven took one such photo at the 1994 German Grand Prix. It shows Paul Seaby, one of the Benetton mechanics, in his cobalt blue fireproof overalls, balaclava[64] and goggles, turning away from Jos Verstappen's burning Benetton, wreathed in spectacular golden flames.

'When Jos Verstappen came into the pits, fuel spilled out of the refuelling hose. Then the whole thing exploded,' he tells me, as I look down at the photograph. 'The explosion lasted about two seconds but, in that moment, I managed to get three or four frames off of my camera. Right place at the right time.'

---

64 Before helmets were made compulsory for pit mechanics.

Well, it seems to me that while you need some luck to shoot such an extraordinary photo, not many people would react to a ball of flame by firing off frames on their camera. I was even able to find video footage of Steven taking the photograph, seemingly unfazed by the startling events happening right in front of him.

Paul Seaby later joked, 'When I first saw the photographs, I had a word with Steve Tee and said, "You could have been putting me out rather than taking my photograph." But I'm glad he took them.' When Paul and his wife first started dating, he gave her a copy and it hangs on the wall in her house next to her family wedding photos.

Multiple award winner Stephen Etherington has worked in Formula One since 1992. When we talked, he stressed the importance of quick reactions. At the start of the German Grand Prix in 2014, Stephen was positioned at turn one and was shooting the leading cars when, out of the corner of his eye, he saw Kevin Magnussen's McLaren clip the back of Felipe Massa's Williams. His photographer's instinct enabled him to spin and capture a perfectly framed image of Massa's Williams, wheels skywards, with the roll bar skidding along the tarmac, sending out a cascade of sparks which settled on the track surface like spilled golden sovereigns.

But according to Darren Heath, honorary fellow of the Royal Photographic Society and veteran F1 photographer, who we met earlier in the 'brake-steer' story, preparation is all important. Darren already knows most Formula One circuits like the back of his hand. He knows where the sparks will fly most dramatically, when and where the cars' exhaust plumes will best show against a dramatic backdrop, which buildings' windows or glossy-floored walkways will create intriguing reflections, and where to wait to capture a desert sunset that most strikingly shows off the beautifully designed Formula One machines. He uses that knowledge, season after season, to create ever more compelling images.

One of Darren's favourite photos perfectly illustrates his understanding of when and where to be. The spectacular image shows the rear view of a Red Bull taking the first corner at the Shanghai International Circuit in 2018 trailing an avalanche of sparks which fill the frame. He explained:

'As the cars exit the straight and pitch into the corner, if you shoot through the fence, you get a fantastic show of sparks, some of which are close to the camera. In many of the larger sparks you can see a reflection of the chain link fencing. People really seem to enjoy the picture.'

When I see Darren at work at a Grand Prix, he always seems calm and still, almost Zen-like. By contrast, Mark Sutton, senior photographer at Motorsport Images, gives the impression of constant motion. I see him everywhere, flitting between photo opportunities like a supercharged bee, but he usually finds time for a quick chat en route.

'Kris, look at this shot!' he told me at the end of the 2017 Canadian GP. I looked at the screen on the back of his camera to see the quite amazing photograph that Mark had taken from the top of the control tower looking down on the podium. It showed, from directly above, a victorious Lewis Hamilton, arms aloft, wearing a maroon cap. In his right hand he held the traditional magnum of champagne and in his left the trophy for the winner of the Grand Prix, the outline of a maple leaf made from anodised aluminium, mounted on a maple wood base with 12 carbon fibre rods. But what made the image so remarkable was that maple leaf blazed out like a golden halo.

'Wow!' I said. 'Is that an effect?'

'No, it's the sun's reflection, I just happened to catch it,' he said with a wide, proud smile. 'My golden moment!' he shouted over his shoulder, laughing as he hurried off to his next position.

'You're the master!' I called after him.

Glenn Dunbar, of LAT and Motorsport Images, gave me a different insight into the work of a professional photographer when describing one of his ten favourite photographs, a picture of Charles Leclerc's Ferrari coming through the first Degner Curve in Suzuka in 2019. It shows the car twisting under the stress of the centrifugal forces as it comes off the kerb, the front inside tyre off the ground and the outer rear tyre squashed down on to the track.

'I'll be totally honest,' he says. 'The shot was inspired by Peter Fox, who got a lovely image of Nico Rosberg at the same place in 2018. So, I thought I'd go to the same place to get that shot of Leclerc.'

Glenn paused for a few seconds and then confided why he particularly liked the image. 'On the way home from Japan I got a call from Charles's PR company asking to use the photograph on his social media account. I have the utmost respect for Charles, as our pictures are often used without permission or compensation, but he was happy to pay, because he loved the picture. Not all drivers are so considerate. Charles Leclerc is an honourable guy.'

Foxy's original photograph, of Nico Rosberg in his Mercedes-AM Petronas, was posted on Twitter by Nico, who asked his 1.6 million followers to identify who had taken it. Foxy's name was soon mentioned and the Englishman's phone lit up.

'When I woke up in the morning and started reading what everyone was saying, it showed the power of an image,' he said. 'The picture captures the visceral G-forces far better than could ever be done with words. That's what photography is all about.'

Foxy used the popularity of the picture to do a limited edition of 20 prints, signed by himself and Nico, and gave 20 per cent of the profits he made to charity.

Another of Glenn's favourite photographs shows Fernando Alonso's orange McLaren Renault flying high over Charles Leclerc's Sauber after Fernando was rammed by Nico Hülkenberg's Renault at the first corner of the 2018 Belgian Grand Prix. Debris explodes from the rear of Fernando's car, water and steam cascading from his broken radiator over Charles's vehicle and, as the video feed from inside Charles's car shows, his visor.

'I'm not a photographer that generally gets crashes,' said Glenn, who followed in his father's footsteps by becoming a Formula One photographer.

'I'm always in the wrong place. It's probably the only crash that I've got in my entire career.' I laughed and patted him on the shoulder.

There is no doubt in my mind that the top photographers make their own luck. They have a sixth sense, doubtless arising from vast experience.

Mark's most famous picture is of Mika Häkkinen's McLaren flying off the kerbs in Adelaide in 1993. All four wheels are well clear of the ground, the gleaming red and white car contrasting with its jet-black tyres highlighted by yellow trim, caught in sharp focus against the background of the crowd. The photo was solely responsible for Häkkinen's nickname 'The Flying Finn' and it is Sutton Images' biggest seller ever.

Mika was in the air for so long that Häkkinen's engineer wondered why there was a blip on the telemetry. No other photographer or TV camera recorded this moment, only Mark, and now it is immortal.

A good Formula One photographer (and they are all excellent) must know the sport inside out. They must be able to predict when and where things will happen, know what track access is available, the gossip from the teams, the position of the sun, how to handle rain and what is happening during the race. They must decide how to invest their time, be it waiting alone out on the track, or perching on a rooftop. Stoicism, determination and infinite patience are needed to get into the right place, season after season, race after race, session after session, from free practice until the circus leaves town. Good relations with the teams and the drivers are essential. Some drivers are easier to shoot than others.

'Lewis Hamilton generally tries to hide from photographers,' Darren Heath tells me from his home in New Zealand during a pandemic Zoom call. 'But Sebastian Vettel is a fantastic driver to photograph. It's as if he doesn't know you're there.'

And what about current world champion Max Verstappen? Vlad gives me his take.

'Max is good to photograph because he just doesn't care. He pays you no attention and he's always himself.'

Photographers also need to cultivate the right contacts away from the track. James Moy, who has more than 20 years of experience shooting F1, gives me a couple of examples.

'To shoot the Singapore circuit lit up at night you need a contact at the Swiss hotel who will lend you a key to a room on the 53rd floor. And if you want a bird's eye view of the harbour and circuit at Monaco you need access to the rooftop of the Hotel de Paris.'

And don't forget, there are times when photographers literally have to fight to get the shots they need. One shot that Foxy took in Abu Dhabi in 2016 is of Nico Rosberg celebrating his World Championship win. Nico, his cap with the Mercedes logo askew on his head, is in the midst of a throng of 15 of his team, his mouth wide open in a primeval shout of triumph. But what makes the photo so special is that it also captures the unbridled joy of his team of mechanics, the real heroes of Formula One according to Foxy, who are no less ecstatic, faces shiny with glee.

The picture looks so intimate you can imagine Foxy standing calmly in front of the celebration, taking his time to reel off a dozen frames. But the reality was a little different.

'Behind me,' he tells me with a smile, 'there were people pulling my hair, my legs, grabbing my camera and trying to get me out the way. When you walk away, you realise just how exhausted you are. But when you come out with great images like this, it's worth it.' In fact it might be said Foxy got off lightly. I know photographers who have had far more sensitive parts of their anatomy grabbed in the media scrum!

The multiple award winner Mark Thompson, or 'Thomo' as he is known, who we met earlier at the Red Bull Energy Station, works for Getty Images, the agency that supplies many of the teams with photographs. Thomo reminds me of the commercial aspect of the business.

'A lot of photographers want arty pictures,' he tells me, 'and there's nothing wrong with that. But when you work for a company like Getty Images you have to get news content, because it's the picture that tells today's hot story that sells.'

Another of the many interesting photographers working in Formula One is the affable and talented Spanish photographer and journalist José María Rubio, who began his career back in 1977 and has attended over 650 GPs. He will often take photographs of Juan, Uli or me in the paddock, which he sends over. At the Saudi Arabian GP in 2022, he took a close-up of me that I found less than flattering, so I jokingly asked him to zoom out a little more in future. Just 20 minutes later, Rubio had printed off a large copy of the photograph and stuck it to the notice board in the media centre with the words 'Wanted: Dead or Alive' printed below.

It was Rubio who took the photograph I have included in this book of an encounter I had with Bernie Ecclestone on the grid at the Indian Grand Prix on Bernie's 81st birthday in 2012. So, thank you, Rubio!

And while the commercial side of the business can never be overlooked, it is the Brazilian photographer Beto Issa, who has worked in F1 for over 30 years, who sums up why most of them are there.

'We photographers look for a unique and exclusive picture,' he tells me. 'A shot when no one else is there. We love to see our creation on the screen or in a magazine. To be able to freeze that moment and create something that will last forever; that is the best feeling for a photographer.'

As the rain poured down on the 2022 Singapore Grand Prix, I noticed Glenn making his way to the paddock exit, jacket hood drawn tight around his head. I pulled out my phone to take some footage of him for my *GP1* show.

I remember him telling me that the worst part of his job was being away from his family. Yet even in the torrential rain, he still smiled and shrugged his shoulders as he headed out to the track. *Perhaps today*, I thought, *he will capture his second crash.*

Monte Carlo or Bust

Hong Kong 1994

I WASN'T more than an occasional Formula One race watcher when I took on the producer's role for the 1994 season, but I was quickly hooked. I watched the highlights of every race I could find and read everything I could about the sport and the personalities involved.

Sam suggested I gave the F1 show a new look and I leapt at the opportunity. Before the first race in Brazil in March 1994, I created a new 60-second 'opening' titles sequence, a 'closer' and numerous 10- to 20-second bumpers.

I spent many, many hours searching for the most exciting, euphoric and heartbreaking moments from hundreds of Formula One races. And I listened to countless albums to find the perfect music to accompany those images. Tough work, but someone's got to do it!

I edited the opening titles to U2's haunting song 'One'. The Edge's evocative guitar riff and Bono's tender, heartfelt vocals asked questions that were never answered. 'Is it getting better? Did I disappoint you? Have you come here for forgiveness?' The track was ideal for shots of the best Formula One drivers in history in their eternal quest for the perfect lap, or reacting to the triumphs and disasters that make Formula One what it is. I felt the hairs on the back of my neck prickle every time I watched the titles go to air.

For the programme closer I used an upbeat and uplifting anthem, 'Moving On Up' by Primal Scream, with a montage of fast cuts of drivers and teams celebrating victories, podiums and pole positions, designed to leave the audience on a high.

A dozen bumpers showed off Formula One. Eloquent close-up shots of drivers' eyes, or their urgent hand gestures to show their engineers how the car was reacting through corners at speed; crash compilations; drivers putting on their helmets or climbing into their cockpits; pit stops, podium celebrations, anguished faces, overtaking manoeuvres, on-board camera shots and the ever-popular montage of driver punch-ups.

I was the producer and I decided what went out on air, selecting the most relevant bumper to go to a commercial break. I felt like a god. When the U2 'One' F1 show opener first aired, everyone in the studio gallery clapped. When the director mixed through to the gregarious Johnny Green, the face of motorsport for the channel, he smiled as he came on air and initially ignored the text on the teleprompter.

'Wow, great new titles! Well done to our producer, Kris Henley! That's enough to get anyone in the mood for a new season of Formula One!' He then continued, back on script, 'Welcome to the 1994 Formula One World Championship and our coverage of round one at the Interlagos circuit in São Paulo for the Brazilian Grand Prix. I'm joined by my co-host, Matthew Marsh, ex-World Touring Car Championship driver and Formula One expert. Welcome, Matthew.'

Matthew also loved the new look, complimenting each short bumper when it aired. There was even an article in the *South China Morning Herald* praising the use of music in the show. The recognition felt great. I had finally found something I could excel at, evoking emotion with video and sound.

Often when I sat in my office on the 12th floor and looked out at the skyscrapers and harbour traffic below, I thanked my lucky stars that I had failed in London but tried Hong Kong.

The success of the new-look *Formula One Show* certainly boosted my confidence. I particularly loved participating in production meetings and having my opinion heard. At one such powwow, after the second race of the season, the Pacific Grand Prix in Japan, which we had covered from the studio, I decided to float an idea I had been considering since my appointment as producer.

'I bet our viewers would love to see Prime Sports at a Formula One race this season,' I suggested.

To my astonishment there were no eye rolls, sighs or expostulations of outrage at this preposterous idea. Instead, most of the people around the oval boardroom table nodded, some thoughtfully and some even enthusiastically. The only such nodding I had previously experienced was when I asked a party of customers on the terrace in Le Jardin if they wanted another round of drinks.

Then Johnny Green, the bubbly presenter, who knew he would also be required to travel, cleared his throat.

'And what better circuit to go to than Monaco?' he declared.

I must confess, I had no idea where Monaco was, but I did know that it was the most exclusive and iconic circuit on the calendar. It was only the fourth race of the season, so there would be little time to set it up. But it was time to raise the stakes again and I backed Johnny up.

'Yes, exactly, Monaco, where else?'

Sam looked down at the Formula One schedule on a piece of paper in front of her. She thought for a few moments.

'Well, I have the budget. I would say you should stick around for Barcelona as well, but we have the Indy 500 that weekend, so Johnny needs to be back in the studio. I'll find an edit suite somewhere close by and you can put together a half-hour pre-show and satellite it back on Sunday morning to run before the race. Leave it with me.'

Nods of approval rippled around the room. I nearly fell off my chair. Johnny and I failed miserably to conceal our delight and high-fived each other shamelessly. So, Johnny Green and I would be travelling to the Monaco Grand Prix, my first in-person experience of a Formula One race.

Sam efficiently organised everything, booking the flights, including a stopover for me in Paris after the race to stay with my best friend Reb for a week before returning to Hong Kong.

Sam also arranged for a British freelance cameraman by the name of Ben Williams to cover the event. He would meet Johnny and me at Nice airport where we would rent a car and drive to Monaco. A hotel in the Principality proved more problematic. The Grand Prix clashed with the Cannes Film Festival, so there was no reasonably priced accommodation available. This didn't stop Sam. Confident she could square away the escalating budget, she booked us into the luxurious, five-star Hermitage Hotel with its stunning views of the circuit and harbour. She also arranged an editor and edit suite in a production company close to the hotel. After Sam confirmed the tickets, I sat inside an edit suite where I was working and took a moment to reflect. I was going to Monte Carlo! How on earth could that be happening to me?

Well, as you already know, it happened because of a pinch of charm, a lot of bluff and a large dollop of blind luck. But maybe, just maybe, I could now permit myself to add one thing to the list. Perhaps a little bit of talent after all.

In a Different Dimension

San Marino, Italy, 2022

I AM standing with Juan and Uli at the Tamburello corner at the Imola circuit, the place where Ayrton Senna died in the 1994 San Marino Grand Prix. As most F1 fans know, on lap seven, while leading the race, hotly pursued by Michael Schumacher, Senna's Williams FW16 suffered a mechanical failure and he crashed head-on into the concrete barrier at over 300kph.

It was the third horrific crash that weekend. Austrian Roland Ratzenberger lost his life in qualifying when a part of the wing broke off and became lodged underneath his car, causing him to crash into the tyre barrier. Rubens Barrichello, Senna's fellow countryman, also crashed spectacularly during the Friday practice session but miraculously survived.

In 2022, 28 years later, there is a metre-high banner fixed to the fence with an image of the beloved Brazilian driver walking away, his iconic yellow helmet in his right hand, his shadow sharp behind him, superimposed on a Brazilian flag. His signature is written across the flag and the word '*sempre*', 'forever' in Portuguese, is printed in capitals below.

Before leaving Hong Kong for my first Grand Prix in Monaco in 1994, the race which followed Imola, I had produced a tribute piece to the man who has become perhaps the most powerful and evocative figure in the history of the sport. It is impossible to overstate the impact Ayrton Senna made on Formula One. Perhaps his early death, aged just 34, contributed to his legend, but there are many reasons for his immortalisation. With 41 wins, Senna is the fifth-most successful driver of all time and he won the World Championship three times. Inside a racing car he was a genius, particularly in wet conditions, and his record in qualifying was unrivalled, achieving pole 65 times in just 162 race starts. His 40 per cent success rate is higher than the two men with more poles, Lewis Hamilton with 103 (36 per cent) and Michael Schumacher with 68 (22 per cent).

He was the arch competitor. One of the first things that sparked my interest in Formula One was his intense rivalry with Alain Prost. I remember James Hunt once observing in a commentary, 'It wouldn't be unreasonable to say they hate each other.' What, I wondered, could cause two drivers who had been highly successful team-mates for two years to come to see each other as such deadly enemies?

Their contrasting personalities and driving styles were certainly a factor. As Prost said many years later, if he was 100 per cent committed to winning, Senna was far more so, to the point where Prost was actively frightened by the risks that Senna was prepared to take. Senna relished driving on the absolute limit, but Prost's more canny, methodical and cerebral approach often gave him the advantage in race management, earning him the nickname 'The Professor'. But perhaps their rivalry was inevitable because they were team-mates in 1988 and 1989 at a time when McLaren-Honda were completely dominant, so there was really no one else for them to compete with.

Ironically it was the older Prost who convinced the McLaren team to hire Senna. They competed reasonably affably during the first season in 1988, Senna just winning out for the World Championship. But Prost began to feel that Senna was getting preferential treatment, particularly from Honda, the engine supplier, which their boss did acknowledge, putting it down to Senna fandom among his young engineers.

But the bad blood really started to flow in 1989 at Imola. The dominant McLarens qualified on the front row, with Senna on pole. The drivers made an agreement that whoever was leading the race into the first corner would not attempt to pass the other, to ensure McLaren scored maximum points. Senna got the better start and was leading when the race was red-flagged after Gerhard Berger also crashed at Tamburello, his Ferrari bursting into flames, leaving him with a broken rib, bruises and second-degree burns.

When the race was restarted it was Prost who started faster and passed his team-mate. Senna was incensed as he considered the non-passing agreement had been settled at the first start and so he overtook Prost, who saw things differently, believing the agreement had been reset when the race was restarted. Senna went on to victory but both men felt cheated.

By the penultimate race of the season, the Japanese Grand Prix in Suzuka, they were barely speaking. The points position was such that Senna had to win the last two races or Prost would be the world champion. Senna qualified on pole by more than one and a half seconds, a huge gap, but this was because Prost, demonstrating his race craft, had secretly configured his car for racing rather than qualifying.[65] It was a good decision and Prost got ahead of his rival at the start and built a six-second lead. But after stopping for fresh tyres, Senna reeled his team-mate back in. On lap 47 Senna attempted to overtake, going for the inside line at the final Casio Triangle chicane.

Before the race, Prost had said that he would 'slam the door shut'[66] if he felt that Senna was going for a gap that did not exist. The cars collided, became locked together and stopped. Prost knew his race was over and climbed out of the car, but Senna, with the help of a push from the marshals, managed to restart his damaged car and keep going.

The Brazilian had to pit to get the damage repaired and then fought his way back into the lead to take the chequered flag, but was later disqualified on a technicality as he had cut the chicane to re-join the race after the collision. McLaren appealed the disqualification,

---

65 He removed the Gurney flap, a small lip on the trailing edge of the wing, to increase his straight-line speed at the expense of cornering.
66 Move off the racing line to block Senna's overtaking attempt.

but the FIA doubled down, upheld the decision, fined the Brazilian $100,000, imposed a suspended six-month ban and labelled him a 'dangerous driver'. Alain Prost was crowned world champion.

Senna was not a man to forgive or forget and his chance for revenge came the following year at the same Japanese venue. This time the relative positions were reversed, so if Prost failed to finish, Senna would be world champion. Senna qualified on pole with Prost alongside him, but the Brazilian complained that pole position was off the racing line and on the 'dirty' side of the track where he knew the grip would be worse. He railed to get the grid switched around, but his protests were ignored.

As Senna feared, Prost got away faster and went into the first corner ahead, but Senna drove straight into him without braking, taking them both into the gravel run-off area and out of the race. This gave Senna his second Formula One World Championship. Some consider this to be the worst incident in Formula One history. Although Senna denied wrongdoing at the time, he admitted a year later that he had done it deliberately. Despite his confession, the record books were not adjusted and the Drivers' World Championship of 1990 remains his.[67]

Senna's competitive obsession was demonstrated when responding to difficult questions from Jackie Stewart, who challenged him about the number of times he had collided with other drivers. Senna didn't give an inch. Impossibly earnest, handsome and emotionally intense, he replied:

'You should know that by being a racing driver, you are under risks all of the time. Being a racing driver means you are racing with other people and if you no longer go for a gap that exists, you are no longer a racing driver, because we are competing; competing to win.'

But as well as being the supreme competitor, Senna was, according to Frank Williams, 'an even greater man outside the car than he was in it'. Spontaneous and charming, he was worshipped

---

[67] At Alain Prost's last race in 1993 their rivalry ended and the two were reconciled and even enjoyed a brief six months of active friendship before Senna's untimely death.

in Brazil and his quotable quotes run to many pages. He was deeply religious and donated millions to educate young children in his home country. He had also become an ambassador for improving safety in the sport and ironically nearly didn't race the day he died after the death of Roland Ratzenberger and Rubens Barrichello's accident.

Standing at the fateful Tamburello corner, I recalled my own memories of that sad day. Prime Sports was broadcasting the World Feed[68] to the Star TV audience, Johnny Green and Matthew Marsh commentating from the studio floor. During the race there was usually not much for the studio production crew to do apart from managing the commercial breaks. So, we were sitting back and watching as the race aired.

Moments before the crash, the director selecting the shots for the live feed cut away from Schumacher's on-board camera to a wide shot of the two cars entering the corner. We saw Senna's car cross the run-off area and smash into the safety barriers before rebounding, front right and rear tyres spinning wildly into the air. It later emerged that the front suspension had snapped back into the cockpit, penetrating the Brazilian's famous yellow helmet. Gasps filled the studio but no one spoke as the horrible scenes played out.

The director in Imola cut between aerial shots of the marshals and medical staff swarming around Senna's car, then away to various drivers as they stood shell-shocked in the pit lane after the race was red-flagged. Nobody in the studio gallery in Hong Kong could find the right words.

Our studio director mixed back to the unsettled Johnny and Matthew for 30 seconds. They both knew something terrible had happened and could only speculate why. I wasn't sure what else they could say, so I intervened and suggested we go back to the live pictures. In the gallery we sat in silence as we watched the medical helicopter land and saw Ayrton's limp body loaded on

---

68 Also known as the International Feed, the primary source of race material provided to the world's TV stations.

board before he was airlifted above the trees en route to Bologna hospital.

'This is really serious,' Matthew Marsh said to me, off air.

The next day Ayrton Senna's death from brain trauma was confirmed and the racing world poured out its grief. A day later, in a dark, lonely viewing room, I was preparing to make the tribute piece, sorting through footage and listening to interviews detailing Ayrton's life when I burst into tears, something I had not done since my father died.

In 2022, Juan, Uli and I crossed over to the Acque Minerali Park on the edge of the circuit to film the Ayton Senna memorial, a life-size bronze of the man in his racing overalls. He is seated on a plinth adorned with reliefs of moments from his career, including the poignant image on the banner. His head is bowed in reflection, a red rose in his hands. Behind, on the fence that separates the park from the track upon which he raced for the last time, hang many of the flags of the world and lovingly hand-made tributes.

One good thing did come out of the tragedy. Senna had led the way in voicing concerns about driver safety. After that heartbreaking weekend, the FIA introduced many of the modern safety devices and regulations that protect drivers today. Accidents are an unavoidable part of the sport, but these days it is not at all unusual to see drivers walk away from crashes that look for all the world as if they would be impossible to survive.

In the 2020 Bahrain Grand Prix, Haas driver Romain Grosjean provided dramatic testimony to the effectiveness of the safety measures, when he was able to stay conscious following his 119mph, 67g impact with metal crash barriers before his car exploded into flames. After a delay of nearly half a minute, when it seemed certain he must be burned alive, the Frenchman escaped from the cockpit and jumped out of the fireball with only burns to his hands, to the intense relief of everyone.

There has been, however, one further death in a Formula One World Championship event, when another Frenchman, Jules Bianchi, died after sustaining severe head injuries in the Japanese

Grand Prix in 2015, before the implementation of the 'halo'. There have been fatalities in associated races, tests and demonstrations and many, many more in motorbike events such as the Isle of Man TT. Motor racing will always be a dangerous sport.

Following in the tradition of many pilgrims to the site, I pay homage by rubbing the bronze tip of Senna's left racing boot, now a golden colour from the countless other visitors who have polished it in the same way. I was once told that Senna was so quick through corners because of his unique way of applying pressure to the brake, his one foot pulsing the brake while accelerating with the other foot.

But he did not make it through Tamburello that day. I look at the monument and read the quote engraved there.

'*Credo di essere molto lontano da una maniera di vivere che mi piacerebbe.*' I don't understand the words, but there is another pilgrim visiting the shrine, a local woman dressed in a yellow Brazilian shirt. I ask her to translate for me.

'I think I am very far from a way of life that I would like,' she tells me.

I thank her and consider the phrase. Did Ayrton Senna want more from life outside of Formula One? Or was he referring to his racing life? Or both?

I consider my own life again, thinking of my family and friends and wonder if, alongside this towering legend, I am not the luckier man.

Moroccan Black

Monaco 1994

A WEEK after the tragedy at Imola in 1994, my sadness had passed and Johnny and I were giggling like schoolboys as we settled into our business class seats on the Cathay Pacific flight from Hong Kong to Paris. We arrived early on Tuesday morning with plenty of time to shower in the business class lounge and board our connection to Nice.

It was my first luxury travel and despite my excitement, I slept well on the long-haul flight. When we arrived at our destination in the south of France at midday, I was feeling great. Ben Williams, the freelance cameraman, was arriving an hour later. I sipped coffee and waited for him, while Johnny went to pick up our rental car.

A squat man with long, wispy blond hair came into the arrivals hall. He pushed a trolley loaded with a water-resistant hard case and a tripod bag with a Digi Betacam camera perched on top. I waved him over.

'Ben! Hi! I'm Kris Henley. Johnny Green has gone to pick up our rental car. We'll meet him in the parking lot.'

'Nice to meet you,' he smiled. We walked out to the meeting place. When we arrived, Ben sat down on the edge of his trolley and made himself comfortable.

'Do you smoke?' he asked.

'I gave up,' I told him. 'But there's a Tabac inside, if you want to get some cigarettes.'

'No, no, I don't smoke cigarettes.'

He hooked a finger into the space in his mouth between his upper left molars and his cheek and pulled out a cling film wrapped ball, the size of a marble.

'I had a bit of spliff left over and I thought it would be foolish not to bring it with me. We are in Monaco after all!'

'Actually, we're in Nice, but yes, it would be rude not to.'

He unwrapped the ball while checking the coast was clear of airport police. He showed me a soft brown globule of Moroccan Black hashish.

'Yuk, that's been in your mouth all flight long?'

'No! I took it out in the plane and kept it in my pocket.'

'Well, that's good enough for me. Skin up!'

To tell the truth, I would have smoked it even if he had chosen to smuggle it in a more sensitive orifice.

It took Johnny longer than expected to meet us. By the time he arrived in a silver Citroen C5, flustered from his ordeal with the French Avis team, Ben and I were completely stoned.

We loaded the car and I volunteered to co-pilot and call out the directions, while Johnny, the only sober member of the team, took the wheel for our drive to Monaco. I'd like to say that due to my faultless map reading we arrived at our destination within the required 30 minutes. But unfortunately, route-planning, along with learning languages, exam technique and any form of dance are not areas in which I excel. An hour and 20 minutes later, it became clear that while we were no longer in France, neither were we in Monaco.

Somehow, I had guided us into Italy, a wonderful country, but not one we had planned to visit that day. In my defence, it's an easy mistake to make in that part of the world, especially if you have taken a few too many hits of Moroccan Black.

By the time we found the Hermitage Hotel, it was late afternoon. A group of bellboys met us in the portico to take our bags from the boot of the car and pile them on to their baggage trolley.

Abruptly Ben's body language and persona changed. Before my eyes he transformed from a chilled-out, easy-going hippy to a crazed headless chicken, rushing around the Citroen opening and closing the car doors and the boot in a blind panic.

'What's wrong?' I called over to him.

'Where's my camera?' he screamed.

'You lost your camera?' Johnny asked nervously. 'Oh shit.'

'Fuck me, I must have left it in the parking lot on the baggage trolley. We have to go back.' Ben sprang into the front passenger seat, shaking his head morosely.

I took the car keys from Johnny and left him to check us into the Hermitage and drove back to Nice airport with an eerily calm Ben Williams beside me. We got back to the airport in just 25 minutes. Fear and desperation do tend to focus the mind. And the international airport was clearly signposted.

Of course, there was no sign of the Digital Betacam camera in the parking lot or perched on any of the baggage trolleys neatly stacked by the airport entrance. We went inside to the lost and found. A pretty, apologetic French teenager told us that there had been no camera handed in, but recommended that we fill in a form describing the lost item with our contact details in case it turned up. She explained in perfect English where we needed to fill out a police report for the insurance and apologised for our loss. She told us that thieves were known to be operating around the airport area.

'That must be what happened,' Ben averred. 'It was grabbed from the trolley when we weren't watching.'

We? I thought. *You smuggle in illegal drugs, then you get a bloke you just met completely stoned* (admittedly with his enthusiastic cooperation), *then you decide to share with him the responsibility for looking after your camera? Audacious, to say the least.*

The full implications sank in when I used a payphone to call the Hermitage Hotel and told Johnny we were down one camera, which meant the number of available cameras to shoot the event was precisely zero. I suggested he started contacting production companies in the area to see if we could hire another, but he was way ahead of me. He had called five already and they all said the same thing. As the Cannes Film Festival and the Monaco Grand Prix were taking place that weekend, no cameras were available for hire in the whole of the south of France.

Ben filled in the paperwork with the Nice airport police so he could make the insurance claim when he got back to England. The value of the Digital Betacam camera was over £20,000 for the body and more for the lens. I wondered why he hadn't handcuffed it to himself. We left the police station in a blur of uncertainty. What were we going to do? We had no camera and a 30-minute show to produce by Sunday. The driver interviews, which we needed to film, were scheduled for the next day.

By the time we got back to the hotel it was too late to reach any more production companies and, in any case, Johnny had run out of numbers to call. Johnny phoned Sam to tell her about our calamity and we decided to go to sleep and get up early to try to fix the problem. We retired to our rooms in varying states of shock, but when I woke at 7am, a handwritten fax message had been slid under my door.

'Oh my God! Who loses their camera on a shoot? Don't panic though, try this mobile telephone number below. I spoke to Sony yesterday and this guy is working on finding you a replacement. Great start! Ha ha. Let me know, Sam xxx.' 'Philippe' was written below with a mobile number.

Philippe answered his phone on the second ring and I began to explain who I was.

'Ah yes, I've been expecting your call,' he interrupted. 'Can you come down to the Cannes Film Festival?'

While Johnny took care of collecting our F1 accreditation and ticket to enter the parking lot, Ben and I drove to Cannes, some 30 miles away.

By 10.30am we arrived at the Sony exhibition stall and there, locked up in glass cases like the priceless Crown Jewels in the Tower of London, were about a dozen gleaming professional Sony cameras. I feasted my eyes upon them. So, this was where all the spare cameras in the south of France were hiding!

Philippe exemplified my theory that the world would be a better place if people would just do a random act of kindness every now and then. Especially for me, who is in constant need of them.

With only a photocopy of Tim's credit card as a guarantee, Philippe let us walk away with a brand-new Sony Digital Betacam camera and use it for five days without charging us a single French franc. He even phoned Sam in Hong Kong to let her know the problem had been solved. Though now as I write, it does occur to me that Sam was in a good position to ask for favours from Sony, who would see Star TV as a potentially important customer.

But for whatever reason, the process went so smoothly that by midday Ben and I were back in Monaco outside the circuit, meeting up with Johnny to collect our event passes.

'So, that's fantastic news about the camera,' Johnny began, 'but we have another slight issue.' He jumped into the back of the car and I noticed he was carrying a white envelope. He took out our plastic passes and the ticket to open the parking barrier in the lot.

'What kind of problem?' I asked, certain that nothing could ruin my great mood.

'Bernie Ecclestone.'

'Bernie …?'

'Ecclestone, the man who decides everything in Formula One.'

'Ah, Bernie, yes,' I said vaguely. I was dimly aware of the name, but did not yet appreciate what it meant.

Bernie Ecclestone, as any F1 fan knows, was the ringmaster of the circus for nearly 40 years. A self-made man, he made his first deals aged 11 selling biscuits and buns in the playground for a tidy profit. Later he traded in auto spare parts, formed a motorcycle dealership and then sold used cars. He raced with some success before deciding, after an accident, to focus on his business interests.

After buying the Brabham brand in 1971, he had the vision to see the opportunity for the competing Formula One teams to take control of the sport. Beforehand constructors typically staged races by paying circuits to host events. Bernie saw that, if the constructors acted in concert, that arrangement could be switched around, so that circuits were required to pay the constructors. So he formed the Formula One Constructors' Association (FOCA) with Frank Williams, Colin Chapman, Teddy Mayer, Ken Tyrrell and Max Mosley and later became its chief executive.

Three books[69] and many millions of words have been written about how Bernie managed to emerge as the de facto supremo of Formula One. He has ardent admirers and impassioned detractors in equal measure. But his success seems to me to stem from his appreciation of the opportunity, his remorseless and ruthless pursuit of power by working harder and smarter than anyone else, and his knack of playing off the interests of the F1 teams, the circuits, the sponsors and later, the broadcasters. He revelled in conflict and uncertainty and was more than happy to wade deep in dubious business practices, rifling through wastepaper baskets to retrieve messages exchanged by business adversaries and 'persuading' hotel staff to show him confidential telexes.

Working with Max Mosley, he later acquired control of the FIA and FOM. Some of his quotes, for example, describing the death of Ayrton Senna as 'good for Formula One' (because of the publicity it attracted) appear to show a brutally dispassionate man. But whatever you think of his doubtful, meticulous and controlling ways, there is no denying he set the high standards that built Formula One into a global phenomenon, making a huge amount of money for himself and many others along the way.

But Bernie certainly didn't achieve that success without being a tough businessman.

'Apparently, he is a bit pissed off with Star TV and so has denied us access to the pits or the grid. When Star TV bought the exclusive rights to F1, apparently Bernie didn't twig that it was transmitting to 48 countries. And there is nothing that annoys Bernie more than not getting every penny out of a deal. The word is, he massively undersold the rights to Star TV. So, we just have paddock passes.'

---

[69] *No Angel* by Tom Bower, *Bernie* by Susan Watkins and *Bernie's Game* by Terry Lovell.

Well, that sounded OK to me, but that was because when I heard the word 'paddock' I still pictured a rolling green field with grazing horses. Ben and I stared with blank faces.

'So,' Johnny explained, 'that means we can interview the drivers in the allocated areas of the paddock, but we can't film in the pits or access the grid, so we won't have a single shot of a racing car to use as inserts for the pre-show.'

'So,' I asked, suddenly panicked, 'we're not allowed on the track either?'

'Only the host broadcaster is allowed track access.'

'Oh.' I could now see how serious the problem was. 'We can't sneak into the garages from the paddock?' I asked naïvely.

'Not unless you want to get kicked out of the circuit and banned from Formula One for life.'

'I'll take that as a "no" then.' Back to the drawing board.

We left our car in the media area of the parking lot, took the lift up to ground level and walked round the sparkling Monaco cliff coast and then dropped down into the harbour area, down a stone staircase.

As I entered the paddock on that Wednesday the turnstile beeped. At least my pass was valid. Despite the setbacks, I felt ready to take on the world.

Crashgating the Party

Miami 2022

ONLY IN America can you take a selfie in front of ten luxury motor yachts without a drop of water in sight. I sat beside the large fake lake that had been built, along with a 3.36-mile street circuit and all the other required amenities in the huge parking lot around the Miami Dolphins Hard Rock Stadium. The 'mirage-like' set-up was part of the project that brought Formula One to Miami for the first time in 2022.

I looked around and spotted the Sky Sports UK News presenter, Craig Slater, simulating the backstroke on top of the hard, dappled-blue plastic that was stuck to a plywood base. From above, it did a convincing impression of the crystal Florida coastal ocean. Even up close it was passable. Five TV channels were waiting to interview Tom Garfinkel, the president and CEO of the Miami Dolphins and the person most responsible for bringing Formula One to Miami.

When my turn came, Tom explained that the original idea had been to race across the Port Miami Bridge by the harbour, but the impact on the port and other bureaucracy made the plan unachievable. When Tom was trying to convince Formula One that the parking lot around the Hard Rock Stadium would be a realistic alternative, he promised the yachts, and yachts they got. It took just 11 months to build the racetrack and surrounding infrastructure.

When it was announced that Las Vegas would be the third USA venue in 2023, it was at last official. The USA was fully invested in Formula One. As if to bless the accession, modern-day deities such as David Beckham, Michael Jordan, Serena Williams, Dwyane

Wade, Matt Damon, Ashton Kutcher, rapper Bad Bunny, Mila Kunis, Pharrell Williams and many other top-tier superstars showed up to give their blessing.

Among the many famous faces that passed by, perhaps the most surprising to me was former F1 driver Nelson Piquet Junior, who I had not seen for a while. I said 'hi' to the Brazilian and he waved and smiled, probably thinking I was a fan, although during my time working in Formula E, I had interviewed him many times before and after he won the inaugural Formula E World Championship.

I felt for Nelson, although I wasn't sure why. For better or worse, he was entwined in the fabric of Formula One. His father, Nelson Piquet, is a three-time F1 world champion with a forthright turn of phrase that frequently lands him in hot water. His most recent transgression was to use a racially charged word to describe Lewis Hamilton when analysing the crash with Max Verstappen at the 2022 British Grand Prix at Silverstone, resulting in an indefinite ban from the Formula One paddock. His daughter, Kelly, who I knew from her time running Formula E social media coverage, is Max's girlfriend.

Seeing Nelson Piquet Jnr in the paddock made me think of 'Crashgate', one of the most colourful stories in Formula One history. In 2008 the team principal of Renault F1 was Flavio Briatore, who started his career as a ski instructor and restaurant manager and then worked in Finanziaria Generale Italia, an investment bank in Milan. There he met Luciano Benetton, founder of the clothing company which became an iconic fashion brand in the 1980s and 1990s, with a network of over 5,000 stores.

In the 1980s, a court in Bergam, northern Italy, convicted Briatore of fraud. One of the more intriguing charges against him was that he engaged a team of confidence tricksters who invited guests to dinner and then systematically defrauded them in rigged gambling games, replete with fictional characters and fake playing cards. The amounts lost by the victims were substantial. To avoid prison, he went into exile in the Virgin Islands where he ran some successful Benetton franchises, before returning after an amnesty was arranged.

Meanwhile, to promote the Benetton brand, the company got into Formula One, initially as a sponsor and then by buying the Toleman and Spirit teams to create Benetton Formula Ltd. Briatore managed the team from 1990 to 1997 with great success, his key move being to bring in a young Michael Schumacher. After Benetton was sold to Renault in 2002, Briatore returned as team principal of the rebranded team, achieving further success with Fernando Alonso leading the Renault F1 team to World and Drivers' Constructor's Championships in 2005 and 2006. When Alonso left for two years, Renault had little success. When he returned in 2008, he qualified a disappointing 15th on the grid at the Singapore Grand Prix, after having performed well in practice. The season was not going well.

Renault planned an unconventional three-stop strategy for Alonso, so he started the race with a light fuel load, hoping to make up positions in the first stint. But when the Spaniard was first into the pits on lap 12 to refuel and fit new tyres, he re-joined the race right at the back.

Things looked hopeless until, two laps later, his team-mate Nelson Piquet Jnr crashed into a wall at turn 17, one of the few areas of the track without a crane close by. So the safety car had to be deployed and at the time the regulations stipulated that the pit lane be closed, preventing other drivers from refuelling and changing tyres. The field now bunched up behind the safety car, wiping out the large deficit Alonso had incurred from his early pit stop and transforming his race position, as all the other cars still needed to pit. Alonso took the lead in the final third of the race and held off Nico Rosberg and his ex-teammate and rival, Lewis Hamilton, to secure a most unlikely victory.

But that was not the end of the matter. At the 2009 Hungarian Grand Prix, Flavio Briatore decided he had had enough of Nelson Piquet Jnr, who hadn't scored a single point for the team. Nelson was fired and replaced with the Frenchman, Romain Grosjean.

CRASHGATING THE PARTY

The furious Nelson Piquet Jnr, possibly encouraged by his father, refused to go quietly. He told the FIA that Briatore and executive director of engineering Pat Symonds had ordered him to crash at that specific time and place during the Singapore GP. The FIA accused Renault F1 of 'interfering with the outcome of the 2008 Singapore Grand Prix, conspiring with its driver Nelson Piquet Junior to cause a deliberate crash, with the aim of causing the deployment of the safety car to the advantage of its other driver, Fernando Alonso'.

Initially Renault threatened lawsuits, accusing Nelson Piquet Jnr and his father of making false allegations to secure Piquet's seat through blackmail. But wiser heads prevailed and later the Renault team issued a statement confirming they would not dispute the recent allegations, and that Briatore and Symonds had left the team.

Renault were disqualified from the 2008 championship and given a two-year suspended ban. Their title sponsor, IMG, withdrew support.

Pat Symonds received a five-year ban and Briatore was suspended from all Formula One and FIA-sanctioned events indefinitely, although both bans were overturned by a French court in 2010. They did, however, both agree not to work in Formula One or FIA-sanctioned events as part of a later settlement with the governing body. The press, of course, lapped it all up, and gave the scandal its 'Crashgate' moniker.

Max Mosley, the FIA president, confirmed that Piquet Jnr would face no action, although he left Formula One for NASCAR the following season. In April 2010, the FIA announced a settlement with Briatore and Symonds and stated that the legal action had been ended. Incidentally, Max Mosley was no stranger to controversy himself, having successfully sued the *News of the World* for defamation, after they falsely accused him of taking part in a 'sick, Nazi-themed orgy'. He did concede that at the time of the allegation, he was engaging in sadomasochistic practices with five consenting women, but no Nazi uniforms or salutes were involved.

So that's all right then.

Restricted Access

Monaco 1994

I HAVE been to the Monaco Grand Prix over ten times and twice to the Formula E Prix, that uses a section of the F1 track, but the greatest thrill was in 1994 when my pass beeped and the turnstile opened, allowing me to enter the Formula One paddock for the first time.

I was hoping to enjoy the moment, perhaps stroll along the harbour and soak up the atmosphere, but instead we immediately came across a pulsing group of cameramen and journalists from the world's press. For some reason they were crammed into the front entrance of Benetton's white hospitality tent.

'Schumacher!' Johnny shouted. 'He's talking now! Ben, how long will it take you to set up the camera?'

'Two minutes.'

'Go for it, we need this interview. I thought he was scheduled for later.'

I didn't really grasp what all the fuss was about, but I took the Prime Sports cube from my backpack and put it on the microphone, plugging in the cable and handing it to Johnny. With the camera up on Ben's shoulder we attempted to join the media scrum waiting to speak to the talented German driver.

There was no way into the fray. Every possible position around the great man was taken. It was like trying to penetrate a hoplite phalanx. Ben was struggling to position his camera above his head and encouraging Johnny to push the microphone through the throng of people to get a quote. Ben had not been to an F1 race before, but as a professional cameraman, he had plenty of experience of media scrums. Then I realised Michael was not speaking English.

'He's speaking in German,' I told Johnny.

'Great, English next,' he assured me. 'The German crews will leave space for us.'

At that moment, Schumacher turned sharply to his left and the five German reporters and their cameramen peeled off like choreographed ballet dancers in the *Nutcracker Suite*. The remaining TV crews spread out, leaving just a small opening for Ben and Johnny at the end of the line.

Michael effortlessly switched to English and each journalist was asking a question, before the next butted in to try to get a useable soundbite for their channel. Down the line it went. Johnny reached in with his microphone to piggyback the interviews and Ben recorded Michael's face, side on at first, but slowly turning towards our camera. As Michael's eyes flicked ever-closer to Johnny for his question, other cameramen and journalists were leaving two by two, satisfied with what they had.

When it was Johnny's turn to speak, I decided to interrupt as something had occurred to me. It seemed to me that the tent was insufficiently glamorous, given the exotic location and the presence of the man who was leading the World Championship.

So, the first words I ever spoke to the German megastar were these:

'Michael, the inside of this tent is not that great visually, would you mind stepping outside so we can get a nicer shot of you with the harbour in the background?'

The temperature inside the tent dropped instantly from balmy to ice cold. Johnny and Ben looked sideways at me in disbelief and the three remaining journalists looked across in astonishment. One of the cameramen even took his eye from the viewfinder to clock the imbecile who had just had the audacity to make such an outrageous request. Yet it was Michael's face that would stay with me for many years. Normally a decent and respectful person, somehow, he managed to convey anger, contempt, embarrassment and disbelief with one glance. His face visibly swelled. I did not need to be telepathic to get the message.

'Who the fuck are you? Are you nuts? Don't you think I have anything better to do than stroll around the Monaco harbour for half an hour so you can get a nice shot?'

'… or not,' I followed up quickly. 'As you wish, here will be fine as well.'

I sensed it was a good time to leave and peeled away, feeling my cheeks start to burn. My move was not as well-choreographed as the German evacuation, but it was done at considerably greater speed.

I'm not sure who Michael's press officer was that day and thankfully our eyes didn't meet. But knowing what I now know about press officers, they would certainly have crossed me off the interview list for a decade.

Johnny apologised on my behalf and professionally asked his questions about how Michael was going to approach the weekend following the tragedy of Senna's death. Happy that I was no longer in his line of sight, Michael gave the heartfelt answer that would open our pre-show to Monaco.

So, within a couple of minutes of entering the paddock, I had set the pattern for plenty more cringe-worthy cock-ups that would characterise my career in Formula One. When Michael had returned to his motorhome, Johnny and Ben joined me. Johnny's eyebrows were raised incredulously.

'Was it really that bad?' I asked.

Both Johnny and Ben nodded vigorously in unison. Johnny took a deep breath and patiently explained the protocol of the interview system.

'So basically, you just wait around with your mouth wide open like a ravenous baby bird waiting for mama to bring a worm?' I said.

'Yes, it's exactly like that,' Johnny confirmed.

'Fair enough.' It was my first hard lesson in paddock etiquette.

Later that day Johnny interviewed Damon Hill, Mika Häkkinen, Johnny Herbert, Jean Alesi, Martin Brundle and Gerhard Berger in similar scrums. By the end of the day, we had good material for the base of the first and some of the second segment of the pre-show.

When there was time between interviews, Ben and I wandered out to the harbour and he took shots of the superb views. When we finished the last interview of the day, we walked over to the quaint town centre to record more material to help me with my edit. The Monaco racetrack threads through the streets beside the harbour and is largely unchanged since the first race in 1950. Most of the facilities are built specially for the race and are rapidly disassembled once the circus leaves town.

Security is tough, run by the Monaco Police, who are the largest per capita police force in the world and can't be sweet-talked into anything. There are plenty of wealthy people among the 40,000 who live in Monaco and they certainly don't want to give potential criminals even half a chance. As I would learn over the next couple of days, it is also extremely tricky to get anywhere in Monaco with a limited-access pass.

The racing schedule was also a little different. Recently, things have changed, but traditionally Thursday was the day that drivers did interviews with the press at most circuits, but in Monaco it was Wednesday. Free practice was on Thursday instead of Friday and on Friday there was no scheduled activity at all.

I assured Johnny I would spend the whole of Thursday searching for a place to film some free practice track action to solve the problem of having no pit or circuit access. Johnny had his doubts it was possible but didn't try to dissuade me.

So, for the first free practice session, Ben and I tried to film from the balcony of my room at the Hermitage Hotel, but with little success. Stunning, though the view of the circuit was, it was difficult to get a clear shot of the cars. The session was stopped at one point and only later did we find out that yet another accident had occurred at the Nouvelle Chicane when Karl Wendlinger's car slid into the water-filled barriers. The Austrian was in a coma for several weeks. Sauber-Mercedes withdrew their other, driver Heinz-Harald Frentzen, from the race out of respect for his team-mate.

As the images from the balcony were unusable, I decided to walk around the meandering streets surrounding the circuit with Ben in search of a better vantage point to film the afternoon session. The tripod and borrowed camera were uncomfortable to carry and we wasted four hours climbing thousands of steps in search of a gap in the buildings. There were few to be found. I even tried holding Ben by the legs as he dangled out across stone walls and fences trying to shoot cars passing at 150mph through tiny gaps. Ben was not happy. I finally conceded that my idea was perhaps not the best. It was impossible to film track action without access rights in Monaco. I hoped the next day would bring a solution to my predicament, but at that moment I had absolutely no idea how.

At 8pm on Thursday I went to the first of my three booked edit sessions at a production company close to the hotel. I had logged my tapes using the camera Philippe had lent us to view the material, so I was well prepared and expected to be wrapped up in a couple of hours.

The editor assigned to work with me was a Frenchman called Jean Paul. But there was a problem. For every word of French that I had managed to learn during my ten years of instruction in the language on an island only 14 miles from the French coast, which was, to all intents and purposes, none, Jean Paul had acquired a similar number of words of English. The English words for 'cut', 'mix', 'tape', 'stop', 'hello' and 'water' had never come to his attention. But then neither had any French words stuck in my sieve-like brain. Apart from '*bonjour*', to be fair to myself.

He was also oblivious to the meaning of hand gestures that one would have thought were universal in communication. He didn't twig that the scissor-like gesture with my middle and forefinger signified a 'cut'. Everything seemed lost on Jean Paul.

Hoping to smooth communications, I spoke to the other French editor who was working in the suite beside us. He spoke some English and together we noted on a piece of paper the important words I would need, with a translation. But this just added to the confusion because I kept losing the makeshift crib sheet under the tape boxes and just wasted more time searching for it.

Before starting the edit, I checked to see if any of Ben's precariously shot footage of free practice one was useable, but the answer was a resounding 'no'. So, we cut down the interviews we had recorded into useable soundbites, while I wrote the scripts for the links for Johnny to record to camera the following day. Progress was slow. In addition to the communications difficulties, Jean Paul required a lengthy cigarette break every quarter of an hour. As I sat waiting, I must confess, I felt my patience drain away.

We made some progress when I left Jean Paul to edit a 30-second montage of pretty shots of the harbour and the streets around Monaco, but by the time we were finished it was 5am. I got back to the hotel at 5.30 and instantly fell asleep, but what felt like moments later, I was awoken at 7am by a call from Johnny, who announced he was keen to make the most of the 'ideal light' and do the opening link for the pre-show from a viewing cove above Monaco. My 'ideal light' would have been pitch black for another six or seven hours, but I forced myself out of bed and into the shower.

Our tight-knit team downed *café au laits* and refuelled at the breakfast buffet before driving up the roads cut into the sheer cliffs to find the perfect spot to set up the camera in a layby. I had already driven along the Moyenne Corniche, the middle of three roads cut into the mountain between Nice and Menton, in both directions, but I was either too stoned, too worried about the stolen camera, or too ecstatic about replacing it, to fully appreciate the dazzling panoramic views across the bay, now glittering with early morning sunlight.

This time, as we climbed the cliff roads, I remembered the scenes from the James Bond film *GoldenEye* where James gets into a flirty race in his Aston Martin DB5 with Onatopp, the sociopathic lady assassin, in her Ferrari F355.[70]

---

70 Although their 'race' does finish in Monte Carlo, in fact the scenes were shot some distance away in Thorenc.

Two black Lamborghinis flashed by as we pulled into one of the few places available to park on the stretch of road and unloaded the camera equipment. Johnny prepared his opening link to let the audience know we were on site in Monaco for the most iconic race on the Formula One calendar, before linking to a tribute package of drivers commenting on the calamitous deaths of Roland Ratzenberger and Ayrton Senna. While he waited, Ben recorded a selection of pans and static shots of the spectacular views. Johnny was right, the light was perfect.

He nailed the opening link, starting with his normal enthusiasm before switching to a more serious and sombre tone to set up the tribute to Ayrton and Roland.

As Ben and Johnny climbed back into the car, I looked again at the glistening sunlight. Everything seemed perfect. Except, that was, for the tiny problem that I didn't have a single image of a Formula One racing car, which might be thought to be kind-of-nice in a programme about Formula One racing cars.

Back at the circuit we recorded more of Johnny's links to camera to cover the commercial break transitions, a variety of extravagant boats bobbing in the background.

Although there was no scheduled activity on Friday in Monaco, the teams and sponsors did set up special interviews and Johnny, who had a contact in the Sasol Jordan Team, had organised a sit-down interview with Rubens Barrichello at 4pm on a yacht moored in the harbour. So, we met Johnny's contact at the dock and took the short boat ride out in search of the Brazilian. The slot was short, but Rubens was quite charming and Johnny asked him about his first podium finish in the Pacific Grand Prix and the start of his second year in Formula One. He also talked about his relationship with his hero, Ayrton Senna, and his own dramatic accident in the previous race. Even though the yacht was bouncing up and down like a cork in a hot tub, and everyone felt a little seasick by the end, the interview was great. Shaky, but great.

I began my Friday night edit a little later than planned. I had no key to the building containing the edit suites and Jean Paul turned up late to find me sound asleep on the doorstep. No apology was forthcoming.

We set to work, but our relationship was souring fast. I began to wonder if he was paid by the hour, because he seemed to be doing far more smoking than editing, which didn't help progress one bit. I was beginning to dislike Jean Paul more with each passing puff. By the time we finished the shift, it was 6am.

I had completed the first of three programme segments in the two edit sessions, so just one down and two to go, with only one session left. I had brought footage on a Betacam 'dump' tape with me from Hong Kong with everything I thought I might need, including the bumpers, opening and closing titles, shots of Senna and Ratzenberger and highlights of the previous year's Monaco race.

At least the first segment looked great. It was a little over eight of the scheduled 24 minutes, leaving space for three two-minute commercial breaks. It began with my opening titles which then mixed to a montage of panoramic and pretty shots of the Monaco harbour and town, cut to a groovy beat. Johnny's 'welcome' link to camera was followed by the drivers' tributes to Senna and Ratzenberger. Then came a piece I had titled on screen 'The Magic of Monaco' that was a collection of driver soundbites explaining why Monaco was so special, with more footage that Ben had recorded. The segment ended with Johnny sat on the yacht moored in the harbour with Rubens Barrichello.

'That's right, we are here in Monte Carlo and where else would we be than on a yacht in the Monaco harbour chatting with none other than this guy, Rubens Barrichello.' Rubens nodded genially and winked at the camera.

'You don't want to miss that, so join us again after the break for more coverage of the Monaco Grand Prix.' I used the podium celebrations to close the segment, but added Rubens celebrating his podium in the Pacific Grand Prix.

But most of the work was still to be done. I was trying to convince myself that if I could get Jean Paul to stop taking cigarette breaks and if I could find some footage of the cars, I could still finish the job before my deadline. But they were two big ifs and I was worried. That night I slept for just two hours before it was time to get up and drive to the circuit for qualifying.

The Pride of Venezuela

Circuit de Catalunya, north of Barcelona, 2012

THE START of the 2012 Formula One season was unusually exciting because the first seven races were all won by different drivers. But the fifth race on the calendar, the Spanish Grand Prix, was unforgettable for Williams fans, those who love an underdog, and particularly for Latin American fans, because of the exploits of the racing star Pastor Maldonado.

Pastor was born on 9 March 1985 to wealthy parents in Maracay, Venezuela. He became friendly with his country's President Hugo Chávez, who organised the support Pastor needed to secure a seat in the Williams team in 2011. The national state oil company, PDVSA, which fronted several of Chávez's initiatives to promote Venezuela, was rumoured to have brought over $40m to the table.

Pastor showed plenty of racing skill when convincingly winning the 2010 GP2 Series championship. But in Formula One he earned something of a reputation for his supposedly erratic driving, which in turn led to an enthusiastic cult following. There is no denying that the Maldonado crash highlights reel is longer than the straight at the Shanghai International Circuit. In his 96 races he retired 29 times and incurred 39 penalties for various offences, 12 of which were for causing a collision. In his honour, his fans built a tongue-in-cheek website which detailed every misdemeanour of 'the Crashtor' and how long, in days, hours, minutes and seconds it was since his last crash.

His critics included Mark Webber[71] who answered an interview question, 'Who was the worst F1 racer?' by saying with characteristic Australian directness, 'Probably Maldonado. He's out of his depth and just shouldn't be there.'

But Pastor didn't care what people thought. Indeed he revelled in his infamy, choosing to drive with the unlucky number 13 on his car in 2014 and posting a picture of a boat that had collided with some rocks, with himself in the foreground and the caption 'just arrived in Monaco'. He also defended himself robustly. 'When Pastor crashes, it's big news,' he said. 'When the other people crash, there is no news. To find the limit, you need to cross the limit. I think I have the big balls to cross the limit every time.'

In a parody of Senna's famous quote, 'If you no longer go for a gap that exists, you are no longer a racing driver,' the joke was, 'If you go for a gap that doesn't exist, you are Pastor Maldonado.'

But when it came to sheer speed, even his critics conceded he was quick and they admired his total commitment to racing as hard as he possibly could. Sometimes he was brilliant. Other times, not so much.

I spent a lot of time with Pastor Maldonado and what I can say for sure is that he is a well-spoken, open and friendly guy. As with all Latin American drivers connected with Formula One, Fox Sports LatAm reported his every move. For more than a season, after qualifying and the race itself, I interviewed Pastor for a channel in Venezuela owned by Hugo Chávez. We had to go outside the circuit, because the channel didn't have the rights to use the regular interviews Juan had already done with him at the track for Fox.

Having a sweaty Englishman and a cameraman accompany him on a sometimes-lengthy walk to get out of the circuit and then cast around for a neutral background to film the interview wasn't ideal, but he was always happy to suffer my small talk in bad Spanish. He was a perfect gentleman, full of self-confidence and rarely in a

---

71 Australian driver in Formula One from 2002 to 2013 who won nine Grands Prix and achieved 42 podiums.

THE PRIDE OF VENEZUELA

bad mood, even after a difficult race. He certainly never looked out of place among his fellow drivers. On the rare occasions Pastor did not want to discuss his lack of pace, his charming wife Gabriela, a journalist herself, was happy to keep the conversation going.

He drove for Williams from 2011 to 2013 and then at Lotus in 2014 and 2015 before the sponsorship money dried up and he was forced to move to test driving and then to leave the sport altogether. While some considered him a liability on the track, he scored a total of 76 championship points over five seasons; not a huge number, but certainly more than others managed in similarly competitive cars.

The Circuit de Catalunya (aka the Circuit de Barcelona-Catalunya after 2013) which is situated near the town of Montmeló about 15 miles north of Barcelona, hosts the Spanish Grand Prix. It is also traditionally used for pre-season testing, because the track layout has long straights and a sufficient variety of corners to enable the engineers to analyse their cars' all-round performance before the season begins.

My 2012 visit was my second to the circuit, as I had travelled there to produce a programme with Johnny Green in 1995. On Saturday afternoon, in dry conditions, Lewis Hamilton set the fastest lap, but his fuelling mechanic broke a technical regulation by failing to fill the tank with the required amount of petrol, thus making the car lighter and giving Lewis an advantage. So, the British driver was forced to start at the back of the grid. This promoted Pastor, who had surprised everyone with his blistering pace in the Williams-Renault, to pole position, the only time he came close to achieving the honour.

Fernando Alonso, in his home Grand Prix, was alongside Pastor on the front row in a Ferrari, and Romain Grosjean and Kimi Räikkönen in the Lotus-Renaults were just behind in third and fourth places. So Pastor, despite his starting position, was not fancied to win. Few believed he could be consistently quick enough to claim the top spot.

When the starting lights went out in front of a crowd of 82,000, Maldonado slipped his clutch and so didn't get the start he wanted.

He instinctively turned to the right to block Alonso, pushing the Ferrari out towards the grass, but Alonso kept accelerating and after a fierce battle down the main straight took the lead.

But Maldonado was not about to give up his chance to become a Grand Prix winner and kept his cool through the first two cycles of pit stops. As a frustrated Alonso was held up in traffic, Pastor emerged from his second stop in the lead, to the delight of his Latin fans everywhere and his ecstatic family watching in the pits.

A slow tyre change dropped him to second place after his third pit stop, but he managed to catch and overtake the race leader Kimi Räikkönen on lap 47. Alonso also overtook the struggling Finn and started to chase Maldonado down, closing on him with every lap. To the astonishment of everyone and despite his deteriorating rear tyres, Pastor held his nerve and fought off the chasing Ferrari to become the first Venezuelan to win a Formula One Grand Prix, over three seconds ahead of Fernando Alonso, with Kimi Räikkönen half a second further back in third.

The victory gave Williams their first win since the 2004 Brazilian Grand Prix (when another South American, Colombian Juan Pablo Montoya won) and came after a terrible 2011 season for Williams that nearly ended their participation in Formula One. The achievement of Maldonado and his team triggered a flood of congratulatory messages from, among others, former champions Damon Hill, Jenson Button and Nigel Mansell.

Meanwhile in Caracas, car horns blasted and banners flew emblazoned with 'Maldonado, Pride of Venezuela' as he was heralded a national hero. President Chávez would, of course, soon call to congratulate him.

On the podium Kimi and Fernando, who understood just what the victory meant to Pastor, lifted him up on their shoulders as he held his arms aloft in front of the capacity crowd. It was Pastor's supreme moment. He was now a Grand Prix winner and nobody could ever take that away from him. For all the ups and downs of his career, I am pretty sure that everyone who contributed to it financially, practically or emotionally felt they got a handsome return on their investment that one ecstatic day. I am privileged to have been there.

And as if that was not enough excitement for one day, the celebrations continued in the Williams garage and ended with a bang, as we shall see.

Animal Farm

Monaco 1994

I PLANNED for the second segment of the pre-show to feature three elements: the Barrichello interview; drivers talking about the sensation of driving at the limit so close to the Armco safety barriers; and a two-minute highlight package I had edited in Hong Kong of Ayrton Senna's win the previous year.

The latter was particularly poignant, as it was Senna's fifth consecutive win around the street circuit and his sixth victory in Monaco, breaking Graham Hill's achievement of five. Graham's son Damon had finished the 1993 race in second place. Johnny Green's link would follow these race highlights and throw to Damon's answer to a question about his father's achievements in Monaco, before a bumper would close the segment. That was the plan. All I needed was Jean Paul's cooperation.

Before the qualifying session began on Saturday, Ben recorded as many drivers as he could either strolling up and down the paddock or walking back and forth from their garages. In Monaco, unusually, the pit lane is a few minutes' walk from the paddock, so the drivers must cross a temporary metal bridge to get there. As our passes didn't allow us to go across, Ben and I were stationed at the base of the staircase on the paddock side to get shots of the drivers before they climbed the stairs. We thought the images might be useful as inserts covering the interviews for the second segment.

We arrived back at the interview pen after qualifying started, to find a worried-looking Johnny. It wasn't hard to see why. The square pen, built from galvanised steel mobile metal fences, was surrounded by a febrile mob of the international press. We had shown up far too late to get a useful position.

Today, the interview pen at a Formula One race is reasonably ordered and civilised. Each authorised television channel is allocated a position in a small group to set up their cameras on tripods outside the barriers. The drivers are led by their press officer into the pen to talk to each group in turn. Each channel usually asks two questions and records the answers to all the group's questions.

Back in 1994, however, there was no organisation at all. It wasn't called the 'pen' by accident, given the dictionary definition of a pen is 'a small enclosure, especially for animals'. Getting interviews in this environment was indeed dog-eat-dog and the devil take the hindmost.

Some people could take the pressure of the pen in their stride, usually self-confident reporters with a name and a big TV network behind them, making it easy for them to attract the drivers' attention. But the smaller fish in the sea of reporters were often humiliated. I have seen grown men with microphones shaking so uncontrollably that it looks like they are tapping out a rhythm on a crash cymbal. I have seen people freeze and totally forget their question, smash equipment in anger, curse live on air and break down in tears. I have done most of these things myself. When I accidentally bashed British driver Paul di Resta on the nose with my microphone, it was, I am ashamed to say, because I was not paying attention to his answer to my question because I was trying to signal to another driver to come over and talk before they left the pen. Very reasonably, Paul didn't take the assault at all well and pushed my microphone back towards me purposefully, while staring me down. Once again, my humble apologies, Paul.

Another reason the pen can be a hostile environment is that sometimes the driver simply doesn't want to be there, although their contracts oblige them to attend and they get fined if they don't. Qualifying laps and races often don't go to plan and problems and disappointments abound. Perhaps the driver just crashed a multi-million-dollar car into the wall for no obvious reason and will shortly have to explain why to his team principal. Or maybe a driver has just been shunted off the track by his team-mate, or indeed done the shunting himself and is not in the mood for explanations.

The pen is where one driver might confront another about an on-track incident, as it is often the first opportunity they get to vent their frustrations. At the Hungarian Grand Prix in 2017, Renault driver Nico Hülkenberg, having been forced off the circuit by Kevin Magnussen, tapped Kevin on the shoulder during his live interview in Danish with Luna Christofi and said:

'Congratulations. Once again, the most unsporting driver on the grid!'

'Suck my balls, mate,' was Magnussen's instant response, before refocusing his attention on Luna.

Juan was interviewing Sergio Pérez right next to Luna at the time and we all had a good laugh when Checo and Kevin had moved on. Years later Kevin said he regretted the remark, not because of what he said, but because he thinks he will always be remembered for those four words rather than the rest of his long and distinguished motor racing career! In a further irony, Kevin and Nico had to make up in 2023 when they became team-mates at Haas.

Many drivers live in a constant state of anxiety that their performance will not be seen as good enough, which can mean losing the job they have yearned for since childhood. So repeatedly answering similar questions from every channel in the world can be gruelling for all involved.

Some channels, depending on the driver's nationality or the team's commercial interests, are given preference in the pen, but in the early nineties, if you were unknown and from a channel covering Formula One on site for the first time, no one would yield their hard-fought place for you. You were on your own. Our late arrival was a rookie error. We should have been there at least an hour earlier to stand even a chance of getting a good spot. We knew nobody and there were certainly no friendly faces, only grim, hard expressions among the jostling members of the world press. Reporters with every right to be there were pressed up against the steel metal barriers, their cameramen, shooting over their shoulders, slightly back and to their side. Behind them, the print media were lining up, ready to lean in with Dictaphones to catch a comment for their news pieces. Behind them were the photographers, hungry for photos, the more chaotic the better.

I was ready to throw in the towel, already thinking of excuses to explain our failure to get a single post-qualifying interview. Perhaps I could blame Bernie and just send by satellite two segments to start the pre-show and let the commentators explain what happened during qualifying as they showed the grid?

No, that would not do. Sam had trusted me and spent a fortune for us to come to Monaco. There had to be a way in. I ruled out the side of the pen where all the German and Austrian crews were jam-packed. Schumacher was the most important person to interview as it looked like he was going to be in pole position. And we needed his answers in English.

I circled the other three sides of the pen with Johnny and Ben following closely. I was looking for a glimpse of daylight amongst the bodies, cameras, microphones and limbs for a gap into which to slide a microphone and a camera lens. I could feel the throng stir as we approached. They all knew full well what we were up to and closed ranks, their backs in tight formation, with elbows sticking out aggressively. There was no way in. Desperate, I begged the friendliest-looking people to make room for Johnny and Ben, but learned only the expression for 'get the fuck out of here' in half a dozen languages.

Then a brilliant, if risky, idea occurred to me.

The drivers came in and out through a gap in the pen which was clear. If we timed it right, once the top drivers we needed to interview were inside the pen, perhaps we could grab that spot and hope for a final comment as they left. It was dicey, but it was our only chance. Ben and Johnny hated the idea but agreed it was the only way to go.

When the pen contained the top ten finishers we were interested in interviewing, I distracted the marshal in charge of keeping the entrance area clear by asking him how many years he had been working for the Monaco Grand Prix. He was surprised by my odd question and asked me why I wanted to know. But while he gave me his attention, Ben and Johnny slipped in.

A couple of drivers exiting the pen pushed them aside, but they were able to hold their position without anyone noticing. Johnny made himself as unobtrusive as he could by squeezing to his right and managed to get short answers from Damon Hill, Jean Alesi, Mika Häkkinen, Gerhard Berger, Christian Fittipaldi, Martin Brundle and the all-important pole-sitter, Michael Schumacher. I had enough material to complete the final segment.

It had been thirsty work, so we popped into Stars 'N' Bars, a few metres from the paddock enclosure, for celebratory pints. In the packed sports bar, I struck up a conversation with a guy called Tom, who turned out to be a producer at the BBC, and was also in high spirits after a successful post-qualifying interview session. After chatting for a while over a few drinks, I told him about the nightmare I was facing in my last edit session with the cantankerous Jean Paul, with no footage of cars to overlay the interviews we had just shot.

'So, you're after a copy of qualifying on Beta SP, basically?' he asked matter-of-factly, after hearing my sob story.

'Well, ideally, but I'd settle for a few shots of the top five drivers' cars at this point.'

'And Star TV are F1 rights holders?' I nodded to confirm. Star TV, although they had allegedly got a good deal from Bernie, had still paid a tidy sum of money for the rights to show material, which included any World Feed shots from practice, qualifying and the race.

'Leave it with me,' he said with a wink.

I'm not sure how Tom got the message through to his colleague but 15 minutes later someone showed up with a 60-minute Betacam tape of the qualifying session and handed it to me. I couldn't believe my eyes. I ordered tequila shots for my new friends at the BBC and celebrated with Johnny and Ben until it was time to head off to my final edit session, somewhat the worse for wear.

I now had all the necessary material to complete the task. But my relationship with Jean Paul was about to take a further turn for the worse.

Gooshbumpsh on the Grid

Zandvoort, the Netherlands, 2022

WITH 45 minutes to go before the scheduled start of a Formula One race, the cars leave their garages and head out for their installation lap[72] after which the TV crews and the rest of the press are allowed to cross from the paddock to the pit lane and on to the grid. It's always an exhilarating experience. I feel like a professional sportsman running on to a stadium pitch for a cup final or sell-out international. The fans burst into life at the sight of the cameras, especially when they are pointed in their direction. They dance, sing, shout and cheer.

The safety car drives around the circuit to check for problems and then parks at the front of the grid. The FOM security staff are first to take up their positions then, for a few moments, the TV crews are centre stage. In front of the safety car carpets are laid out where the drivers will stand during the national anthem. The trophies are displayed and brass bands, orchestras or dancers perform.

At the beach-fronted Zandvoort circuit where the 2022 Dutch Grand Prix was held, the paddock is split into two areas, one for engineering and one for hospitality. Uli and I went on to the grid through the gate between them. In the main stand above the grid, Dutch fans had turned up in multitudes to cheer for their idol Max Verstappen. Banners supporting the world champion hung from the

---

[72] The first lap of the day, that starts and ends in the pit lane, was historically used to check everything in the car was working properly, but nowadays is more for the driver to get a feel for the car and the surface and to enable the engineers to gather any information required for last-minute fine-tuning.

front of the stand and Max's father, Jos 'the Boss', also featured in the fluttering signage.

The tipsy fans, known as the 'Orange Army', are a remarkably disciplined force. Every so often they would, on command, wave hundreds of carefully distributed red, white and blue pennants, transforming the stand into a giant animated Dutch flag. When the flags were put away, the shock of orange shirts, hats and cloaks was again revealed.

Uli and I were waved through the grid entrance by Steve from security, who nodded as we passed. The crowd were in full voice, belting out a rendition of Dmitri Shostakovich's 'Waltz No. 2', followed by the Pitstop Boys' hit 'Super Max', then a spectacular version of Queen's rousing anthem 'We Will Rock You'. The stand shuddered from the rhythmic stamping of their feet. Someone had managed to smuggle a smoke bomb into the stand, despite them being banned, and it sent a defiant orange spiral high into the air.

The installation lap complete, it is now time for the cars to leave the pits for a second time and head out on to the circuit, this time on their way to the grid. Pit crews, who may have received information from the drivers about problems or required adjustments, hurriedly make their way to the pit lane and out on to the grid, carrying or pushing trolleys stacked with carefully checked equipment. This is a tense time. A faulty or missing piece of equipment can easily mean the difference between a 25-point race win and a dreaded DNF.[73]

Spare tyres, perhaps 'intermediates' or 'wets', depending on the weather and the race strategy, are carried on trolleys in heat blankets powered by petrol-run generators. Wheel guns are attached to air lines; cooling-fan hoses to iceboxes. The chief mechanics supervise their team. Senior race engineers talk by radio to their strategic engineers already in position on the pit wall.

The first cars begin to arrive, slowing down at the back of the grid before the engines are switched off. The mechanics rush to meet their drivers, jack their cars up on to carbon fibre wheelie boards and

---

73 Did Not Finish. So no points at all.

push them through the growing throng of people into their place on the grid. The buttons on the steering wheel are double-checked to make sure they have been set correctly and a final inspection of the front and back wing settings is performed.

The heads and eyes of photographers and cameramen are constantly moving as they scan for the best action to shoot. As the racing cars are pushed down the centre of the grid, crews, reporters, celebrities, guests and camera operators move aside or, if distracted, are pushed out of the way by mechanics. I am alert, scanning my surroundings, looking for hazards that might put Uli in danger. Although any grid cameraman is aware of what is going on around them, sometimes accidents happen. Collisions are not uncommon and nor is tripping over a piece of equipment on the floor. At times a car will only appear at the last second as the crowd parts to let it through. So, I keep Uli safe with a gentle guiding hand on his shoulder.

As the race start approaches, the grid becomes increasingly chaotic. Like any dance, it works if everyone knows the steps, but since the sport has opened up there are more new people on the grid to get in the way, perhaps taking a selfie in front of their favourite driver. They are unceremoniously pushed out of the way. Some teams handle the newbies more gently than others. Red Bull mechanics smile politely as they move people aside. Ferrari mechanics, however, are renowned for showing little empathy towards anyone who even gets close to interfering with their procedures. I learned about Ferrari's approach the hard way when I was first required to stand in for Uli as cameraman in the pits in Saudi Arabia in 2021 and was, unnecessarily (as I thought) yanked out of the way by a Ferrari mechanic.

'What is that Ferrari guy on?' my photographer friend Glenn Dunbar said. 'He's pushed me three times!'

But to be fair, I did later see the very same mechanic save another photographer from potentially serious injury when he somehow got himself directly into the path of Carlos Sainz as he entered the pits. So, it's perhaps understandable the Italians' motto is to 'push first and don't bother asking questions later'.

As the cars line up, the world's press flock around the most newsworthy drivers, with pole position the most popular. The energy from the crowd escalates further as the excited onlookers gaze down upon the gladiators from their not-at-all cheap seats. Then the drivers climb out of their cockpits, remove their helmets and balaclavas and acknowledge their fans, before returning to their own personal rituals that help them to stay 'in the zone'.

Max Verstappen was on pole in Zandvoort and talked calmly to Helmut Marko, then Christian Horner. I was staggered by how unruffled the Dutchman was while his adoring fans chanted his name in a state of delirium. Christian's press officer, Mark, pointed at me and then at the Red Bull team principal, indicating that he was offering a quick interview. I declined by shaking my finger, then thanked him with a thumbs-up. Our camera was not live, so the interview would be wasted. Juan, elsewhere on the grid, was talking with the commentary team using the LUCI app on his phone. In any case, I had done a 15-minute one-to-one with Christian in Hungary and asked him just about every question I could think of!

This is a good time to look around for celebrities or former drivers to try to catch a soundbite or two to use in the *GP1* magazine programme to add colour before the race highlights segment. Uli and I backed away from Max and went across to Charles Leclerc, who was alongside the Dutchman on the front row. I usually take a photograph of the Ferrari driver in his balaclava for my own collection, part of my own ritual before every race.

Many drivers listen to music to drown out the craziness that surrounds them. It helps them to concentrate on the job that will soon see them go from 0 to over 120mph in about five seconds as they compete into the first corner.

Daniel Ricciardo passed me with his headphones on, nodding his head rhythmically, doubtless in time with the hard-core heavy metal or hip-hop music that he prefers before a race. Uli filmed the Australian as he went to his place on the grid and started his stretching routine, crouched down on the grass and leaning against the wall between the track and the fans. The Australian was in his own world, smiling, his default facial setting.

Some drivers like to be pumped up by their music, like Daniel. Pierre Gasly listens to French or American rap, but others prefer more chilled-out music. Kimi Räikkönen says he listens to Finnish music before a race, however that sounds! Esteban Ocon likes rousing film scores. Each to their own!

Uli and I wandered back to the front of the grid and high-fived our Dutch friend Roy Janssen who was grinning inanely as he walked by, steering the Viaplay cameraman who was tracking backwards, shooting Mervi Kallio as she interviewed Valtteri Bottas in their native Finnish.

As Roy walked past, I smiled as I recalled something he said to me when I did a piece about Broadcast Rental, the company he works for. They are responsible for much of the communications infrastructure that enables a Grand Prix to be broadcast, running cables from their mobile facilities in the TV compound to commentary booths near the track and to the antennae that receive signals from the RF cameras filming in the paddock and pits.

Frank Steenbeek, chief operations officer of the company, explained how it all works. Roy spoke of his role, looking after the client, making sure the equipment in the TV compound is working, laying and pulling cables and setting up and de-rigging the equipment. Uli filmed Roy on a hill near the antennae overlooking the paddock and I asked my friend what the best part of his job was.

'De gooshbumpsh,' he told me in his thick Dutch accent.

'Goosebumps?' I asked. I speak fluent 'Roy', so I knew what he meant.

'What d'you mean by "goosebumps", Roy?'

'Every time I walk on to ze grid wij a client and I see all je cars and the je driversh, and je people cheering, I get gooshbumpsh just being der, every single time.' He smiled his wild, crazy smile, bringing one muscled forearm up in front of the camera, with the other upturned hand miming the hairs sticking up on end. Uli, Roy and I all laughed heartily. I knew immediately I had the perfect quote to close the piece.

On the grid in Zandvoort I, too, had goosebumps just listening to and watching the crowd. Carlos Sainz passed by, looking ridiculously suave and sophisticated. He reminds me of a racing driver from another era with his chiselled jawline and luxuriant jet-black hair.

Lewis Hamilton was chatting with New Zealander Angela Cullen, his assistant, minder, physiotherapist and friend. Pierre Gasly was facing his personal trainer who was randomly dropping two tennis balls from just below the top of Pierre's head, sometimes one and sometimes both at the same time. Pierre was catching them every time long before they hit the ground, showing his lightning reaction speed.

I smiled as I remembered a comment our main commentator Fernando Tornello had made live on air during a previous race transmission, when he said that ESPN Disney had their very own Pierre Gasly who does the same as the Frenchman, but with bottles of beer instead of tennis balls. Fernando had once seen me accidentally knock a full bottle of Corona from a table during a dinner in Mexico and then move with uncharacteristic precision and speed to catch it before it hit the ground!

It was time for the Dutch national anthem and the drivers were making their way to the front of the grid to hear the Dutch singer and songwriter Floor Jansen perform 'Het Wilhelmus'.

The mechanics stood respectfully still beside their cars. I must admit, I was not showing the same deference as I had just begun interviewing Irishman Eddie Irvine, the former driver who had spent four seasons at Ferrari with Michael Schumacher as his team-mate. I asked him what he thought about being back on the grid. He told me that it wasn't the driving that he missed, but seeing his old friends, Stefano Domenicali, Mattia Binotto and photographer Peter 'Foxy' Fox with whom he used to share a room. The national anthem ended but Eddie had more to say, insisting that his team Ferrari, despite their difficult season festooned with tactical mistakes, driver errors and reliability failures, were 'brilliant', had the fastest car on the grid and were definitely going in the 'right direction'. Once a Ferrari man, always a Ferrari man, I guess!

I had one more question for the Northern Irishman as the engines were being fired up on the grid.

'What about Max Verstappen? How good is he, Eddie?'

'He's the one guy I'd compare to Michael Schumacher on pace. No team-mate can get close to him. Now he's not making mistakes, that is hard to beat.'

I thanked Eddie as the drivers returned to their cars to prepare before the formation lap.[74] It was time for the press to leave the grid and security were on the case.

With the drivers back in their cars, balaclavas, gloves and helmets back on and visors down, the mechanics hurry back to the pits in case there is an incident at the first corner of the Grand Prix. This is the moment when Uli and I always fist-bump.

'Recto final,' Uli says and we both laugh at our inside joke. '*Recta final*', meaning 'final straight', is what he should say, as only the driver interviews, closing links and news pieces are left to do. '*Recto final*' however, is what I said for quite a while before Uli confided, giggling, that 'recto' meant 'rectum'. Goosebumps give way to a feeling of relief.

No two grid experiences are quite the same. In some, like Monaco, Interlagos and Spa, you feel the overwhelming sense of history and nostalgia. Others heighten your senses with the stunning surroundings, like the lights in Singapore, the setting sun in Abu Dhabi or the iconic BIC Building in Bahrain. At Austin or Miami in the United States, there are so many celebrities about, it feels like a Hollywood party. I even got to chat briefly with Brad Pitt at the 2022 Austin GP and scored a selfie that secured major bragging rights.

---

[74] The pre-start lap the drivers do, in grid order, to enable them to warm up their tyres and so reduce the risk of accidents once racing starts.

Others circuits are special for other reasons. The atmosphere in the Hermanos Rodríguez Autodromo in Mexico is one of a wild party. The energy radiating from the passionate 'Orange Army' at Zandvoort is perhaps even exceeded by the Italian 'Tifosi' in Monza cheering as the air force jets fly overhead, trailing the red, white and green colours of the Italian flag. Then there are the die-hard fans at Silverstone or Hockenheim dressed in their raincoats, unabashed by bad weather. And weirdest and most wonderful are the Japanese fans, with their outlandish outfits, hats with working DRS back wings, or hand-built half-metre-long headgear of replica cars. And the Japanese fans are certainly the politest. You will never hear anyone boo in Suzuka.

But Roy is right. The best way to describe the Formula One grid is 'gooshbumpsh'.

The Art of Silence

Monaco 1994

I HAD somewhat sobered up when I arrived at the production company. Jean Paul was already there so we started cutting the Rubens Barrichello interview into a three-and-a-half-minute piece. By one o'clock in the morning, the second segment was complete. I used shots of the harbour to mask the untidy jump-cuts in the Rubens interview and the newly acquired qualifying shots to cover the drivers talking about racing around Monaco. With the 1993 race highlights, bumpers and links, it came to seven minutes.

But progress was slow. The tequila shots and my lack of sleep didn't help and you would have needed a fibreglass pole to vault the language barrier. Most annoying of all, I was frequently left twiddling my thumbs while Jean Paul took yet another smoking break. At last, my patience evaporated and I decided to remonstrate with him. With little option, I made my complaint in mime. First, I did my best impersonation of a cigarette smoker with my index and middle finger raised to my mouth. Then I pointed at my wrist to indicate that time was running out. Then I waved my hands dramatically in the air to indicate, sensitively I hoped, my frustration.

Now it is just conceivable that Jean Paul may have interpreted my finger gesture as a V-sign. Jean Paul may have been aware that the origin of the impolite gesture is said to date from the Battle of Agincourt, when English longbowmen mocked the defeated French army by waving these two fingers, which would have been cut off to prevent them from using their bows again had they been captured. If he was, it can only have added to the unintended offence.

However he interpreted my little mime, after a short but tense silence, Jean Paul countered with a performance of his own. It, too, involved a fair amount of body language, but embellished with sound effects. These consisted of a somewhat loud, even screeching tirade, accompanied by an expansive set of hand gestures and gesticulations, amongst which, the two-handed, middle-finger gesture featured, somewhat different from the British version, but meaning pretty much the same thing. I certainly formed the impression he was not complimenting me on my production, linguistic, diplomatic or miming skills.

For some reason I decided that this was a good time to locate the missing piece of paper with the translation of the key editing phrases. He stared at me contemptuously, then grabbed what I was looking for from under a tape and slapped it down on the table in front of me, fired off another tirade that I guessed meant: 'Here is your stupid piece of paper, you English dickhead! What do you expect to find on there to help you explain your gross insults and insufferable incompetence?'

I ran my finger down the list: 'cut – *coupé*'; 'in point – *point d'entrée*'; 'out point – *point de sortie*'; 'mix – *mix*'; 'record – *enregistrer*'; 'interview – *interview*'; 'footage – *séquences*'; 'audio only – *audio uniquement*'; 'pictures only – *images uniquement*'; 'can I take the tape out of the machine please? – *puis-je sortir la cassette de la machine s'il vous plaît?*' and so on.

If that was indeed what he was implying, he had a point. There was no phrase saying, 'Sorry if I offended you, can you please forgive me?' or 'Let's agree to disagree on the finer points, but let's work together and finish this, please, so we can all go home. Please.'

Jean Paul spun around and stormed out of the edit suite. I expect he needed a cigarette more than ever to calm himself down. I thought I would give him a few minutes before going after him. I was contemplating my plan of action when the door opened again. But it was Johnny, not Jean Paul standing at the door.

'There's a pretty disgruntled bloke outside pacing up and down and ranting to himself in French,' Johnny said. 'Tell me that's not your editor?'

'Well, I'm not sure if he just quit or not. I haven't understood a word he has said since we started editing.'

'Anything I can do?'

'Can you edit?'

'Ah, no.'

'How's your French?'

'Non-existent.'

'Do you know where we can find a translator?' He understood the question was rhetorical.

'Is that the voice-over?' I asked, pointing at the tape in his hand.

'Yup, there's an intro to follow my segment opening link, then a bit about Martin Brundle, then the top six drivers in reverse order, then a closing round-up. Five minutes exactly as you asked. With the interviews, that should be perfect for the last segment.'

'Awesome, Johnny boy! Now I just need to mime Jean Paul down from the ledge, finish the edit, send it back by satellite and we're done!'

'Good luck!'

After Johnny left, I went outside to clear the smoky air with Jean Paul. I gave his fellow countryman Marcel Marceau a good run for his money, miming for my life. I movingly portrayed remorse and entreaty with the praying-hands sign, dropping dramatically on to one knee. I shrugged my shoulders attempting to convey 'I wasn't thinking' but it came across more like, 'I don't care.' I shook my hands frantically to try to withdraw the shoulder shrugging, but that confused matters even further. Which kind of assumes total confusion can be further confused, which I'm not sure is possible.

Things were hopeless. Everything was lost. There was just one option left, one final, hopeless throw of the dice. I can imagine no other circumstance in which I would even have contemplated such an appalling course of action, but I was desperate.

It was time for the 'man stuck in a glass box' routine.

I went to work, pressing my hands against the imaginary surface, to each side, above my head and behind, my eyebrows raised, my mouth forming a bewildered 'O'. Jean Paul looked on, still very angry. But after ten seconds or so he was still angry but also a touch bemused. Then after a few more moments, his face softened a fraction and gradually the anger drained away. When I shifted into the 'and now the box is getting smaller and I'm getting squashed' bit, at last he smiled, something I hadn't seen him do since we met. At last, we shook hands and went back inside.

The last few hours were a brutal slog, but Jean Paul resisted the urge to smoke any more cigarettes. It was about eight o'clock in the morning when, after an awkward embrace, I finally took my leave of Jean Paul. We parted amicably enough, though I must say I can't recall receiving a Christmas card from him.

But though I didn't make a lifelong friend, in my hand was the precious master tape of the pre-show in three segments, mixed with music, ambient sound, interviews, camera links and voice-over. The final segment ended with Johnny's voice-over of the lap that secured Michael Schumacher's pole position, followed by an interview with the happy German.

'After the break, we continue our coverage of the Monaco Grand Prix,' were Johnny's final words. I was proud of our work. Now I just had to transmit it to the crew and commentators back in Hong Kong.

What could possibly go wrong?

Lost in Lewis's Eyes

Milan 2019

ONE-TO-ONE INTERVIEWS with drivers are the best kind of material an F1 programme producer can have to complement track action. They provide exclusive material for your channel and draw in fans who want to get to know the drivers. A one-to-one must usually be arranged at least three weeks in advance with the driver's press representative. I try to do one at each race, but before the summer break, when there are more *GP1* shows to fill, or before our 'home' Grands Prix in Mexico, Miami and Brazil, when we are on the air much longer, I request several drivers and a couple of team principals.

It's easier to get time with some drivers than others. Not surprisingly, given his stellar success over the last decade, the hardest to reach is Lewis Hamilton. On behalf of our channel, I ask for a slot early in the season and, after sending a few polite reminders, usually get a confirmation towards the end of the year.

Lewis is Juan's favourite driver although, of course, he remains professionally neutral on air. But he has a good relationship with Lewis, so it is always with great excitement and anticipation we prepare for his chat with the seven-time world champion.

But in 2019, we were offered an additional slot with Lewis before the Italian GP. I had done a feature on Petronas[75] earlier that year and as part of the deal they offered us, at short notice, an interview with Lewis on the Wednesday before the race. Juan was

---

75 Mercedes' lubricant supplier and title sponsor.

scheduled to arrive too late, so I stepped in as Juan's understudy. I hoped Lewis wouldn't be too disappointed not to see the main man.

Uli and I drove straight from the airport to the centre of Milan, parked the hire car and walked to A'Riccione Terrazza 12, the rooftop bar and restaurant. We were early, but I wanted to check out the location. We walked up the stairs to the terrace to meet Charlotte, my contact at the marketing agency, Crunch.

'Hi Charli, how's it going?' I said, kissing her, Italian style.

'Oh hi! You're a little early, but you will be setting up over there.' Charli pointed to an area in the restaurant that had been cleared of tables and chairs.

'Perfect.'

Charli was busy with the TV crew that would interview Lewis after Sky Italy, who were set up to go first. I walked to our spot and started visualising where to put our main camera and GoPro to best capture the beautiful restaurant décor and ensure a good view of the Petronas logo that was on a large TV screen on the wall.

Unlike Juan, who would have sat alongside Lewis, my place is behind the camera, so I placed a chair for myself near where Uli would shoot from and then, after thoughtful consideration, one for Lewis. It was then I heard a loud 'psssst' from over my shoulder. I turned to see an angry-looking Sky Italy cameraman waving his arms frantically. I was standing in the background of his shot. Even though they were not yet recording, their presenter Mara Sangiorgio was scowling at me before her grimace melted into a warm smile as Lewis appeared and sat down on the stool in front of her. I put my hand up to the crew to apologise and Uli and I cleared out.

Satisfied that all would be well, Uli and I had time to walk down to the Duomo Di Milano to take a few shots for the introduction to our feature. As Uli busied himself around the cathedral and piazza, I sat down on a bench and went over my preparation.

This was not the occasion for my usual casual approach, so I had spent several hours meticulously researching Lewis's stellar career and carefully crafting questions artfully designed to get him to talk about the secrets of his success. They had already been checked over by Mercedes, who had agreed to them, apart from the last, which was:

'Lewis, you're an Arsenal supporter. I understand you were a pretty good footballer and cricketer and you also practised karate. Do you think you could have made it to the top in another sport if you had dedicated yourself to something other than motor racing?'

Mercedes reckoned that Lewis had never played cricket, so asked for the reference to be taken out, which seemed a little nit-picky to me, but I rephrased the question.

Our time slot was approaching, so we returned to the restaurant. Sky Italy were packing up and the other crew were finishing up with Lewis. I asked Mara how her interview had gone.

'*Spettacolare! Tutto bene!*' she said with a relaxed smile, her interview safely in the bag. I, on the other hand, was a little nervous. I had interviewed quite a few world champions before, but face-to-face with Lewis Hamilton seemed a little different, especially as I had asked him an ill-informed question or two over the years, which had received the irritable response they deserved.

I sat down next to Uli and read through my questions one last time. The room went quiet as Lewis reappeared and was directed to the comfy armchair in front of me. I shook the legend's hand and thanked him for his time as he picked up the microphone. He looked at me expectantly.

'We're in Monza, Lewis! A track you must love,' I began confidently. No need to be nervous. Perfect planning prevents poor performance, as my father used to say.

'You came second in your rookie season here and then won on five occasions,' I told him, feeling proud of my newly acquired knowledge. I had even written down the years he had won and for some reason decided to start reading them out.

'2012, 2014, 2015 …' I saw his eyes glaze over, but I had come too far to stop. '2017 and 2018.' This took forever to say, but at last I got to the point. 'My question is what are your strongest memories of Monza?'

'Honestly,' Lewis said, 'I have a terrible memory. I remember a little of my first race in 2007 and last year, but that's about it.' Silence reigned. A tumbleweed blew past.

Nervous now, I looked down at my security blanket, the list of questions on my phone. Aah, here was a good one.

'You hold the record for the most wins at different circuits with 26, Lewis, which shows your versatility as a driver. Which of those circuits do you like best and why?'

'I'm not really interested in records or statistics,' said Lewis. Which was a shame, because my next three questions were all based on meticulously researched statistics.

It was official, he hated me. But then things took an unexpected turn for the better.

'But there's plenty of circuits I do love …' he said. Perhaps taking pity on me, he opened up. He told me how much he loved Milan, a city he had visited to compete in karts when he was younger and still does, for Fashion Week. He spoke of his love for Monaco, his memories of watching his idol Ayrton Senna drive the circuit and how he felt when at last he realised his dream of driving the circuit himself. He prefers, he said, circuits steeped in history, such as Monza and Silverstone, to the more modern builds. He was now talking to me, so I began to listen rather than looking down at my questions. Nobody else from Mercedes was listening so I decided to go off script.

If F1 drivers share a characteristic apart from their love of racing, perhaps it is the intensity of their eyes, and none are more intense than Lewis Hamilton's. When he looks directly at you, you feel his life's experience. It radiates from within.

As he talked, I wondered if his real gift was to live so intensely in the moment. Whether driving at over 200mph around a racetrack, or talking to an understudy, he is always present. Perhaps that's why he isn't interested in his own incredible racing statistics. He focuses on the present and his plans for the future.

So, I relaxed, abandoned my prepared questions, and started talking to Lewis as I would to a friend. He told me about *The*

Game Changers, a documentary he did with Arnold Schwarzenegger, James Cameron and Novak Djokovic, among others, about athletes who eat a plant-based diet. I told him I would love to try to change my diet and he encouraged me to do so. He chatted about Neat Burger, his fast-food vegan restaurant, and highlighted his love for animals and his uneasiness about how they are treated to feed the world. He talked about his collaboration with fashion designer Tommy Hilfiger to make 100 per cent sustainable clothing, showing me the trainers he was wearing, containing no plastic, leather or suede. I tucked my feet under my chair. I doubted there was much leather or suede in my shoes either, but they definitely contained plenty of cheap plastic.

We moved on to Lewis's early years in karting and I asked about how he toured the country with his father, with a go-kart sticking out from the boot. He fondly recalled his stepmother sitting in the back of the car with his baby brother Nicholas in her arms, and talked about both joys and hardships as he built up his experience, week in week out, putting in the hard work. He spoke about overcoming struggles at school with dyslexia, always being put in the lowest classes and the prejudice he faced. But he said it shaped him to be a fighter.

I wanted to take Lewis back to his early years in Formula One.

'Lewis, I know you like to live in the moment and look forward, but can I ask you about when you claimed your first World Championship in Brazil in 2008?'

'Of course, what do you want to know?'

'It was so dramatic to watch. I can't imagine what it must have been like for you from inside the cockpit. Did you have any idea what was going on during that final lap? When you passed Timo Glock, did you know you had won the championship?'

'What you have to understand,' he replied, 'is when you're in a race you don't know where everyone is. You're lapping people, but often have no idea who you're lapping, what lap they're on or even what tyre they're on until you get close. I had no idea Timo was ahead of me. My sole focus was the car ahead. I knew I had to finish in fifth and when Vettel got past me I was sixth, but I couldn't get close to him because my tyres had gone off. So, when I came into the last corner, I was thinking that I'd lost the championship by one position, for the second year running. I came across the line thinking I'd lost.'

Lewis smiled and his eyes twinkled. He didn't need to say any more.

It is impossible not to respect this man who has overcome barriers that would be, for anyone else, insuperable. In 2021 he became the fourth Formula One driver to be knighted after equalling Michael Schumacher's record of seven world titles, joining Jack Brabham, Stirling Moss and Jackie Stewart, who only have six titles between them. He may have had to fight harder and longer for his success and for his knighthood than anyone but in his dark, revealing eyes you can clearly see both determination and an inner peace.

My final question was about the sports he played at school. He had indeed played cricket after all, so that was another sensational scoop! But he did say that racing was really the only thing he ever wanted to do.

Lucky for the rest of us.

Rubbish Performance

Monaco 1994

AT LAST, I could relax a little. I just had to find the TV compound and send the pre-show back to Hong Kong by satellite at 10am. The feed was booked for a 40-minute window. Talking of feeds, I was even hungrier than I was tired, so I decided to go straight to breakfast when I got back to the Hermitage Hotel. I loaded up my tray at the buffet with fruit juice, coffee and a large helping of bacon and eggs. I put the precious Betacam tape cassette on the tray and thoughtfully covered it with a napkin, just in case anything sticky or liquid got loose.

I hadn't slept more than a few hours in days, so once my stomach was full and the blood rushed to digest the food, I fell into a deep sleep face down on the table.

At 9.20am I woke up. It took me a few seconds to realise where I was. What had been a busy restaurant last time I looked was now eerily empty, not a soul to be seen. I looked down at the table in front of me and blinked. My breakfast tray was gone and with it the master tape! I felt the bacon and eggs in my stomach lurch.

Four days of hard graft and a huge amount of expense had disappeared. My backpack was still beside me and I searched it frantically, but the tape was not there. Just the camera and highlight tapes I had brought with me.

I went into the kitchen, but there was nobody there. I sprinted to hotel reception only to find a long queue of impatient guests waiting to check in or out. There was nobody in the concierge and just a couple of bellboys hovering around the door. I had less than

50 minutes to get to the TV compound, which was already tight. I irrationally thought of calling Jean Paul, but I didn't have his phone number, he wouldn't understand a thing I said and he wouldn't be able to offer a solution if he did. We hadn't had time to make a spare copy. I returned to the breakfast area and went back into the empty kitchen.

How the hell did these people clean everything up so quickly? I found a door that went out to a patio at the back of the building where a young man with a wet, dirty apron was drinking a coffee. Having spent plenty of time washing dishes myself, I recognised '*le plongeur*' as the French say, enjoying a break after his morning's exertions.

Luckily, he spoke decent English, so I explained my dilemma, pulling out a similar Betacam tape from my backpack to show him what I was looking for. He shrugged but followed me back into the restaurant so I could show him where I had left the tape.

Finally, he offered the only plausible answer.

'In ze garbage, per'aps?'

We checked the large plastic dustbin in the kitchen, but it was empty with a clean bag loaded.

'Where is the old bin bag?' I asked in desperation.

'Bean bag?'

'The bin bag! The other bag, you know, the fu ... the bag that was there before?' I was coming across as quite rude to this man, who was only trying to help.

'Ah, bin, like dustbin. Bin bag. Ah yes, I understand.' Really, it was no time for an English lesson.

'Out ze back,' he continued. 'Come, I show you.'

He led me to a large black rubbish disposal unit on wheels and I opened up the top. And, of course, there was not one, but over a dozen large bulging rubbish bags inside, like the vile brood of a giant evil-smelling black slug, all identical and side-by-side. There was no clue as to which was the most recent arrival.

In a panic I tipped the container on to its side with a loud bang and started randomly ripping open the bags and sifting through the disgusting mess of scrambled eggs, vegetable peel and who knows what else. The dishwasher muttered something and disappeared. I was expecting him to return with the hotel manager or a couple of security guards but instead, bless him, he brought some empty rubbish bags and gamely began clearing up the horrendous mess I was making. I ripped open the last of the bags, in a state of hysteria, but of the tape there was no sign.

'Bin bags,' he said brightly, proud of his newly acquired vocabulary.

The sweat was running down my face and prickling uncomfortably under my shirt. I was breathing fast and struggling to focus. The stress and lack of sleep of the last few days had caught me up, overtaken and was disappearing far into the distance. I slumped down in a bag of old vegetable peelings ready to burst into tears.

'Is this it?' The dishwasher asked calmly. He picked something out from a pile of melon rind. I couldn't believe my eyes.

'That's it! That's it! You found it. You beautiful Frenchman.' I took the tape from his outstretched hand and hugged him. Opening the tape's plastic cover, I was half expecting to find the master tape missing, but there it was, untouched by the sticky fruit juices. I looked down at my watch. It was nearly 9.45 and I was at least 25 minutes from the TV compound.

I took out my wallet and tipped the dishwasher 30 francs for his help. Apologising profusely for leaving him to clean up my mess, I told him I had to go.

'Bin bags,' he said, waving cheerfully as I left.

Rather than risk getting stuck in traffic in the car or, more likely, lost en route, I decided to make a run for it. Racing out the front of the hotel, I dropped the master tape into my rucksack and turned left, skirting the racetrack in the vague direction of the paddock. I knew how to find the TV compound from the circuit entrance. I put my head down and ran.

First, I rushed helter-skelter down a dead end, realised my mistake and doubled back. Then I saw some concrete steps which I ran up, but from the top I could see I was way off course. I bounded back down the steps cursing to myself. I asked a likely looking resident for directions and spent a precious minute listening to detailed instructions which I instantly forgot. I tripped over a kerb and the treasured tape shot out of my rucksack over the back of my head and went skittering across the road, narrowly avoiding the wheels of the oncoming traffic. I took my life in my hands running across the road to retrieve it.

I was sweating buckets and after an all-nighter in a hot office and a romp with the breakfast detritus, I could tell how bad I smelled, which is never a good sign. I was just starting to despair again when between two buildings I glimpsed the heavenly sight of the circuit entrance. I knew my way from there and headed for the accreditation centre (on the outside of the circuit where passes, parking and camera stickers are issued) and then it was just a breathless five-minute jog before I saw, from above, the TV compound with its satellite dishes. I skipped down the granite stone steps and turned into the reception area. The sweat was running down my face and I was gasping for air when I found my contact, Steve. I have never been so pleased to see anyone in my life. Now I was worried I was going to run over the allocated time slot, but Steve was relaxed. When he was satisfied that Star TV was receiving video and audio, he rewound my master and pressed 'play' on the Betacam machine. I half-expected to see the ferric-oxide tape come spewing out of the slot and spontaneously catch fire, but instead I saw colour bars on the monitor and heard the test tone. Steve gave me the thumbs-up.

I collapsed on to a chair and watched my pre-show play out as it was transmitted across the world. When it finished, Steve spoke to someone at Star TV who confirmed that the programme had arrived safely. I repeatedly asked Steve if he was sure. The fourth time he grabbed my shoulders, looked deep into my eyes and told me that yes, everything was fine.

In a daze I ejected the master tape from the machine and put it back into my rucksack, then wandered down to the harbour, found an empty bench and fell asleep again, before being awoken

20 minutes later by a Monaco policeman who told me I couldn't sleep there.

When I caught up with Johnny to tell him that the programme had been successfully sent (I left out the fiasco with the rubbish bins) he said he had good news too, but suggested, with a wrinkled nose, that I should go and 'freshen up' in the paddock restrooms before he revealed it. I was only too happy to oblige. As I patted my face and torso dry with a paper towel, he told me we had been invited by his contact at Jordan, the guy who set up the Rubens Barrichello interview, to watch the race from a terrace in a building just above the Chapelle Sainte Dévote corner. It's the first tight right-hander that the drivers take as they leave the grid before flying up the section of Beau Rivage where cars pick up speeds of 150mph before braking for Massenet. On that terrace, I experienced my first taste of the 'high life' in every sense. We sipped Möet & Chandon champagne and I looked down on the exciting action, happy that our work was done for this Grand Prix at least.

In a respectful gesture by the authorities, they left the first two grid positions empty and painted them with the Brazilian and Austrian flags as a mark of respect to Ayrton Senna and Roland Ratzenberger.

Then, for the first time, I heard the live sound of 24 Formula One cars, an orchestra of V8, V10 and V12 engines, roar off the start line and, as the leaders came through the first corner below our terrace, I saw Damon Hill's front left tyre clip the back right of Mika Häkkinen's McLaren, sending the Finn backwards into the run-off area. A few corners later Hill had to retire with a broken front suspension. In fact, only 11 of the 24 starters completed the Monaco Grand Prix that year.

I nibbled finger food, drank more champagne and was on the highest of highs as Michael Schumacher took the chequered flag for his sixth Formula One Grand Prix win and fourth consecutive victory of the 1994 season. When word came back from Sam in Hong Kong that the show had aired and been exceptionally well received, Johnny, Ben and I congratulated each other ecstatically.

Sebastian's Slowest Lap

Zandvoort, the Netherlands, 2022

ON THE Thursday before the 2022 Dutch Grand Prix Juan, Uli and I were walking with Albert Fabrega down the main straight towards the final corner of the Zandvoort circuit. Albert is the brilliant, humorous and charismatic Spaniard who sometimes works as a technical commentator and co-presenter with Juan. On race weekends he also appears on the Spanish channel DAZN, F1 TV and other media outlets. Before he became a TV and media personality, Albert was team manager of the Chinese Formula E team NextEV and before that team coordinator with HRT Formula One.

His trademark is to explain complex F1 engineering concepts with a witty, endearing and deadpan delivery style, which he can do in English, Spanish or even Catalan if you prefer. To enhance his explanations, he often uses intricate models and props constructed in his home in Barcelona.

After the 2020 Australian GP was cancelled due to the pandemic, I met with Albert at his hotel as we had arranged to go in search of face masks. He was finishing a podcast episode, so I went up to his hotel room to wait. On his bed was a full-sized go-kart that he had planned to use on air to explain Dual-Axis Steering.[76] It didn't surprise me to see a go-kart taking up most of his double bed. I could even imagine Albert sleeping tucked in beside it. Two

---

[76] A new system introduced by Mercedes to adjust the alignment (toe) angle of the front wheels. It was banned after 2020.

large empty suitcases were a clue as to how he had brought it with him from Spain.

'How much did you pay in excess baggage to bring that?' I asked. He smiled and shrugged his shoulders.

'Don't ask! It would have been worth it if they hadn't cancelled the race.'

Albert told me of his plan to increase his online following by creating video content. As he is one of the most energetic and proactive people I know, I had no doubt he would do exactly that.

We arrived at the final corner in Zaadvoort and walked up the banking to record a link to camera, explaining the changes to the circuit since its last Grand Prix in 1985. Albert and Juan have good chemistry on camera and they joked as they explained how the new banked corner would allow the drivers to arrive at the corner with DRS open and travelling 20kph faster, allowing more overtaking opportunities on the main straight.

To illustrate the 18-degree banking on the corner, Albert dug into his pocket to find a coin. He then knelt, held the Euro on its edge, and with an expectant look on his face, let it roll rapidly down the bank. Uli expertly panned and zoomed to follow the coin all the way to the grass inside the track.

'That was a Euro,' the Spaniard joked when Uli panned back to him. 'I'd better go and find it!' The link ended with Albert chasing after his money and Juan laughing as he looked on.

It was time to move further around the circuit and find more points of interest. It took us five minutes to reach turn 12, where we had been told 'fake gravel' had replaced the pebbles that had been thrown on to the track the previous year when drivers went wide, causing stoppages.

I was expecting to find a plastic photo of gravel stuck to the outer edge of the kerb, like the fake water in Miami, but of course a veneer of plastic would have been obliterated by the first hot tyre that touched it. Instead, the gravel trap beside the kerb was sealed with a generous helping of clear resin. The shiny finish was slippery so it would deter the drivers from cutting the corner.

SEBASTIAN'S SLOWEST LAP

Albert and Juan tested how secure the stuck stones were and considered the perils of a cluster being kicked up into the air. Just then Sebastian Vettel appeared, walking towards us with his team on their customary track walk.[77] Uli began to film as Sebastian tested the slipperiness of the new gravel feature with his rubber-soled trainers.

He noticed us setting up the camera and stopped briefly to say hello, swapping pleasantries before continuing on his way. Juan and Albert then recorded their link to camera, mentioning Sebastian's arrival at the scene.

I watched the four-times world champion walk off in the direction of the final corner. Then I noticed him running away from his race engineers up a bank towards the perimeter fence. I thought perhaps he was going to answer a call of nature, but he was actually heading up towards a fan. He stayed talking with her for a few minutes before coming back down, now holding a small brown paper bag in his hand.

'That must be Sebastian's drug dealer,' I joked to Uli.

The German showed his engineers what he had been given as he walked away. On our way back towards the paddock, we spotted the lone fan and I called her back so Juan could ask her on camera what she had given to Sebastian and what their conversation had been about.

'I made a diary of everything I love about Sebastian,' she said.

'Have you met him before?' Juan asked.

'Oh yes, he always takes the time to talk to me, he is so lovely.' Her eyes glistened with tears of joy.

She had been waiting for two hours, hoping he might pass by. I wondered how many other fans had waited for their heroes and called out their name, only to be ignored. Not so Sebastian Vettel. He is such a nice guy that I have decided to work on my own diary of everything I love about him.

---

77 When a team walks around the circuit to observe the layout, note any changes and discuss strategy.

Nousnous Violet

Monaco 1994

EVERY LAP of my first on-site shoot had been a tough struggle, but I had made it to the chequered flag and sat proudly on the top step of the podium. Although actually there is no proper podium in Monte Carlo. The drivers go to the royal box for the ceremony. Here would be the perfect place to leave the story of Monaco 1994, but unfortunately the joker, who had been absent for just a few short hours, made yet another appearance that I can scarcely omit.

The night following the race, Johnny, Ben and I went for a further round of celebration until the early hours. They were on a flight to London at 10.30am but although my flight to Paris wasn't until 1pm, we had to travel to the airport together and drop the camera off at Cannes, so we left the hotel around 7am. I had passed yet another night with little sleep.

Philippe, true to his kind nature, took back the camera, barely checked it and wished us luck on our travels. What a guy!

After we dropped the Citroen C5 off at Avis, I said goodbye to the boys and with four hours to kill, decided to put my bags on a trolley and check out Nice airport. I had borrowed two suitcases from my flatmate Wanda although, I have to say, they didn't quite chime with the image I was trying to project as a professional TV producer in the most exclusive location on the planet. But they did accurately reflect Wanda's extrovert, cheerful personality, as they were both bright pink with a cartoon of a cheerful purple teddy bear printed on the sides. It certainly makes sense to have distinctive luggage if you travel a lot, making it easier to spot and less likely to be taken by mistake. But, no, they would not have been my first choice.

But baggage aside, I felt a little strange. The week had been super stressful and I had partied hard with little sleep so I was beginning to hallucinate. I felt both euphoric and exhausted and was no doubt still a little tipsy from the previous night's celebrations.

I took a good look around the boutiques and shops and noticed a miniature Ferrari 412 T1 in the window of a store. I blinked to make sure it was real. It would make a great present for my young nephew, who was already taking an interest in Formula One. I could send it by post to Jersey from Paris. I parked the trolley and went inside to buy the toy. But when I came out, I did a double take. The trolley was still there but my bags were gone!

I fell to my knees in despair. Why me? I just couldn't catch a break. In a panic I checked my backpack. Thank the stars, at least my passport and money were there, but all the Betacam tapes and my clothes for the Paris trip were in the bags. My distress was so obvious that a French guy, around my age, came over, introduced himself as Claude and asked if he could help. Embarrassingly I blubbered as I told him what had happened.

'I am so sorry,' he said, all sympathy. 'Let's report this to the police. I'll help you with translation.'

So, it was back to the now familiar airport police station, where I had been with Ben six days earlier reporting the stolen camera. We began filling out the paperwork as Claude acted as interpreter with a portly French officer.

'He asks what the suitcases look like,' Claude told me.

'Um, pinkish, well, actually, bright pink.'

'Pink ...? *Rose*,' Claude translated for the officer who looked me up and down before rattling something off to Claude in French.

'Any other distinctive markings?' Claude asked me.

'Well, yes actually,' I swallowed. 'They both have a large purple cartoon teddy bear on the front.'

'A purple cartoon teddy bear?' Claude repeated, making sure he had heard correctly.

'It's a long story.'

Claude relayed the information to the police officer, who raised his eyebrows. No doubt he had dealt with a fair number of pranksters in his time.

'*Un nousnous violet de dessin animé?*' The officer repeated the words slowly while he wrote, glancing up from time to time to eye me suspiciously.

Claude hung around until the report was made. He really could not have been kinder or more patient. I thanked him profusely before we parted ways.

It was getting close to my flight time so I decided to give up on my bags and check in. I walked to the desk, fished out my passport and there, poking out from either side was … my boarding pass! I had already checked in. I must have done so in a sleepless haze. And, of course, attached to the boarding card were two luggage receipts. My bags hadn't been stolen at all. I had already checked them on to the flight! Sleep deprivation coupled with excessive alcohol can do funny things to a man with something missing from his brain. I couldn't believe what I had done, but the relief was overwhelming.

As I took my seat on the plane, I noticed my new friend Claude half a dozen seats behind me. I waved and smiled at him sheepishly. Once seated, I fell into a deep sleep and only woke up when the wheels touched down in Paris. When we disembarked, Claude caught up with me on the concourse. We bumped fists and walked together towards the exit.

'*Que jolie!*' he said. 'Same flight! Crazy!'

'It was so nice of you to help me out, thank you,' I said. Claude was still all sympathy.

'Who steals bags in an airport? I mean, who does that?' I forbore to observe that actually no one had. Not from me, anyway. But Claude's deep well of helpfulness was not exhausted. He offered me a place to stay, but I assured him I had made plans with a friend in town. We arrived in baggage reclaim and waited.

'Don't wait here just for me, Kris,' he said. 'You 'ave no reason to wait. One good thing about losing your baggage!'

'Oh no, don't worry. Very happy to wait with you for a while. I am in no hurry.'

The carousel started up. Claude immediately spotted his elegant-looking bag when it emerged, but just a few bags later my two pink, purple-bear-adorned monstrosities burst out from behind the flap at the top of the conveyer belt and slid and flopped noisily down on to the carousel. A more conspicuous entrance would be hard to imagine. They gleamed pink and the bears supplemented their wide smiles by appearing to wave. Claude would surely see them; he had spent the best part of ten minutes trying to describe their design to the baffled police officer.

Claude walked towards the carousel, eyes fixed on the conveyor belt. He stared directly at my bags and appeared to do a double-take. I winced, looking for a place to hide. How the hell was I going to explain this? But instead, he picked up his bag and turned to me.

'You know what we should do?' he said. 'We should go for a drink. I know a place close by.'

Over Claude's shoulder I could see my two suitcases, rotating ostentatiously.

'I would love to, Claude,' I stammered. 'But I haven't slept properly in nearly four days. Another time.' To make my escape I mumbled something about visiting the toilets.

Claude looked back at the carousel. My increasingly isolated bags continued to revolve, gleaming brightly, the stars of the show in the limelight; luminescent, bright and radiant.

But miraculously Claude never made the connection and accepted we must say '*au revoir*'. He gave me his business card and told me to call him if I fancied a drink while I was in Paris. We parted with Gallic hugs and I watched, with relief, as he finally disappeared into the arrivals hall, while I skulked in the general direction of the toilets. It was ten minutes before I dared to approach my luminous suitcases. The last thing I could face was running into Claude and having to explain how my luggage had miraculously reappeared.

But I concluded from my trip to Monaco, that even in the face of crass stupidity, bad luck, language barriers, access barriers, lost luggage and misplaced belongings, simple acts of kindness can change your day from being a nightmare to one that you can just about muddle through. I know. I've muddled through my whole life.

Away with the Fairways

Hong Kong, late 1994

AFTER THE madness of Monaco and a further week of hard partying in Paris, my return to the studio for the Barcelona Grand Prix was somewhat deflating. I remember feeling cut off from the action as we watched qualifying, although my problems were insignificant compared to those of Andrea Montermini, the Italian test driver who replaced Roland Ratzenberger but lost control of his Simtek S941, smashing into the barriers and breaking his left heel and right foot. These were difficult times for Formula One. It was undeniable that driver safety was a huge problem.

It was also the first time we saw Scotsman David Coulthard on the grid, when he stepped up from test driver to replace Senna at Williams, sharing the remaining races of the season with Nigel Mansell.

Schumacher scored his second career pole on Saturday when he was half a second faster than Williams-Renault's British driver Damon Hill, who was himself only one-thousandth of a second ahead of Mika Häkkinen in third, a statistic that blew my mind.

The race was won by Hill, his first of the season, but it was pole-sitter Schumacher in the Benetton-Ford, in search of his fifth consecutive victory who was the story of the day, driving most of the race stuck in fifth gear. Remarkably, he still managed to secure second place ahead of Mark Blundell, who claimed his team's last-ever podium in the Tyrrell-Yamaha. Michael's impressive driving included a pit stop, so he got the car going again by manipulating the clutch and accelerator to get it back up to speed. It is still considered one of the best drives of his long, illustrious career.

Damon's victory was a much-needed boost for the Williams team still mourning the catastrophe in San Marino. The thrilling season went to the wire in Australia with only one point between Schumacher and Hill.

The pre-show for the Monaco Grand Prix was a great success, but a decision was taken shortly thereafter that Prime Sports should focus its investments on local sports in the Asian market. So, with outside broadcasts for future Grands Prix less likely, I settled back into the routine of covering Formula One races from the studio, re-editing what little promotional material and features I was sent from teams like Williams and McLaren and combining it with past race footage to create something original.

The *Formula One Show* was now ticking over nicely and continued to generate good viewing figures. In a conversation with Sam, I mentioned how much I had enjoyed covering Monaco and a few days later she told me about a new opportunity. In 1994 the Asian Professional Golf Association was formed and Prime Sports decided to produce programmes covering the APGA Omega Tour the following year. A total of 18 72-hole tournaments were scheduled across Asia and the Middle East. My role would be to build a team of cameramen to accompany me to the events and produce a one-hour highlights show of each tournament.

The budget was generous and it was an obvious career step, given I would have sole responsibility for producing the programmes. Although Monaco had been exhausting, I had thoroughly enjoyed the excitement of the outside broadcast and there was the enticing prospect of business-class travel to countries I had not yet visited. I had a choice to make, but first I would complete the 1994 F1 season.

As it approached its climax, we pulled off a coup by arranging an exclusive interview with Damon Hill at the Peninsula Hotel in Hong Kong, when he stopped over on his way to the season's penultimate race, the Japanese Grand Prix. Going into the race Michael Schumacher led by five points, so Damon needed to beat his rival to have a realistic chance of challenging the German for the World Championship in the last race in Adelaide, Australia.

Johnny, the camera crew and I were setting up beside the pool on the eighth floor of the hotel that looked out over the stunning Hong Kong harbour skyline. A jacuzzi in the corner of the pool bubbled away quietly. When Damon and his press officer arrived, we made our introductions. Damon was in good spirits despite the pressure he was under. As he seemed so relaxed, I tried my luck and asked:

'Damon, we'd like to show how chilled out you are despite the pressure you face over the next two weekends. Any chance of you stripping off and jumping into the jacuzzi with Johnny so we can do the interview there?' He didn't reply immediately, so I continued, 'You know, with the Hong Kong skyline in the background?'

'I didn't bring my swimming shorts,' he said, rather stiffly. 'And I don't think your viewers want to see me naked.'

'Poolside and clothed it is, then. I'll get some chairs.' Another bust. In my defence, I was only trying to do what has become commonplace these days, getting more up close and personal with the drivers. You could say I was years ahead of my time!

In late November the Prime Sports motorsport crew were allowed out of the office to cover the unofficial Formula Three World Championship in Macau, where the drivers battle it out and try to attract the attention of the Formula One teams. Being just an hour's ferry ride away, it certainly counted as sport in the local market and we were live on air for six hours each day covering all the action, including touring car and Porsche categories as well as motorcycle races. It was there I got to meet my hero, the great Murray Walker, who Sam had contracted to commentate on the F3 races around the famous street circuit.

I ran into him outside the commentary booths near to our makeshift studio. I thrust out my hand and introduced myself, as nervous as a schoolgirl meeting her favourite pop idol.

'Oh hi, Murray, I'm Kris Henley, the producer. It's an absolute pleasure to meet you. I have been a huge fan of yours for ever.'

'Thanks, nice to meet you too.' I don't know what I was expecting, but for some reason I was astonished when he spoke with exactly the same voice I had heard a thousand times before on the TV.

'You're the producer, you say? So, you must be the man I talk to about "producing" my fee?'

Okay, it was something of a quote, but not in the class of 'there are seven winners of the Monaco Grand Prix on the starting line today and four of them are Michael Schumacher' or 'the lead car is unique, except for the car behind, which is identical', or 'IF is a very long word in Formula One; in fact IF is F1 spelled backwards.'

But hey, nothing comes for free and certainly not from the voice of Formula One himself.

'Payment, yes, of course, we're not here only for the love of the sport, right Murray? Payment is Sam Hague's department,' I told him. 'I'll introduce you shortly.'

'Sam Hague. Great, I'll be around the commentary booth when she gets here.' Then he was gone. Striding up the hallway, shaking people's hands as he went. A true character. I was really going to miss motorsport.

By the end of the season and with many misgivings, I handed over the Formula One baton to a new producer. I left the roar of F1 engines and prepared to focus on the much quieter sport of golf, where I would get to visit fantastic cities and picturesque Asian golf courses.

I didn't know it at the time, but golf would become my speciality for the next 15 years, as I produced programmes about the Asian, South American, European and Web.com tours. For a while, my time in the Formula One circus was over.

Liar, Liar, Car's on Fire

Hong Kong 1994

MY FIRST season in Formula One was memorable not only for the fierce competition and the tragedies, but also for controversy, which gave our presenters and the commentary team plenty to talk about. Accusations of foul play abounded, mostly directed at Benetton and Michael Schumacher.

Before his death, Ayrton Senna had been suspicious of the Benetton team and characteristically made his feelings known. For one thing, the Benetton cars spent less time in the pits than the other teams. At Hockenheim, in the German Grand Prix, Jos Verstappen, Michael Schumacher's team-mate, came into the pits on lap 15 for refuelling and fresh tyres. When the fuel hose was disengaged it sprayed fuel into and over the car and half a second later the Benetton, with Jos Verstappen in it, exploded in flames, thick black smoke instantly filling the air.[78]

Murray Walker, commentating, permitted himself an 'Oh, my goodness me' before exhorting everyone to stay calm, as the fire officials mobilised. The flames were out within eight seconds and Verstappen, apart from slight facial burns, was unharmed. The investigation which followed found that the Benetton crew were not using the required fuel nozzle filter, so they were able to refill the car more quickly and gain about a second. Except when they set fire to their driver, of course.

---

78 This was when Stephen Tee took the photograph of the fire. See 'Snappers'.

The next controversy arose at the start of the French Grand Prix after Schumacher flew past the first two cars on the grid to move from third to first place. Some observers suspected that traction control[79] was being used. The system had been permitted but was outlawed after the 1993 season.

After the Brazilian Grand Prix, the FIA ordered Benetton, Ferrari and McLaren, the teams that had finished first, second and third, to hand over their engine management systems' source code. Ferrari complied immediately, but Benetton and McLaren dragged their feet and missed the deadline, incurring a $100,000 fine.

When the FIA was finally able to examine the systems, launch control software was indeed found in the Benetton and appeared to include a hidden trigger system. But the team claimed it was there for testing purposes only and was not used in races, and in any case, they said, it could not be activated by the driver. The FIA were unable to prove their case, so the matter was dropped. But the doubts remained.

In the British Grand Prix at Silverstone, Schumacher was given a five-second stop-go penalty[80] for improperly overtaking Damon Hill on the formation lap. But he failed to serve the penalty in time and so was given the dreaded black 'disqualification' flag, ordering him off the track, which he also ignored. Schumacher was consequently fined, formally disqualified and handed a two-race ban that the team served in Italy and Portugal.

The German also finished first at the Belgian Grand Prix but was again disqualified, this time for excessive wear on the plank underneath his car, which had lost a lot more than the permitted 1mm during the race. But despite these setbacks, Michael still claimed eight Grand Prix wins, ten podiums, 92 points, eight fastest laps and six pole positions that year.

---

79 Traction control is an electronic system that enables the maximum amount of power to be applied to the drive wheels without them spinning. It guarantees maximum acceleration on any given surface.

80 A mandatory pit stop without tyre change or refuelling.

But Damon Hill was not about to give up and there was still all to play for in the Drivers' World Championship. The cool Brit left Hong Kong for the penultimate race in Japan needing to win the race and claim maximum points. And that's exactly what he did. Under extreme pressure and in torrential rain, Damon reduced his five-point deficit to just one after a race that was stopped and restarted. The result was decided with an aggregate race time over the two legs and Hill claimed victory over Schumacher by 3.3 seconds.

So, with Schumacher just one point ahead, all depended on the final race at the Adelaide Street Circuit. On race day, I was in Hong Kong asking a production assistant to cue up the season's highlights feature while Johnny and Matthew Marsh were hyping up the classic encounter with their banter on the studio floor.

When the race began, the camera crew, Johnny, Matthew and I were glued to the monitors to watch the conclusion to the riveting season. Nigel Mansell had surprised everyone by returning to the Williams team after his surprise spell in IndyCar racing. He proved his class by qualifying on pole.

Mansell was slow off the line and Schumacher flew past him. Hill went past Mansell on the inside, following the German into the first chicane. Schumacher retained the lead with Hill following, but the Brit was unable to put pressure on the leader. On lap 18, the championship contenders pitted at the same time for fresh rubber and more fuel. The positions remained the same when they exited the pits.

Schumacher and Hill began pulling away from the rest of the field but by lap 36, Hill had found enough speed to put the German under pressure. Schumacher then made a most uncharacteristic mistake, running wide at turn five and careering across the grass, hitting the wall hard with both his front and rear right tyres, slowing the car down and causing Hill to brake to avoid him as the Benetton staggered back on to the track.

I sat forward in my chair and gasped. Through the glass I saw Johnny and Matthew do the same on the studio floor. The crew 'oohed' and 'aahed'.

Schumacher's car was surely damaged, but only he knew for sure. In hindsight, Hill could perhaps have waited to see the extent of the damage and then tried to overtake a little later, but because Schumacher had lost speed there was a clear gap. As Senna said, 'If you don't go for a gap, you are no longer a racing driver,' and Damon Hill was certainly a racing driver. He went for it, trying to pass on the inside of the right-hander at turn six.

Schumacher then veered right in a last-gasp attempt to hold on to his first championship. His back right tyre collided with Hill's front left, flipping the Benetton up on to two wheels, before crashing back down and ramming head-on into the tyre barrier.

The gasps in the studio turned to screams and shouts of outrage. Allegiances were made clear as Hill fans blamed the German and Schumacher fans blamed the Brit. Schumacher was out, but Hill was able to make it back to the pits, although his front-left wheel was not in contact with the ground, which could only mean that his suspension was broken. Patrick Head, veteran technical director at Williams, immediately knew the car would not be able to continue. Hill shook his head in frustration, but the championship was decided. Millions of fans around the world felt this was blatant cheating by Michael Schumacher but millions more disagreed, including, crucially, the stewards at the FIA, who called it a 'racing incident'. Michael Schumacher became the first German to claim a Formula One world title and would go on to add six more.

Nigel Mansell won his 31st and final Grand Prix that day, but that memory was overshadowed by the 'racing incident'. It was a fitting end to one of the most contentious seasons in Formula One history.

That was the third Formula One title decided by a crash in six seasons. Surely it would be the last? Of course not, this is Formula One! In 1997 Michael Schumacher was again involved and, remarkably, the Drivers' World Championship would yet again be decided on the last race, round 17, at the European Grand Prix, in Jerez, Spain. Michael Schumacher, now driving for Ferrari, was leading the championship with 78 points. Williams driver Jacques Villeneuve was on 77.

In qualifying, each driver was allowed 12 timed laps and the fastest determined their grid positions. Astonishingly, Villeneuve, his team-mate Heinz-Harald Frentzen and Schumacher set precisely the same time of 1:21:072. As Villeneuve did it first, he was given pole and Schumacher, who registered the time second, was beside him on the front row. When the green light came on, Schumacher was characteristically quick off the line and led into the first corner, with Villeneuve slipping back to third. Frentzen allowed his team-mate to pass and by lap 48, Villeneuve was less than a second behind the German. At the right-hand Dry Sac corner, Villeneuve saw an opportunity to overtake Schumacher and dived down the inside, braking later than the Ferrari driver and moving ahead on the track. Then Schumacher, knowing he was not going to be able to catch Villeneuve if he passed him, turned into the Canadian driver.

But this time things did not go to plan. Instead of damaging the Williams' suspension, Schumacher's front wheel hit Villeneuve's left radiator pod, causing no damage. Villeneuve was able to continue, while Schumacher beached himself in the gravel.

Martin Brundle immediately offered his opinion of the incident as he commentated with Murray Walker.

'That didn't work, Michael. You hit the wrong part of him, my friend.' The two McLarens passed the Canadian driver on the final lap as Mika Häkkinen claimed his inaugural Formula One victory and David Coulthard finished second. Villeneuve let them go, happy to finish third and claim the Drivers' World Championship.

But nothing escapes scrutiny in F1. The incident between Schumacher and Villeneuve was looked at by the governing body and blame was unanimously attributed to the German. Schumacher was stripped of his second-place finish in the World Championship and his actions were criticised by the media all around the world, including in his home country. Even the Italian press, who can nearly always be relied on to side with Ferrari, broke ranks.

Sky Dive

Hong Kong 1997, Los Angeles briefly, Paris, London, 1997/98

ON 1 July 1997, the United Kingdom handed sovereignty of Hong Kong back to China and my TV career was at an all-time high. I was feeling pretty good. I was travelling all over Asia, the Middle East and Europe, often in business class and sometimes in first. I was financially secure, managing a production team, and my self-confidence sky-rocketed. This bus conductor had punched his last ticket and would not be seen dead on public transport again.

I began to wonder what else I could achieve given a chance. Better still, what opportunity could I make for myself? Should I become an executive producer? A TV director? Why not a rock star? I had ventured down that path in my teens, playing guitar in a three-piece band in Jersey called Joe the Lion. But despite winning the island's Battle of the Bands a couple of times, which meant recording-studio time and paid trips to meet the record labels, we were not signed. But that was then and this was now! Perhaps, like the Blues Brothers, it was time to revive the band?

But then I had a better idea. In fact, come to think of it, every idea anyone ever had was better than that one. Except for this one. Why not aim for true stardom? Why not move to the United States and become a movie star? *Yes*, I thought, that was a great idea. After all, Americans loved British actors. Look at Hugh Grant, the quintessential, happy-go-lucky, dippy Englishman. I could certainly do that. With my Mel Gibson mullet and British accent, I was surely a shoo-in. I couldn't wait to tell Sam about my plan. I burst into her office and she nearly jumped out of her seat.

I explained my plan in a somewhat disjointed fashion, finishing with, '... So in conclusion it's, New York, New York!' I ended with a few showgirl high kicks to demonstrate my range as a performer. Sam did a fine job of keeping a straight face, which I took to mean she was behind me all the way.

A few weeks later, having said a sad farewell to all my Hong Kong friends, I boarded a flight to New York via Los Angeles. But my acting ability was exposed immediately, when I failed to convince an unsympathetic immigration officer that I was only going to the US for a holiday and had no plan to work without a permit. He deported me with an embarrassing 'entry refused' stamp in my passport. The next day I was in Paris staying with my best friend, Reb. I was a bit annoyed, but the sun was shining and I still had my career in TV to fall back on. When summer fizzled out, I travelled back to London, where I stayed with my friends Jo and Lucy in Clapham.

After more than a decade of travelling in search of the perfect place to live, I had sniffily rejected many of the world's finest cities as suitable places. Some I gave serious consideration, but others I merely breezed through before turning up my nose. Among those that failed to make the cut were: ruthless Bangkok; overbearing Kuala Lumpur; sterile Singapore; isolated Perth; prissy Adelaide; shady Melbourne; deceptive Sydney; backward Auckland; stagnant Christchurch; synthetic Honolulu; hostile Los Angeles; peculiar San Francisco; bitter Dubai; berserk Manila; gruesome Delhi; surly Paris; austere Edinburgh; overdramatic Barcelona; morbid Madrid; bewildering Amsterdam; inhospitable (to me) Dublin and soulless Hong Kong. And now I had a new item for the list, unreachable New York. Come to think of it, I could now add all the towns and cities in the United States of America.

I hadn't made my mind up yet about London. Sometimes, usually when I was sat in a beer garden in the summer sunshine, I was convinced it was the best city on the planet. But then at other times, particularly when it was raining, it seemed the most dismal.

But I decided to give it a go. I applied for jobs and with my now genuine and pretty impressive-looking résumé, backed by a glowing reference from my rock, Sam Hague, it was not long before I was offered a contract with the ever-expanding BSkyB (later Sky) satellite station based in Isleworth. It seemed ideal at this point in my career. But I was in for a shock.

At Prime Sports in Hong Kong, I had become a moderately big fish in a smallish rock pool. A decent-sized bass perhaps. There were bigger fish around, but none that really meant me any harm. I had felt safe, secure and confident in what I was doing.

But BSkyB in the late nineties was a different habitat entirely. The company, backed by Rupert Murdoch's power and financial muscle, was on a mission to revolutionise sports coverage. To take on the likes of the BBC and ITV, they radically upgraded the sports fans' experience, adding a far wider, much-improved range of events. There were many more live games of football[81] from England, Scotland, Italy and Germany, with dozens of ex-players and media pundits adding authority and authenticity. There were also club rugby matches, four-day golf tournaments and American football. The cricket fan could at last enjoy uninterrupted ball-by-ball coverage including tours. There were bigger boxing contests. And all the action was brought to the audience by experienced, refreshed presenters and attractive, dynamic new talent, providing analysis based on deep knowledge of their sports. With more cameras and camera crews, better graphic content and much higher production values, they transformed the way people watched sport in Britain.

The station was run by able and ambitious directors and producers, with a clear vision of how they would shake things up: mostly hardened northerners, super-confident experts in their field and, having launched in 1990, now with plenty of experience of the

---

81 Soccer if you are an American.

new approach. They consumed junior producers in vast numbers and just let them sink or swim.

It didn't take me long to realise that my Hong Kong experience was not going to count for much in this new world. If I was going to get anywhere in this well-established hierarchy, I would have to fight it out with an army of similarly placed juniors. This was no puddle, it was a boundless ocean, fully stocked with giant squid, great white sharks, killer whales, man-of-war jellyfish, electric eels and venomous stingrays, crowding and circling, trying to eat, squash, sting or electrocute anyone in their path. I felt more like Nemo the clownfish than anything higher up the food chain. The hard-won confidence I had built was soon sucked out of me. I didn't really understand what was happening at the time. I was just trying to hold my breath and avoid sinking into the depths.

My first experience of BSkyB's ground-breaking approach to production was when I was sent to Blackpool in July 1998 for the darts World Matchplay. In the late seventies a few blokes with impressive beer-bellies gathered in a pub and threw their 'arrows' between gulps of ale with a few locals crowded in, and a couple of BBC cameras to cover the 'action'. So, I was confused when I was told that my role was simply to produce the one-minute closing title sequence to complete the coverage each day. I pictured myself putting together a quick montage with a (very) wide angle of the fat blokes necking their beer, a few close-ups of three-dart finishes, rounded off with a celebration shot. Surely it would take no more than an hour to edit? Then I could start necking the beers myself.

How wrong I was! Since BSkyB had begun showing darts in 1994, the pub game and its players had undergone an extreme makeover. Drinking on stage had been banned in 1989, but the large crowds were encouraged to consume and consume they did. Cameramen were dotted around the auditorium picking out the drunken antics of the fans, often in outrageous fancy dress, as they cheered, screamed, booed and celebrated.

Cameras flew over the crowd on crane jibs, glitter bombs exploded and music blared from multiple speakers. Every imaginable angle of the 'action' was captured by the large production crew, slow-motion cameras following the trajectory of every dart thrown. You could now see that the dart did not fly parallel to the ground, but rotating flights down, point up, until it magically levelled itself in time to dive into the board. All the angles were covered. The players came into the arena like World Wrestling Federation superstars, accompanied by their own theme music, saluting the packed amphitheatre.

The commentator was 'the voice of darts', the irrepressible Sid Waddell, who brought an added dimension to the coverage. Sid was a sporting wordsmith with his trademark Geordie accent and great sense of humour. His quotes included, 'it's the greatest comeback since Lazarus', and when Eric Bristow had completed a clean sweep of titles, the immortal line, 'When Alexander of Macedonia was 33, he cried salt tears because there were no more worlds to conquer ... and Bristow's only 27!'

So, the simple edit I had in mind was far from it. It took me all day, every day, because there was so much footage to choose from. I think I did a good job though, setting the 'closer' cut for the final day to the Hootie and the Blowfish song 'I'm Going Home'. After it aired, the on-site producer told me that the head of the channel had called to enquire who had produced the piece, as he thought it was very good. I beamed with pride. It was the first encouragement I had received since I started work at BSkyB. Come to think of it, it was also pretty much the last.

It's easy to forget the impact Sky has had on the coverage of Formula One. During the pandemic it was impossible to travel to Grands Prix and our interviews were conducted on Zoom. But I did have the pleasure of sitting down in front of the TV to watch all the 2021 races and most of those in 2022 from the comfort of my home before travelling to four of the last five races.

The Sky UK team really know their stuff, led by the witty and charismatic David Croft, supported by Martin Brundle who, having achieved nine podiums and competed in 158 Grands Prix himself, brings unparalleled knowledge and expertise. The rest of the team make huge contributions from their own unique angles. There are former world champions like Damon Hill and Jenson Button, expert analysts and pit and news reporters. Their coverage of the sport is simply the best in the world.

Sky began covering Formula One from the racetracks in 2012 and, as they did to other sports, immediately stamped their mark. The paddock knew they were coming for a while and I, like many others, was wondering what would happen. Would they be pushy? Would they keep to themselves? Would they raise the bar as they had done elsewhere? Would they make the sport more exciting and accessible? The answer to all those questions was a resounding 'yes'.

Doubtless a lot of their technical crew members had been setting up for days beforehand, but I first saw the Sky Sports F1 HD channel crew enter the paddock in Melbourne, Australia early on Thursday, 15 March 2012. It was a sight to behold as they swarmed through the turnstiles and into the paddock. I watched from Ferrari's hospitality suite, where I was delicately sipping an espresso. It was like watching a meticulously planned military coup. The deployment included editors, heads of channel, pit reporters, presenters, producers, executive producers, camera operators and assistants, all carrying hundreds of thousands of dollars' worth of equipment. There was no doubt they meant business and had come to shake things up. The only comparable thing I have seen is when Netflix arrived for their second season with a much bigger budget, after the overwhelming success of the first season of *Drive to Survive*.

But back in 1998 my next assignment was working on the NFL Europe American football series. We covered live games and produced features for the weekly highlights magazine show. Then I moved to the boxing department where I had the great pleasure of working with British, European and World Boxing Association featherweight champion, Barry McGuigan. Barry was always great fun to be around. He indulged my requests for him to send funny audio messages to my flatmate, Lucy (the Cordon Bleu chef) who had a crush on him.

'Hi Lucy,' he would say into our home answer phone, 'it's me, Barry McGuigan. I know you have a serious crush on me. Well, you're only human! Lots of love! Bye.'

I travelled to talk to undercard fighters in their humble homes and run-down gyms as they prepared for their next fight, hoping it would get them closer to a lucrative title challenge. Barry would join me when he was not doing more important shoots. His interviews were always far better than mine, as the fighters worshipped him and would open up about their dreams and their hopes to pull their families out of poverty.

I cut together shots of these tough, hungry, often humble, sometimes angry young men wrapping their fists with grubby bandages, skipping themselves to exhaustion, having medicine balls dropped on to their muscular stomachs before leaping up to hammer battered, tattered punching bags. We filmed them running, shadow boxing and sweating through the pain. The features went down well and there was talk of a permanent job if I could keep up the good work.

Then the boxing schedule went quiet, so I was moved on to the sport that really mattered to BSkyB, Premiership football. The department was the jewel in BSkyB's crown. In 1992 the company had had £2 billion of debt and there had been serious doubt about whether there was a market for subscription television in the UK. But after Rupert Murdoch grabbed the Premiership rights, subscriptions flowed into Isleworth and the company never looked back.

Unsurprisingly, the team working on Premiership football lived, slept, ate and breathed the sport whereas the Manchester United side from 1977 was pretty much where my knowledge of football ended. I managed to bluff my way for a while, compiling edits from several games into news pieces or highlights shows. Then I was asked to produce short highlights packages of games as they were airing live. These were shown at half-time or after the game, so they had to be paced to give the pundits enough time to make their observations. I would go in at weekends or Mondays and sit with an editor, cutting as the game happened. There was obviously a deadline and things could get tricky, especially if a couple of goals were scored towards the end of a half.

The producers demanded the edits as soon as the final whistles were blown. This kind of pressure, I could handle. If you had a good editor, and all the BSkyB editors were good, it wasn't a problem and I got through these months with little trouble. But it was a harsh culture. There was little camaraderie and no praise for a job well done.

One Sunday I was asked to do the replays during a live Premiership game. Little did I know the composition I would be asked to play that evening would heavily feature the missing keys in my brain.

I assumed the job would be similar to my previous experience in Hong Kong. I would run the highlights from the three recording Digi Beta machines when requested by the producer. But there were a couple of crucial differences. Instead of being in the gallery with the rest of the crew, I was put in a small separate room connected to the producer and director via an intercom system that I had never seen before. There was no editor to assist me. And, of course, I didn't know the first thing about football.

I'm pretty sure the presenters were Richard Keys and Andy Gray and the commentators were Martin Tyler and Roy Hodgson. I don't recall the teams, but during the build-up to kick-off, I was making sure all three Digi Beta tapes were recording the live pictures. I was ready. There was a cackle down the intercom and the producer spoke to me for the first time.

'Kris, cue up the Wenger shot please, we're coming to you next.' Ah, now here was a tiny problem. I had never heard of Arsène Charles Ernest Wenger, the famous Arsenal coach. Instead, what I heard was 'Kris, cue up the wanker shot, please.' I thought maybe it was some sort of joke, but the producer's voice was deadly serious, so I needed to ask him to repeat himself.

Second tiny problem. I hadn't had a chance to find out how the intercom worked. Yes, there was a microphone sticking out from a flexi-cable on a console and a row of black switches with small lights and letters that made no sense at all. I couldn't find anything remotely like a shortened word for 'studio' written on the labels, so I pressed the first button in the line.

'Can you repeat please?' I stammered.

'This is Steve in Edit 4. Repeat what?' replied an unfamiliar voice.

'Sorry, wrong button, forget that.' I pressed the second switch in the line.

'Can you repeat that please?'

'This is Steve in Edit 4. Repeat what?' he repeated sarcastically.

'Sorry, there are two switches for you.'

'Who is this and who are you trying to talk to?' he said a little more sympathetically.

'Kris, a freelancer, I'm trying to get through to the studio.'

'What studio?'

'The Premiership.'

'Which game?'

'Kris! The Wenger shot, we need it now!' shouted the producer.

Well, he hadn't said 'wanker', that was for sure. Was it 'winger'? What 'winger' is he talking about? Which team? The game hadn't even started.

'The Wenger shot,' the producer said, firmly. In a panic I pressed all three of the next switches along on the intercom simultaneously, following the logic that one of them had to be right.

'What is the winger shot?' I ventured.

A cacophony of voices came back at me. Four in total. The first asked me what I wanted. The second was Steve in Edit 4 again, presumably just trying to help but only making matters worse. A third told me not to use the intercom as they were recording a voice-over. But the loudest reply was the producer.

'Arsène Wenger, the Arsenal coach!'

At least now I knew the studio was either switch three, four or five. I picked the one in the middle. At last, a lucky break.

'But Arsenal aren't playing,' I said as my heart began to beat out of my chest.

'He's sitting in the crowd, you plonker, go back five minutes on the tape and cue him up, quickly.'

I was in a blind panic and the game hadn't even started. I stopped one of the Digi Beta tapes and rewound using the shuttle feature, when the door swung open and two guys stood in the doorway.

'Stop messing around with the intercom, I'm trying to do a voice-over,' said the angrier-looking of the two.

'Hi, I'm Steve from Edit 4,' said the more sympathetic one.

'Sorry, I don't know how the intercom system works.'

'It's really not that difficult,' said the man attempting to do the voice-over. 'A light shines on the button you have to press.'

'Kris! What are you doing in there?' shouted the producer.

'See the light?'

'I see it now, thanks.'

I hadn't seen the light because I was too close and it was recessed in the panel.

'Don't touch button three again!' the angry voice-over guy shouted menacingly before he left.

I pressed the correct button and answered my producer.

'Just cuing it up, sorry.'

I turned to Steve from Edit 4, who was still standing in the doorway.

'Do you know who Arsenal Wenger is?' I spluttered.

'Arsène Wenger? Yes, of course I do. Who are you again?'

'I'm a freelancer who doesn't know much about football. Can you please help me, I don't know what he looks like.'

'Wenger! Hurry!' the producer shouted down the line. He was getting irate.

'See, I need it now. Apparently, he's in the crowd.'

Steve from Edit 4 helped me locate Wenger and paused the tape ready to go. I pressed button four on the intercom.

'Wenger standing by,' I said into the microphone.

'We're finished with that, Kris. What the hell are you doing in there?'

'Sorry, I had a technical issue.'

'Get your shit together. You are going to have to react a lot quicker than that.'

'Sorry.'

I looked back at Steve from Edit 4.

'I'm not sure I'm qualified to do this job.'

'Well, I'd love to stick around and help you, but I am in the middle of an edit. If you're really stuck, come and find me, I'm in …'

'Edit 4, yes, thank you Steve.'

I needed to apologise to my producer, but I pressed the wrong switch on the intercom again.

'Sorry …'

'Are you retarded? I told you we are doing a voice-over here. Don't make me come down there again, for fuck's …' He hung up.

I peeled a green 'DUB' sticker from a tape label that I found on the desk and I stuck it above the correct button four. At least I now knew the director's intercom switch, which I guess was progress of a sort.

'Kris, cue up some fan shots, I need 30 seconds. One minute back.'

'Roger.'

I realised I hadn't restarted recording on the tape that I had cued for the Wenger shot, so I pressed record on that deck, now recording over part of the Wenger shot from that tape. I stopped the second tape deck and rewound. The images flew back three minutes.

'Come on!' the producer shouted over the intercom. 'I need it now.' I panicked again and spun the tape forward. Too far forward. I lined up a crowd shot and informed the producer. In my panic, I accidentally stopped the third machine from recording.

'Crowd shot ready,' I said trying to sound like I now had things under control.

The director came over the intercom and counted me in.

'Three, two, one, roll tape.'

I pressed play and the crowd shots appeared. But in my panic I had cued up a later crowd shot than the one I had intended and after 24 seconds the shot ran out. The screen went black, on my monitor and on air.

'Fuck me!' came the voice down the line. 'I told you 30 seconds! Are you stupid?' the producer screamed. 'We just went to black!'

Now there are a few things you really don't want to do if you are a premium TV service. Apart from accidentally broadcasting something grotesque or illegal, 'going to black' is the cardinal sin. Millions of your paying subscribers settling down at home to watch an exciting game suddenly find themselves staring at a blank screen. They gawk for a moment or two. Perhaps pick up the remote control or walk out to check the fuse box. Then the TV splutters back on with the presenters looking somewhat flustered. It just isn't the way to look professional. For the director, going to black is like losing a finger.

He was not happy.

'What the fuck are you doing in there?' he began. 'You just made me go to black! When we ask for 30 seconds, we want 30 seconds, not 29, 28 or 20-fucking-4.'

I was too humiliated to respond.

'Okay, let's see if you can do one simple thing. We are going back to Arsène Wenger. Do you think you can cue that up?'

Now, that I could do, or so I thought. Up and down I went until I realised what I had done. I had recorded over the top of it.

The director was screaming now and I was on tilt. I finally found Wenger on one of the other tapes and cued it up. But it was too late. Again.

Now the producer really laid into me. The game had started and I was all over the place. An early goal was scored and I realised that I had stopped all three tapes. I had no replay to show.

'Cue up the goal, two angles,' came the inevitable voice down the line. I took a deep breath and spoke.

'I wasn't recording on any of the machines, I'm really sorry.'

What came back down the line was mostly foul language and a few words of advice to find another profession. I had failed completely in my role as football replay guy and the game was only 15 minutes old.

And the nightmare continued. I pressed fast forward on air and by 40 minutes in, both the director and the producer were screaming at me simultaneously. By the time the half-time whistle blew, the intercom had gone silent and I didn't hear from either the producer or the director again. Obviously, someone in the studio had taken over. I sat in the room and didn't know what to do. An apology wasn't going to cut it. I couldn't go home until the game was over, but I knew I wouldn't be working for Premiership football at BSkyB again.

When the game was over, I didn't wait around. I couldn't see that further humiliation was going to help. I packed my things, crept out of the building and caught a train back to central London.

Remarkably, a few days later I was called back in to work on the boxing and nobody mentioned the incident to me again. But I knew that word was out about my meltdown during the sacred Premiership football and so, in that unforgiving culture, I had no future.

It was time to move on.

Digging deep for answers and even deeper for intelligent questions! Clockwise from top left, George Russell, Bernie Ecclestone, Max Verstappen, Nico Hülkenberg, Lewis Hamilton, Daniel Ricciardo, Lando Norris, Max again. Centre Pastor Maldonado.

'Checo! Checo! Checo!' Vladimir Rys snaps Sergio Perez's perfect somersault into the Red Bull Energy Station pool after the 2022 Monaco GP. (Vladimir Rys)

Bottoms up in Hockenheim. Steve Etherington's fast reaction captures the moment Felipe Massa's world turns upside down at the 2014 German GP. (Steve Etherington)

Maple leaf halo. Mark Sutton climbs the control tower to immortalise the moment the sun glints on the winner's trophy after Lewis Hamilton's victory at the 2017 Canadian GP. (Mark Sutton, Motorsport Images)

I reflect on words of wisdom from the Iceman Kimi Räikkönen at the 2013 Canadian GP. (Emily Davenport, Motorsport Images)

Donuts with no hands and just one foot. Fernando Alonso shows off his incredible skills in a souped-up go-kart at the 2021 Abu Dhabi GP. (James Moy)

Benetton ablaze. Steven Tee keeps snapping as mechanic Paul Seaby is engulfed in flames after Jos Verstappen's car catches fire at the 1994 German GP. (Steven Tee, Motorsport Images)

Nico Rosberg's Mercedes under stress at Suzuka at the 2018 Japanese GP. (Peter 'Foxy' Fox)

Darren Heath uses his deep knowledge of F1 circuits to capture the sparks reflecting the chain link fence spilling from Max Verstappen's Red Bull at the 2018 Chinese GP. (Darren Heath)

The legendary and much mourned Ayrton Senna, with Ron Dennis, in a moment of triumph after a fifth consecutive victory in Monaco in 1993. Damon Hill and Jean Alesi look on. (Peter Nygaard, Grand Prix Photo)

Guenther Steiner, Team Principal of Haas Formula One Team, who shot to fame with his show-stealing appearances on Drive to Survive, lights up the paddock with his smile and colourful vocabulary. (Peter Nygaard, Grand Prix Photo)

The ESPN Disney dream team in Monte Carlo 2022. Ulises Panizza, Juan Fossaroli and me. (Ulises Panizza)

'You have made history, man!' Sebastian Vettel congratulates Lewis Hamilton on equalling Michael Schumacher's seven titles at the 2018 Turkish GP. Checo behind. (Beto Issa)

Lewis Hamilton at the 2019 Monaco GP in front of Sebastian Vettel's Ferrari holding the helmet he designed in tribute to Niki Lauda who had just died. (Peter Nygaard, Grand Prix Photo)

Daniel Ricciardo's trademark smile is missing when Joshua Paul captures the Australian's sombre side with a 1913 Graflex camera at the 2015 Italian GP. (Joshua Paul)

The smile is back! Daniel Ricciardo sports his own version of MotoGP legend Valentino Rossi's 2008 Mugello helmet at the 2022 Monza GP. (Jiří Křenek)

Clockwise from top middle, Diego Mejia, Charles Leclerc, Vin Diesel, Sebastian Vettel, Brad Pitt, Mika Häkkinen. Right middle, me as the crash test dummy. Left of that, sad moments at Imola. Centre, always the clown.

Careering Around

St Etienne, France; Buenos Aires 1998

SINCE MY brief interest in Manchester United in the late seventies, I hadn't been much of a football fan and my mild antipathy was reinforced by my BSkyB experience. But I will always support the national team in big tournaments and so on 30 June 1998, my friend Andy and I went to St Étienne in the south of France to watch England play Argentina in the World Cup, my first experience of a live football game.

As it happened, Argentina had recently been on my mind. While I was living in Hong Kong, Reb was in Paris, where he met a guy from Cork called Jason Murphy who then moved to Buenos Aires and, in 1995, opened an Irish bar which, with startling originality, he called The Shamrock. It took a year to take off but became a roaring success. People queued around the block to get in. So, when I decided that I had no future at BSkyB, Reb and I talked vaguely about doing something similar. But I was yet to be convinced.

As Andy and I settled into our seats in the Charles Paret north stand of the Geoffroy-Guichard stadium in St Etienne, I noticed my friend nod to someone in the row behind us and then shake his hand. He was a tall, thin man with short dark hair and angular features. His face looked familiar.

'Who's that?' I whispered, turning to Andy.

'Uri Geller,' he told me, as if I was a fool for asking. For those who don't know the name, Uri created a sensation in the early seventies when he claimed to have what today we would call 'superpowers' which enabled him, through 'the power of his mind', to bend spoons just by rubbing them, describe hidden drawings and make stopped watches start. These amazing gifts he claimed and then denied, came to him from aliens. Either that, or he was an alien sent to Earth from a spaceship. You get the picture.

Uri was mercilessly debunked on the *Johnny Carson Show* when he was asked to demonstrate his powers under controlled conditions, which, of course, he couldn't. Regardless, back then, as now, there was no shortage of gullible people (like me) ready to endorse his unworldly ability.

He went on to make a good living trading on his notoriety and continued to claim paranormal and psychic powers.

'Uri Geller? The spoon-bender, watch-starter, Uri Geller?' I asked my friend, sneaking another peek backwards.

'Is there another?'

'So it is. How do you know him?'

'Everyone knows him.'

I looked at my watch. Unfortunately, it was working fine and, as I didn't have any spoons, or paper and crayons to put him to the test, I settled into my seat. As predicted (doubtless by Uri) the game was an epic encounter.

I sang along with the somewhat uninspiring terrace songs and even joined in the strange motif consisting of nine rhythmic handclaps followed by the scream of, 'Ince!' or the name of whichever player the fans particularly wanted to single out for approbation.

At the other end of the stadium, the Jean Snella south stand, the spectacle was glorious. The sky-blue and white scarves and flags of the Argentinian fans waved relentlessly in the sunlight and dancing in the hypnotising rectangle, thousands of pieces of paper fluttered in the air above them. And what uplifting terrace anthems! It made 'Jerusalem' seem like a funeral march when every Argentinian man, woman and child in the stadium began belting out '*Es un Sentimiento, No puedo Parar*'[82] as their team came out of the tunnel. These, I felt, were true football supporters, vivacious,

---

82 It's a feeling I can't stop.

passionate and proud. Many years later I learned that my friend and colleague Juan Fossaroli was also in the stadium, although not with his fellow Argentinians, as he had acquired his ticket at the last moment. Perhaps we brushed shoulders.

I cannot say I felt the English fans stood up well to the comparison. Plenty of beer-bellies and buzz-saw haircuts were in evidence and the mood was more one of aggression than passion. But my national pride held firm and I joined the eruption of protest when David Seaman conceded a penalty that was duly converted. I punched the air when Alan Shearer equalised from the other penalty spot. I watched in awe as the 18-year-old Michael Owen confirmed his arrival on the international stage, picking up the ball just inside Argentina's half, battling past Jose Chamot and then zooming past Roberto Ayala. I screeched in ecstasy as he drilled the ball past Carlos Roa to put England ahead. Then I put my head in my hands when Javier Zanetti equalised on the stroke of half-time with a brilliantly worked free kick.

When play restarted, I joined in as the crowd booed the referee and hurled insults at Diego Simeone who managed to provoke a young David Beckham to lash out, for which offence he was sent off. England were left with the near-impossible task of holding out for the rest of the half and extra time with ten men. But hold out they did. By the end I had a lump in my throat the size of a squash ball, genuinely proud of the courageous fight the team had put up. But as our heroes rubbed their tired muscles on the field below, all I could hear was negativity and defeatist talk all around me. The England fans had bad memories of penalty shoot-outs. Argentina won the toss and chose their end to have the shoot-out. And no wonder; the crowd looked like a vibrant living organism, raining positive energy down upon their players below.

Sergio Berti was first up for Argentina and coolly placed the ball into the right side-netting, beating David Seaman at full stretch. Shearer equalised, blasting the ball into the roof of the net. I clapped nine times and shouted 'Shearer!' When Hernan Crespo made his way into the penalty area, I heard Uri Geller speak clearly above the crowd.

'Seaman will save this penalty,' he said, with flat certainty.

In the quiet moment his voice carried and instantly the atmosphere changed. At last, hope surged through the English fans. And when Seaman did save the side-footed effort, the English fans went ballistic, particularly those who had heard Uri's prediction. Andy, helped by me and a few other supporters, lifted the skinny man high on to our shoulders and we hugged his gangly legs. He was now our leader, our talisman, our guru. Uri, the all-seeing one. With his alien powers now recruited to the cause, how could we fail?

'What next Uri? What next?' we shouted.

'Ince will score,' Uri assured us, still perched on Andy's shoulder. We waited with absolute conviction that Ince would bang it home for England.

Disaster! Betrayal! Treachery! I thought my eyes deceived me when I saw Roa save it easily, diving to his left. We all looked at Uri accusingly. How was this possible? We dumped him unceremoniously back into his seat. He was yesterday's news. And while allegedly he could make stopped clocks start, he couldn't turn them back. A few moments later, England were out of the World Cup.

But I must admit that as the downhearted mass of English supporters plodded out of the stadium, I was smiling to myself. I, at least, had taken something positive from that game. I wanted to be with the Argentinian crowd.

Within a few days my decision was final. I would head off to Argentina and see if we could start the bar Reb and I had talked about. Within a week or two Reb and I were in Buenos Aires looking at potential locations and trying to find investors.

Reb, who is like a brother to me, was completely broke at the time, and so was I. So, we approached our actual brothers to ask them to invest. But they, neither the type to let brotherly love cloud their business judgement, asked to see our business plan, which was inconvenient, as we didn't know what one of those was and we certainly couldn't be bothered to find out. So those brotherly Dragons were 'out'.

CAREERING AROUND

But Reb is a charmer and already knew people from his first trip to Buenos Aires. It wasn't long before we were put in contact with Carmen, a wealthy, older woman who had always wanted to own her own bar but didn't know how to go about it. Who better to guide her than two clueless English drunks? And so The Lock Inn was born. Carmen invested just enough cash to get us started and left the bar to us. At first things went pretty well. We filled the bar at weekends, but trade was slow during the week. There were three issues and two insoluble problems.

The first issue was that the bar was in the wrong area for the time (although it later became a popular spot). The second was that we were inadequately funded and the third was that we had no experience in the bar trade, or of running any kind of business. There was also a Brazilian cocaine addict who lived in a broken-down car parked outside the bar, which kind of sent the wrong message to our potential clients. Carmen, kind soul that she was, offered him food and beer one day. In no time he was calling in regularly, stealing the money from the tips jar and demanding his free beer and food. When we refused, he threw our heavy glass ashtrays at us. That problem was solved when a government tow-truck removed the car from the street with him inside. But while the issues could perhaps have been resolved with application and hard work, the two insoluble problems remained. Namely Reb and I, who were far more interested in drinking the stock than selling it.

Then, one slow night, three armed men came into the bar. One put a gun to the head of one of our customers and another seized my chef's knife, that I used to cut the lemons, and held it to my throat. But they were to be disappointed. As I said, business was slow and when they looked inside the till, they made no effort to hide their disgust at our tin-pot operation and lack of business acumen. They fleeced our customers, but they were mostly broke too, so the villains left with scarcely enough cash to cover their travel expenses. They did, however, steal my knife, which I was quite upset about, as it was the most valuable thing in the bar.

Perhaps the bar trade was not really our thing. We soldiered on for a few more months, but the writing was on the wall. My mind was made up for me when Terence O'Rorke, the producer I handed over to when I left the APGA Omega Golf Tour, emailed me. He asked if I was interested in producing the TV coverage for the new professional golf tour, the Tour de Las Américas in South and Central America.

Terence explained that a new network called PSN was producing the programmes. He said they were generous with their budgets, that I could fly business class and use an edit suite at a top production company in Miami. While I was in the US I would be provided with a house and a convertible car. Oh, and the salary was ridiculously high and paid in US dollars. I weighed up the decision for all of two seconds. I had served drinks and I had been served drinks and, frankly, being served is better. I still had the little problem of my exclusion from the United States to overcome, but after a lot of effort and some help from Jason's dad, who had a well-connected friend, I was granted a visa.

I have had my fair share of luck and my ace-in-the-hole was in overdrive when I met my one-in-a-million wife Agustina, now mother of my two lovely children, Benjamin and Isabella. When I was approached to join the TLA golf tour, Agustina was pregnant, so a regular salary was just what was required.

I produced the first year's highlights magazine shows for PSN. It was only after the channel was closed for running a money laundering operation that I twigged why my pay and conditions were so generous.

But no matter. Although my salary dropped when I switched to producing the show for ESPN and the Golf Channel, I was still doing well.

The next decade was golf tours and pay cheques in US dollars, which went a long way in Argentina. It wasn't long before I was able to buy an apartment in cash. Which is literally what you have to do in Argentina, as the banking system doesn't work.

So how did I get back into the world of Formula One?

CAREERING AROUND

It was on a golf course, the Jockey Club in Buenos Aires in 2001, that I met Juan Fossaroli. At first, I didn't pay attention to the slim, blond, long-haired Argentinian holding a microphone standing beside me on the 18th green. I was too busy formulating a question in my shaky Spanish on the off-chance that the newly crowned Argentina Open winner, Angel 'Pato' Cabrera, would give me a break.

In all my years of interviewing sports personalities, few have refused to talk to me, which is surprising given my track record of asking ill-informed and foolish questions. After all, I once asked the American golfer Chip Beck what it was like to be named after a golf shot. He laughed heartily and said:

'That's a good one, yes, I've never thought of that.' I have to say I find it extremely hard to believe it had never come up before, but there we are. Then he said:

'Do you have any serious questions?' But sadly, on that day, that was all I had.

For some reason Cabrera always ignored me in the pre- and post-round interviews. Perhaps he didn't like my terrible Spanish, or maybe he just didn't like the look of me. Or maybe he's just not a nice person. His conviction in 2021 for assault, theft and intimidation might suggest the latter, but who am I to judge?

Yet that day he was swinging freely and won the Argentina Open by two strokes. 'Pato' (the duck), so nicknamed for his gait, waddled over to the media scrum to discuss his victory. As usual he avoided eye contact, refusing me the opportunity to ask a question. Hearing me curse under my breath, Juan, the blue-eyed Argentinian, offered to help.

'You can film my interview if you like,' he said. 'Just put your microphone and camera in when I ask the questions. It will be okay. I have *"onda"* with him.' I later learned that *'onda'* meant 'rapport' or 'a good vibe', but at the time I honestly thought he meant they jointly owned a Japanese car!

And that was that. Juan asked good questions and I got the soundbites I needed. A random act of kindness from a stranger always has a lasting effect on me and Juan was instantly in my circle of trust. It turned out that my new friend owned a production company that specialised in golf and motorsport, so I began to use his editing facilities and hire his cameras and cameramen to cover my TLA events. We were soon good friends.

One evening in the Argentinian summer of 2002, I invited Juan to my birthday party. Agustina and I had cooked up a plan to introduce him to our English friend, Cathy. I told Juan about the lovely lady we wanted him to meet, but at the last minute Cathy was unwell and sent her apologies. When he arrived, Juan began chatting to a woman he thought was Cathy and he was most impressed. In particular he was blown away by her impeccable Spanish.

'How come your beautiful English friend has managed to learn perfect Spanish when you can't string two words together?' he asked me. It turned out he had been talking to my wife's cousin, Carolina, who is, of course, Argentinian. Eight months later Juan and Carolina were married and now have three children.

By 2011 Juan's career in Formula One was on the up. He progressed from cameraman to behind-the-camera producer, to interviewer, to main pit reporter, then presenter and ultimately the face of Formula One for Fox Sports, who had exclusive rights to show F1 in Latin America.

At that time, golf's Tour de las Americas was running out of steam and sponsorship was drying up. I had travelled to countless courses and produced hundreds of golf highlights magazine shows, so I was ready for a new challenge. My opportunity to get back into Formula One came when Juan approached me during the 2011 season. His previous producer had departed after a dispute about which was the best döner kabab restaurant in Istanbul escalated into 'irreconcilable differences'.

I leapt at the chance. But ever since I have been most careful to let Juan have the last word about where we dine.

Ulises the God of Love

IT WAS great to return to the world of Formula One. I had missed the roar of the engines and the sheer excitement of the scene. And now I had access not just to the paddock and TV compound, but also the pits, media centre and the grid. Bernie had no beef with Fox LatAm.

I went to most of the remaining Grand Prix races in 2011 and when Juan asked me to commit to the 2012 season, I was delighted. Meanwhile, Juan's cameraman had also moved on, so there was another vacancy to fill. Juan asked me if I knew someone who met two requirements. First, they had to be able to do the job and second, I had to be happy to share a room with them when required. I immediately thought of my good friend Ulises Panizza.

I met Uli when I first came to Argentina in 1998. Whenever I ran into him, at parties, *asados* (Latin American BBQs) or in late-night bars, he greeted me with the widest, most open smile you could imagine. It was impossible not to like the pint-sized, handsome, happy-go-lucky Argentinian with his designer stubble and kind brown eyes. His laughter, over which he has absolutely no control, is more infectious than measles and he is streetwise, calm under pressure, and practical.

Uli told me he was a cameraman when I first met him, but as he also told me he was a chef, DJ, barman, welder, delivery man and had several more dubious activities on his résumé, it was only when I was short of options for a golf tournament in Mexico that I asked him to fill in.

He was excellent. He learned how to follow a golf ball in the air in one afternoon, which, believe me, with the broken tripod, ancient camera and the cheap lens I supplied, is impressive. I figured that if he could follow a golf ball on a cloudy day, he could shoot a Formula One car exiting the pits or a driver standing in front of him, so on my recommendation, Juan hired Uli and he became a part of the team.

I wouldn't say I knew Uli that well beforehand. Most of our encounters took place in loud bars, barbecues or parties, so I can't say we discussed South American politics, quantum mechanics or our favourite Renaissance novelists. In fact, I soon learned that Uli has never read a book (maybe this will be his first?), but that didn't matter at all. He may not be book-smart, but he is well versed in life experience. He wears his heart on his sleeve and is even more of a people-person than me. He also supplemented one of my many failings with the memory of an elephant and is a delight to be around.

But I would be less than truthful if I said I was completely confident Uli would meet Juan's exacting standards. He loves a party even more than me, but in the years of working in F1 he has always been completely reliable. Apart perhaps from the time he disappeared after a night of passion in Spa and ran sheepishly down the paddock just moments before the deadline. Oh, and the time he fainted during an interview with Checo Pérez after a (very) long weekend in Ibiza.

But that's not to say he hasn't got himself into a few scrapes. Before Uli began his international career freelancing for Fox in Formula One, he had not spent much time outside Argentina so, while he was streetwise in Buenos Aires, he still had a bit to learn about the wicked ways of the wider world. I would often receive random texts late at night when I was tucked up in bed.

'Kris, the strip club won't accept Argentinian pesos, do you have any Malaysian ringgit? You have no idea how beautiful this girl is!' Or: 'Kris, I lost my phone!' To which I replied: 'How are you sending me this message?' To which he replied: 'Don't worry, I found it. I'm hammered.'

As I was falling asleep in Shanghai in 2012, the third race of Uli's first season and the night before qualifying, I received this message:

'I've been kidnapped by the Chinese mafia.'

I replied that he should tell the kidnappers to demand his ransom in Argentinian pesos, not US dollars, or we wouldn't be seeing each other again. He didn't reply, so before long I fell asleep.

I woke up around 7am when Uli came back into our room to tell his tale. Uli and a Mexican F1 journalist called David had been drinking in a bar, where they met a friendly guy who, after a while, suggested they move on to a karaoke place a few blocks away. When they arrived, the generous stranger ordered top-shelf whisky, food and drinks before unaccountably disappearing into the night, leaving Uli and David with the outrageous bill of US $800. Protests fell on deaf ears and two very large doormen ushered them into a side room pending payment. Uli was penniless, so David had no choice but to cough up and became another victim of this popular racket. I was in no position to judge, as I had fallen for it myself years before in Hong Kong.

It wasn't until October of that year that Uli's hard partying came close to causing a real problem. It was the Tuesday morning after the Japanese Grand Prix and, having driven up from Suzuka to Tokyo the day before, I was having breakfast in an annex to the lobby of our boutique hotel in Shibuya.

The previous evening Juan and I had returned to the hotel after dinner, but Uli had gone out to meet a friend. I was surprised not to see him in our room when I woke up the next morning but assumed he had stayed over. We were heading to South Korea later that afternoon for the next Grand Prix, so I guessed he would turn up.

While enjoying my coffee, cereal and fruit, I was reading an article about the previous race which speculated, accurately as it turned out, that Fernando Alonso's luck was running out. Fernando had begun the race in Japan with a 29-point lead in the championship, but after a collision with Kimi Räikkönen at the first corner, he spun out, so was now just four points ahead of Sebastian Vettel, who had won his second race in a row. Sebastian went on to win the next two as well, just pipping Fernando to the championship that year.

My attention was taken by a disturbance in the lobby and I looked up to see Uli, who I would normally have been pleased to see. But today he wore an expression that was at once glassy-eyed and panic-stricken. More remarkable still was his entourage. It consisted of a dishevelled but athletic-looking young man in a McDonald's uniform, three tall, smartly dressed Africans, a geisha girl and four tiny Japanese police officers, all in a state of considerable agitation. The chunk of melon on the end of my fork dropped to the table, followed by my jaw.

'What the fuck?' I mouthed to my friend.

It was many hours before we pieced together what had happened. When Uli first started travelling with us he didn't have a credit card of his own, so after his long night at the karaoke, he thought it might be handy to have one for emergencies, which he borrowed from a (very!) good friend back in Buenos Aires. And indeed, that night there had been a crisis of gigantic proportions, because after a night of hard drinking, Uli found that he was a little peckish and, rather than walk the block or so to the hotel where free (to him) breakfast was being served, he decided to pop into a McDonald's and order himself an egg McMuffin to consume on the short journey home.

When he went to pay, for some reason the cashier asked Uli to provide identification. Given that the name on the card was not Uli's, identification would not have helped and in any case, his passport was back at the hotel. Fearing that the card might be confiscated, which would place Uli in a tricky situation and with his judgement somewhat impaired by the night's excesses, he grabbed the credit card and walked out of the restaurant. But after a few moments Uli realised that the McCashier was shouting after him. When Uli broke into a run, the McCashier, with all the agility of a McNinja, leapt effortlessly over the counter and started to give chase.

Uli ran for it in the direction of the hotel, but he had chosen the wrong man to run from. Uli, sadly, is no athlete, but the lithe McNinja was and so he caught up a few metres from the door, launched himself at my friend and wrapped his sinuous body around Uli's tubby torso.

Uli cried out for help, and it must have been a most piteous sound as the three African gentlemen issued from a nearby nightclub (where they were employed to drum up business), followed by a geisha girl of mature years, resplendent in full traditional dress. This unlikely quartet of civic-minded individuals came to offer Uli their assistance. But neither the intimidating presence of the three large doormen, nor the softer entreaties of the geisha could persuade the McNinja to release his iron grip.

Eventually a passing policeman noticed the kerfuffle and intervened, whereupon, at last, the McNinja let Uli go. The confused policeman, possibly feeling a little threatened by the large crowd, called for back-up. After voluble exchanges in various of the world's languages, the group, which had now swelled to nine persons from at least three continents, decided to walk to the hotel to check out Uli's ID, which is where I happened upon them.

Uli went to our room to get his passport and I called Juan from the front desk. When the senior policeman analysed the credit card and the passport, it was not hard for him to discern that they did not match. The philanthropic Africans and random geisha were then dismissed along with the McNinja, although the latter still appeared rather animated. Then Uli was marched off to the police station for further questioning. Juan and I tried to accompany Uli, but were told by the police to stay behind.

Five hours passed with no sign of Uli and we were running out of time to catch our flight to South Korea, so I packed Uli's personal effects, gathered the camera equipment and checked out of our room. Having considered our options, we decided to go to the police station to see if there was any news. As we went in, we immediately heard peals of Uli's signature laughter and when we saw him, he was delightedly hugging one of the police officers, who was returning the hug with a wide smile. The three others from the hotel were also laughing and patting him on the back. Apparently, Uli had finally reached his friend in Buenos Aires by phone, who was able to explain that the card was not stolen, so Uli was free to go. There's just something about Uli that's impossible not to like. He can make friends with anyone.

As we walked back to the hotel, Uli reached into his pocket and sheepishly pulled out a half-eaten egg McMuffin which he finished off with relish. Which explained why the McNinja had chased him. He hadn't paid for it!

But as Uli said, for a free egg McMuffin, a day with the Japanese police was totally worth it. And, of course, being Uli, he made four new friends. I was amazed that the McNinja wasn't booked to go on holiday with Uli and the geisha girl, but he was probably too tightly wrapped around my friend to see his irresistible smile.

But those incidents aside, Uli was off to the races in every sense. At first, he was a little intimidated by the notorious Formula One media scrum and failed to get a good enough position to shoot the drivers at the post-practice interviews. So, on the third occasion I gave him a little encouragement by pushing him into the fray between two cameramen. A powerful-looking Austrian cameraman, Michael, whose shot was compromised by Uli's camera lens thrusting into his frame, looked down at Uli and said forcefully: 'Use the zoom!'

Those three words, implying you didn't have to get close to the driver to get the shot you wanted, became something of a meme among cameramen in the paddock, uttered in a deep, gruff, guttural voice to let another cameraman know if they were getting in the way. It has been repeated countless times. Yet this was the only time anyone was remotely aggressive towards Uli as, despite not speaking fluent English, he was always willing to try. He went down brilliantly in the paddock on his charisma alone, and he and Michael are now the best of friends.

Uli greets everyone with his trademark smile and treats everyone with the same unwavering respect, whatever their reputation or position in the paddock hierarchy. First, he made friends with all the misfits and geeks, then the caterers and mechanics, then with everyone else.

ULISES THE GOD OF LOVE

In his downtime in the paddock, it was not uncommon for Uli to have a group of people around him, showing them videos he had collected of people engaged in bizarre or horrendous activities. When people averted their eyes in disbelief or disgust, Uli laughed with such uncontrolled abandon that you simply had to love him.

One such video starred Uli himself. I did mention that he had been involved in various dubious activities before settling on his career as an F1 cameraman. When I first got to see exactly what that involved it certainly had an impact. Looking at it purely from a professional perspective, the production values were excellent – as far as pornographic videos go. I made this assessment in five seconds when I watched a video he thrust in front of me, before realising who and what I was watching. I clamped my eyes shut, put my fingers in my ears, screamed and scarpered. I can say no more, other than apart from Uli, two other things essentially Brazilian were involved: a bolo de rolo dessert and a voluptuous beauty. Let's just say that Uli got to have his cake and eat it.

Anyway, it wasn't long before all the cameramen and many other key figures in the paddock had been treated to at least ten seconds of Uli's antics and, I am sorry to say, more than a few watched the whole thing. But rather than damage his reputation, it made him into something of a folk hero, which perhaps is a relevant comment on the sophistication of the gentlemen of the press.

Uli has gone on to become a leading light in the community of cameramen. He organises the annual Cameramen's Night Out at the White Horse in Austin, Texas. I am proud to say I was the only producer who was deemed good, or should I say bad, enough to attend. It certainly wasn't because of my prowess as a cameraman, that's for sure.

Batigol

Monza, 2022

ON THE Friday before the 2022 Italian Grand Prix, Juan, Uli and I were pushing through the paddock turnstiles at the Monza circuit when Juan received a WhatsApp message. It was from ESPN's special guest for the weekend, the footballer Gabriel Batistuta, confirming his time of arrival at the Stazione de Monza from his holiday home in Florence. The plan was for him to appear on camera with Juan during our transmission over the race weekend.

It fell to me to pick Gabriel up from the train station, so I dropped my bag in the media centre, grabbed a coffee in the Pirelli suite and went to see the F1 broadcaster and media accreditation liaison officer Sheila Pattni to pick up Gabriel's paddock and pit lane access pass. Sheila was excited to learn that one of her childhood heroes was coming to Monza and in return for processing his pass 'at short notice with incredible efficiency' as she said, she would need me to introduce Gabriel to her to get a photograph of herself with the legend to hang on her wall.

Sheila's excitement at Gabriel's anticipated arrival was echoed by the group of journalist friends I ran into before leaving the paddock. When they saw whose pass I was holding and learned I was on my way to pick him up, they too were obviously impressed.

'Batistuta is coming to the paddock!?' someone said in an awed whisper.

'You're going to pick him up now? Can I come with you?' asked another.

'Will he be doing interviews?' ventured a third. 'I have his international shirt with me at the hotel. If I bring it in tomorrow, can you get him to sign it for me?'

'Guys, I'm just the chauffeur, not his personal manager,' I replied. They showed their appreciation by booing me as I left the paddock and headed towards the media car park.

Not being a big football fan, I have to admit I really didn't know much about Gabriel at the time, other than that he had long flowing locks in the nineties and was a hero in Argentina. Yet it occurred to me I should do a bit of research, as we would be in a car together for at least half an hour. I reached for my phone and googled him to find some talking points.

I soon learned that Gabriel Batistuta, or 'Batigol' as he is known, is one of the greatest strikers of all time, scoring 56 goals in 78 appearances for his country (second only to Lionel Messi) and 204 for the Italian club Fiorentina in Florence. As I scanned down the long list of his achievements, I noticed that he had also played for both River and Boca, the biggest rivals in Argentina. There couldn't be too many players who had done that! Perhaps I could ask him about that as an icebreaker.

I found a parking space right outside the Stazione de Monza and sent my location to Gabriel's WhatsApp. About 20 minutes later, he emerged from the building and I waved him over. We shook hands.

'*Gabriel! Hola, como va? Como fue tu viaje?*' I asked, smiling.

He told me his trip was fine but he had been delayed by people asking for selfies in the station. Like Maradona before him, he was worshipped in Italy as well as Argentina. He put his bag into the boot and climbed into the front seat, making room by sliding the seat right back.

When settled and strapped in, he turned to get a closer look at his 'chauffeur'.

'How was Florence?' I asked as I reversed erratically out of the parking spot. 'Did you hook up with any of your old team-mates at Florentina?'

'Fiorentina,' he corrected me, looking back to make sure I wasn't about to imperil his life. After a short pause my passenger had a question for me.

'*Quien sos exactamente?*' the goalscoring legend asked me. 'Who are you, exactly?'

I didn't know if Juan had told Gabriel anything about me, so I said I was a producer who had been working with Juan for over 20 years. This intrigued Gabriel, who was immediately curious to know why an Englishman with a sketchy grasp of Spanish was working for ESPN Disney in Argentina. I explained how Juan and I had met in the late nineties on a golf course and how he had supplied me with camera crews and editing facilities for my golf shows. But Batigol was not sure he had got to the bottom of it and probed further. I explained how we had been working together in Formula One since 2011 and my role as Juan's understudy and right-hand man. But Batigol was still not satisfied. At last I mentioned, casually as I thought, that our wives were cousins.

'Ahhhh, okay! So you're family,' he said, smiling broadly, as if a particularly tricky knot had just unravelled in his hand. I was, frankly, a little miffed at the implication I owed my job solely to family connections, but Batigol's attention had wandered and he was now answering a message on his phone.

When he finished, I decided to try out some of the knowledge I had gained from Wiki and asked why he had retired from playing for Al-Arabi in Qatar. He told me that the injuries he suffered led to intense pain in his legs to the point where he wanted to have them amputated. I looked at him to gauge whether he was serious or not. He was. I later learned that only a complex surgery had relieved him from the agony he experienced.

As the World Cup was approaching, I asked his opinion on the Argentinian team. I listened attentively as he critiqued players I'd never heard of, nodding sagely. Then I hit him with my best piece of Wiki-gleaned information. 'There can't be too many people who played for both Boca and River, Gabriel. Out of interest, how did the Boca fans react to you after you swapped teams?' I asked.

'They warmed to me after I became the league's top goalscorer and we won the championship,' he said with a wink. This made me laugh. We were now chatting away easily.

Gabriel Batistuta, Batigol. What a legend, I thought. We arrived at his hotel where he dropped off his bag and freshened up while I waited in the car. I had this chauffeur role down to a tee, just missing the peaked cap. After 15 minutes, my passenger got back in the car.

'So why did you go to Argentina in the first place?' Gabriel asked as we pulled out of the car park. This was a story I had told in Spanish many times, so I confidently began recounting my go-to anecdote.

'*Fui a ver Inglaterra contra Argentina en el Mundial de Francia en 1998 …*' I was off and running, recounting the story related in the previous chapter. I told him about the rather depressing English fans and the animated, passionate Argentinian supporters and how by the end I decided I wanted to be with the singing crowd in white and sky blue.

I even recounted moments from the game itself. Michael Owen's amazing goal. Beckham being sent off. The penalty shoot-out after extra time. I then remembered that Juan had also been at the same game, so I mentioned that incredible coincidence. He was looking out the window now, and said something that I didn't hear at first, so I asked him to repeat what he had said.

'Yes, I was there, also,' he said.

'Oh, really? Where in the ground were you watching from?' I asked, taken aback by the coincidence.

'I was on the pitch.'

I closed my eyes tightly and cringed. Of course he was! He scored the first goal from the penalty spot! I now remembered the English fans booing him as he celebrated at the other end. I babbled my excuses. By the time we arrived at the circuit, Gabriel had joined the growing list of people who had reached the conclusion I was a complete idiot.

That night, I watched Batistuta's career highlights on YouTube. 'Impressive' is an understatement. He fully deserved his nickname,

'Batigol', and his other one too, 'El Angel Gabriel', heaven sent to play football.

And I deserved the nickname my wife gave me early in our relationship: 'the Old Computer'. My hard drive, I'm afraid, is full.

Electric Dreams

2014–18

EVERY YEAR, as the F1 season draws to a close, it's not unusual to hear people in the paddock announce, portentously and with a tear in their eye, that we should prepare ourselves never to see them again because, unlike Arnold Schwarzenegger, they won't be back. Their anticipated departure from the scene may be because of contractual issues, or because their employer is losing broadcasting rights, or has made budget cuts, or decided to invest elsewhere. Others say they have tired of the continual travel that is part of circus life. A few even claim to have lost their passion for Formula One. But nine times out of ten those very same people will turn up the following year and usually for a fair few seasons after that.

At the end of the 2014 season, it was the turn of our crew to doubt our F1 future when we learned Fox Sports LatAm had lost the exclusive broadcasting rights to the Spanish multimedia group Mediapro. Uli and I announced these sad tidings to anyone who would listen. Juan, as always, kept his cards closer to his chest.

But during the last race in Abu Dhabi we heard that Fox had negotiated a deal with Mediapro to transmit half the Grands Prix live. This didn't save me from the F1 chopping block, but it meant that Juan and Uli would travel to the races and manage the reduced workload between them.

Since May of that year, I had occasionally been covering the brand-new motorsport of Formula E and my banishment from F1 freed me up to focus exclusively on the new series.

The concept of an all-electric, international street-racing motorsport competition was first fleshed out on a napkin in a Parisian restaurant in March 2011 when Antonio Tajani, then a vice president of the European Commission overseeing the automotive industry, met with Jean Todt, president of the FIA, and the Spanish politician, businessman and sometime chairman of Queens Park Rangers Football Club, Alejandro Agag. During the conversation about the future of the industry, Todt suggested the FIA should create an all-electric racing championship.[83]

Agag who, with our old friend Flavio Briatore had been responsible for bringing Formula One to Spain, knew his way around the motorsport scene. With a shrewd eye for an exciting business opportunity, he realised that electric-powered car racing could be highly attractive to some of the sponsors from the auto industry who were expressing concern about the environmental impact of traditional petrol-based motorsport. He immediately put himself forward as the series promoter.

The interest of the auto industry was not wholly philanthropic. If they could demonstrate fast, attractive, robust electric cars, it would provide the perfect way to counter the perception that they were slow, geeky and impractical. The image problem had to be addressed because it was preventing the growth of what would ultimately be a huge new market as the world migrated from petrol or diesel to electric-powered cars. But there were other benefits for potential sponsors. As well as promoting their company brand in association with the emerging market, the spur of competition might well help those involved to develop better electric-based technology more rapidly, further accelerating market growth.

But it was a huge step from the dream to reality. Agag had no cars, no teams, no drivers and no racetracks. But within a year the first Formulec EF-01 prototype was built, which encapsulated the new 'Formula' and demonstrated it was possible to build a fast and exciting electric car. In just three years the ABB FIA

---

83 Autosport.com. Article by Alejandro Agag.

Formula E World Championship was launched. And it flew off the grid.

My first experience of the all-electric-powered single-seater motorsport competition had come in May 2014 when I found myself driving from London to the Donington Park circuit – the new Formula E headquarters – to cover the inaugural presentation of the teams and cars.

As I glanced down the entry line-up on my arrival, I saw a who's who of talented drivers, including some I knew from Formula One. There was the German 'Quick Nick' Heidfeld who drove for Prost, Williams, BMW, Sauber and Renault and holds the distinction of making it on to the F1 podium a record 13 times, but without achieving the top spot. Also on the list was Italian Jarno Trulli, who drove in F1 from 1997 to 2011, placing 11 times, including a triumphant win in Monte Carlo in 2004. Although he usually had to drive slower cars, he was renowned for his fast laps in qualifying, which earned him a good grid position, which he then defended with great skill and tenacity, enabling him to hold off faster cars for extended periods. This often resulted in a queue of (doubtless) frustrated drivers behind him, often referred to by commentators, pundits and fans as the 'Trulli train'.

I also knew Jean-Eric Vergne, known as JEV, who had won the British Formula 3 championship in 2011 and then had a spell in F1 with Scuderia Toro Rosso from 2012 to 2014. Later he would become the first person to win back-to-back Formula E World Championships in the 2017/18 and 2018/19 seasons. There was the Swiss driver Sébastian Buemi, who I had chased around for interviews at Le Mans and other World Endurance Championship events, but who also raced in F1 and went on to be highly successful in FE. I once misidentified him in an interview as French, which didn't go down particularly well. Then there was an actual Frenchman, Charles Pic, who drove two seasons in F1, and the Brazilian Lucas Di Grassi, who was destined to become the inaugural winner.

There were also plenty of famous names: Nelson Piquet Junior, son of Nelson, who we met earlier; Nicolas Prost, son of Alain;

Marco Andretti, grandson of the 1978 world champion Mario; and Matthew Brabham, whose grandfather, Sir Jack Brabham, claimed three world titles. And there was Bruno Senna, nephew of you-know-who.

My job on that first trip to Donington was to interview the new drivers and team members mainly in English and Alejandro Agag in Spanish. I was also going to record my first ever links to camera in Spanish which would air that evening on the Fox Sports news show, *Nitro*.

I have to say the prospect of presenting in Spanish made me more than a touch nervous. When I arrived in Argentina in 1998, I was determined to learn Spanish, but my resolution faded when I realised how ridiculously difficult I found it. I did try, first decorating my bedroom wall with post-it notes on which verb conjugations were written large in red ink. But while the little papers mostly stayed stuck to the wall, what was written on them never stuck in my brain. So, I enrolled on a two-week introductory course, but that ended in humiliation when the teacher, Señorita Gutierrez, told me, echoing my performance in A Level physics, I had got worse during my period of education. So, it seemed only reasonable to ask for my money back, but I asked in my version of Spanish, so she didn't understand. Perhaps if I could free up some space on my hard drive by losing all those eighties song lyrics, I would have room left for a new language?

Then I married Agustina, my lovely Argentinian wife, but she was educated in an English-speaking school, so that didn't much help my progress. Nor did socialising almost exclusively with expats.

But the fundamental problem was the same as in my schooldays. I'm a tiny bit thick. One of the missing keys on that broken keyboard in my head is in the area of etymological, phonological, semantic, syntactical and grammatical comprehension, particularly in foreign languages. I hope that you can see by my use of those long words that I have mastered my mother tongue, or at least, how to use the thesaurus on Google.

It took agonising years to be able to converse in Spanish at all. After 25 years I can, at last, understand and communicate comfortably in a day-to-day chat with a patient listener, but as soon as the conversation wanders into specialised areas, I find my linguistic command sadly lacking.

I am constantly ridiculed by my Argentinian friends. They keep a list of words and phrases that I mispronounce or just get completely wrong. I once tried to ask an Argentinian driver during a live transmission, what he thought of his *'conpañero'* (team-mate), but instead asked him what he thought of *'el pajero'* (the wanker). The picture then shook around wildly as the cameraman was unable to control his laughter.

On another occasion, Juan was backing into a parking spot outside a restaurant and I tried to warn him that it was an *'estacionamiento para discapacitados'* (a disabled parking space). But what I actually said was *'el estacionamiento para decapidados'* (parking for the beheaded). Ever since, Juan mimes an imaginary head under his arm whenever the subject of car parking comes up.

So, when it came to recording my first lines to camera in Spanish, I had justifiable cause for concern. To add to the tension, the Formula E host broadcaster, Aurora TV, supplied me with a cameraman, Peter, but just for 90 minutes. Peter made it extremely clear from the outset that he was eager to get on with his own commitments.

By the time he had begrudgingly shot my interviews and some general footage of the cars, we had just five minutes left of my allocated time to record my opening and closing links to camera. The pressure was on, but remarkably, it took me only three attempts to nail the 30-second opening link and just one take to do the 15-second closer. Peter kept grimacing and looking at his watch, but for once I didn't crumble under pressure. I can't say the links were perfect by any means, but they were comprehensible enough. When I was finished, Peter handed me his camera card and waited impatiently while I fumbled about trying to download the footage to my computer. The moment the download was complete, he snatched the card and left.

When I listened to my links, I realised I had made a mistake. When I said, 'Formula E', I had pronounced the 'E' in English, rather than Spanish. Going back to Peter and asking him to re-record did not seem an option. So, being the perfectionist that I am (?), I re-recorded 'Formula *Eh*' on my phone and dropped the corrected audio into the master before sending the material off via WeTransfer to Buenos Aires. Back in my hotel, I went to the lobby bar and sat back to relax, confident the job was well done. Was there no end to my talents?

But later that night, I received a mocking voice message from Juan.

'Formula what?' he laughed on the voice message attached to the video. 'What is Formula *Eehh*? Not even close to how you say it in Spanish.' From that moment, whenever Juan utters 'Formula E', he always pronounces it 'Formula *Eehh*'.

But although my career as a Spanish-speaking news correspondent was not off to the best of starts, I was looking forward to the new challenge. My job for the next four seasons was to interview the drivers and team members on the Friday, then produce the pre-live and post-shows on the Saturday. My old friend Edmundo 'Natt' Nattkemper, who I had worked with many times on both golf and motorsport, was to be my trusty cameraman.

Natt is a workhorse. During the second season, he was indispensable, producing *Sound of the Future*, the half-hour magazine commissioned by Formula E to promote the franchise. In addition to race day coverage, we went behind the scenes and did 'fun' features with the drivers, with just two days to shoot enough material to fill the show. Natt was brilliant at recording as much relevant footage as possible, giving plenty of options for the editor in Buenos Aires.

In contrast to the Formula One operation at that time, access to the Formula E drivers was easy. At a Formula One Grand Prix, you were busy for four days, with driver interviews on Thursday, free practice one and two on Friday, qualifying on Saturday and the race itself on Sunday. Formula E was done in less than half the time. On Friday we covered all the team and driver interviews for news and features. Sometimes the drivers were allowed a 'shakedown' session, when the car's reliability and electronic systems were checked on the track.

On Saturday it was practice, qualifying and the race. The drivers even fitted an online race into their already packed schedule. Sometimes there was a repeat of the Saturday programme on the Sunday if it was a 'double-header'.

Back then, it was difficult to get Formula One drivers to do anything out of the ordinary as, under Bernie Ecclestone's regime, the approach was to shroud the superstars of the sport with mystique. But in Formula E you could propose just about anything for the pre-arranged one-to-one interviews and the drivers and teams would enthusiastically try to make it happen. Boat or jet-ski rides, surfing, playing poker in a casino, tennis, golf or basketball were all taken up enthusiastically. The drivers showed their competitive side as they played Connect 4, chess or table tennis, or drove remote control cars around the paddock, or played pool, or darts, or any other activity that was easy to set up and not too far from the Formula E garage.

Aurora took on the production of *Sound of the Future* in season three when Formula E appreciated that, to realise its full potential, the show required not one but four crews, and went on to arrange even more elaborate shoots with the drivers. I was proud we had built up the show to the point where it was taken forward with such commitment.

Under less pressure to deliver large volumes of material for *Sound of the Future*, Natt and I continued to cover the FE scene, doing the features with the drivers. But now it was less frenetic and I could hold conversations in a variety of relaxed settings.

Formula E came up with a clever approach to build the sport and make it easy for teams to participate without having to invest in designing and building new cars. Initially each team was supplied with Spark-Renault SRT 01E cars with an electric motor developed by McLaren, a Dallara-designed chassis, a battery system produced by Williams Grand Prix Engineering, Michelin all-weather tyres and a Hewland gearbox. The plan was to allow the teams progressively to replace modules of the standard issue with their own manufactured parts, which they did, raising the bar each season.

For three seasons, two first-generation (Gen1) Formula E cars were required by each driver to complete a race, because the battery technology was not advanced enough to last. But by season four, the Gen2 Formula E car had overcome that problem. When the cars first raced in 2014, the engine of the Gen1 Formula E car had 150kW of power and a top speed of 225kph (140mph). In the 2022/23 season the Gen3 Formula E car had an electric motor capable of delivering 350kW of power and a top speed of 322kph (200 mph).[84]

By season four, nine manufacturers were competing, including Jaguar, Nissan, BMW, Audi, DS (Citroen) and Mahindra, confirming Formula E as a competitive platform for global car manufacturers.

Formula E also brought a fresh approach to fan engagement, pioneering such ideas as Fanboost, which allows the watching public to vote to give an extra boost of power to their favourite drivers. So now fans could influence the outcome of an EPrix. In season five they introduced Attack Mode, allowing cars to leave the racing line and pass through a zone to 'fire up' and be rewarded with a timed power boost, gaining an extra edge for a few laps.

By season six in 2019/20, Mercedes-Benz EQ and TAG Heuer Porsche were on board and the grid expanded to 24 drivers. Driver's eye cameras, embedded in the padding of the driver's helmet, were introduced, a technology adopted in Formula One in 2022. In season seven Formula E was officially granted World Championship status by the FIA, joining Formula One, World Endurance, Rally and Rallycross Championships.

One incident sticks in my mind from the inaugural Formula E race in Beijing. We were broadcasting live from the pits and the final corner was close by, so with only a few laps remaining I decided to go there to see the action. On the penultimate lap Nicolas Prost was leading down the straight in his e.dams Renault ahead of his good

---

84 Source. FIAFormulae.com

friend Nick Heidfeld in a Venturi. The German looked to the inside line, but locked up and was unable to challenge. Di Grassi was in third and I watched the chasing cars pass, waiting for the leaders to return for the final lap.

When the cars reappeared, Prost was still leading, but now Heidfeld, who had saved some energy, was close in Prost's slipstream. Heidfeld pulled out to the inside line, drawing alongside Prost. The Frenchman then tried to 'close the door' as is common when fighting for a win, especially in the dying stages of a race. But he was far too late, and the cars' front wheels collided, breaking Heidfeld's front right suspension. Before my eyes Heidfeld was now a passenger in his own car, his steering destroyed. As he crossed the kerb at the bend, his car literally took off, and then, clipping one of the barriers, executed a 540-degree axial spin before smashing down, cockpit first, on to the run-off track.

The incident was so spectacular and violent that my first thought was that Nick could not possibly survive. Would this be the end of Formula E before it had even really started? I grabbed the metal fence and watched in horror as Heidfeld's wrecked car lay like a flipped tortoise, its rear wing lying some distance away. Nicolas Prost's car had also stopped just off the track and Lucas Di Grassi passed by to win the first ever Formula E race, a result that seemed highly unlikely just a few moments before.

But then, to my great relief, I saw some movement under the car and Heidfeld, amazingly unharmed, wriggled head first out of his destroyed machine. There was something he wanted to say to his friend Nicolas Prost and he ran over angrily to confront the e.dams driver. I watched them exchanging words and gestures, but thankfully no blows, as I followed them back to the pits.

The series was off to a dramatic start and instead of destroying the sport's credibility, the crash, filmed by Aurora, became part of the epic promotion package. When I got back to the pits, Uli was filming the two drivers as they walked back to their garages, Juan commentating live about the dramatic end to the first race. Formula E was here to stay.

The vision for Formula E was clear from the outset, differing in some important ways from the established world of Formula One. Apart from the obvious sustainability angle, the series was raced on the streets of some of the greatest cities in the world, bringing the party to the people, rather than asking them to travel to circuits which are often far from the main population centres.

The formula was developed to reduce the differences between the cars, placing, for example, limits on the power output of the engines, to make for more competitive wheel-to-wheel racing and to give more drivers a chance of winning. The vision was to showcase the capabilities of electric cars and hasten the transition to a better, cleaner future. The way the sport was marketed, of which Natt and I were a small part, certainly made its mark. A lot of the ideas developed in Formula E were brought into Formula One when Liberty took over.

There are critics of the fundamental idea at the heart of Formula E and some Formula One fans, perhaps seeing the series as a threat to the sport they love so passionately, are actively hostile. I was a firm believer in Alejandro Agag's persuasive vision for the green motor racing category. But when I returned to the Formula One paddock there was no shortage of sceptics. When I bumped into a racing 'purist' the conversation would usually go something like this:

'Hey Kris, I hear you're covering Formula E now?'

'Yeah, bit of F1, but all of the FE races.'

'Let me ask you this. Electric cars run on electricity, right?'

'Right.'

'And how is electricity produced?'

'Well, you can get it from solar cells, hydroelectric dams, wind farms and nuclear power stations.'

'Surprisingly knowledgeable of you.'

'Yes, I literally just finished a feature on the topic.'

'That explains it. But tell me, how much of the energy we use is created from renewables?'

'Um.'

'Well, let me tell you. It's less than 40 per cent worldwide. The rest comes from fossil fuel.'

'But the UK uses less fossil fuel than that, right?'

'It's still nearly half. So, tell me, how is Formula E environmentally friendly when the manufacture of an electric car uses twice as much fossil fuel energy as a normal car?'

'Ah, well, the thingy, the footprint. Once the car is produced, they have a much lower carbon footprint.'

'You sure about that? What about the 33 per cent inefficiency when electricity is transmitted over the grid, and what about battery disposal? That's an environmental disaster in itself.'

'Well, yes, but …'

'And aluminium for the bodies of electric cars? Transforming bauxite into lightweight aluminium takes a huge amount of fossil fuel.'

'Can I stop you there! Leonardo DiCaprio finances a team. Yes, Leo! Surely a superstar celebrity can't be wrong??'

'Who?'

So, as ever, nothing is quite as simple as you hope it might be. But since its debut in the grounds of the Olympic Park in Beijing in 2014, Formula E has grown into a global entertainment brand. As many as 80 drivers from Formula One, Le Mans, Macau and IndyCar have raced and my friend, WEC WTCC world champion José María 'Pechito' López of Argentina has competed over three seasons. But not everyone has bought in. Red Bull's racing team consultant Dr Helmut Marko, for example, says he is not interested in Red Bull entering a team into the series, 'because we're racing purists'.

But Formula E is here to stay. After consuming well over $100m in its first few years, the sport now has big cash reserves and is poised to generate profits, almost breaking even during the pandemic. Valuations for the Formula E franchise are variously estimated to be heading towards $1bn, which is as good a guarantee as you can have that it will have a bright, electric future. In April of 2021 Formula E even spawned a spin-off, Extreme E, which races spec silhouette (that is, cars which look like productions models) electric SUVs in remote parts of the world such as the Saudi Arabian desert and the Arctic to raise awareness of aspects of climate change.

I was sad to leave Formula E after four seasons, but in 2018 the rights for Formula One were again with Fox LatAm and so I was summoned back to the circus. They must have missed their clown.

Run For Your Lives!

Circuit de Catalunya, north of Barcelona, 2012

AFTER HIS historic win in the Spanish Grand Prix, Pastor Maldonado completed the press conference for the World Feed and then came straight to Fox Sports LatAm in the interview pen. Juan and I patted him on the back to congratulate him before he expressed his gratitude to his team and sent his love to his South American fans, particularly those in Venezuela.

As the proud Latino talked to the rest of the world's press, Juan and I waited with Uli, who was calmly smoking a cigarette in the paddock near the entrance to the Williams garage.

It wasn't long before Pastor arrived and went into the garage with team owner Sir Frank Williams, his daughter Claire and the celebrating mechanics and engineers.

It was less than a month after Sir Frank's 70th birthday and he was overcome with emotion. He was widely admired in the racing community for his pivotal role in developing the sport, the extraordinary success he achieved, his sheer enthusiasm for racing and the way he dealt with the most terrible setbacks.

Born in 1942, he was obsessed with motorsport from a young age. He persuaded his mother to give him £80 to buy a souped-up Austin A35 saloon, which he entered in his first races. Soon he fell in with a group of racing friends which included Old Etonian Piers Courage, the heir to the brewing business and an aspiring racing driver. They formed a close partnership.

Having spent his school holidays with a friend whose father was a car dealer, Frank learned to wheel and deal and was soon able to support his racing passion by buying and selling parts and later, single-seater racing cars.

He started his first racing team, Frank Williams Racing Cars, at the age of 24 and managed to enter his first car into a Formula One race at the age of just 28. Later he formed Williams Grand Prix Engineering and won his first Formula One race in 1979 at the British Grand Prix at Silverstone with a Cosworth-powered Williams FW07 driven by the Swiss driver Clay Regazzoni. From then on Williams became a dominant force in Formula One, winning nine World Constructors' Championships and seven Drivers' World Championships between 1980 and 1997.

What makes his story even more remarkable is that in 1986 he was driving a hire car in the south of France and had an accident which broke his neck and his spine, injuries that confined him to a wheelchair for the rest of his life. He continued to run the team through its glory years and then through the 2000s when race wins were harder to come by. Earlier in his life he had to deal with the death of his friend and business partner John Courage and later that of Ayrton Senna while driving for his team.

Sir Frank acknowledged the congratulations for his 114th Grand Prix win. Lewis Hamilton joined the long line of people who showed their support at the Williams motorhome. In the garage Sir Frank soaked up the love from the jubilant team he founded in 1978.

I will never forget how happy he looked, smiling in his wheelchair, celebrating what would turn out to be the last racing victory of his extraordinary life. He was so obviously happy still to be in the business and thanks to Pastor Maldonado, he was a winner again that day. He died in November 2021 at the age of 79.

Looking into the Williams garage from the pit lane, the car belonging to Bruno Senna was on the right, stripped down on metal stands, with no wheels or nose cone. Bruno had retired from the race on lap 12 after Michael Schumacher struck the rear of his car.

The left-hand side of the garage was clear, except for some fuel barrels at the back, as Pastor's car was undergoing post-race checks. The team occupied that area and Uli began filming the festivities.

The atmosphere was ecstatic. It was a long overdue victory for a team that had been struggling.

Juan, who had already interviewed Sir Frank, saw the opportunity to ask a few questions of his daughter Claire, the director of marketing and communications for the team and later the de facto team principal. With the microphone in one hand, Juan plugged the three-pin XLR connector into Uli's camera and let the cable trail on the floor as he asked Claire if she would say a few words. Claire came towards us, smiling happily as she spoke. I was standing behind Uli listening to what Claire had to say and watching the celebrations to my left.

It was then I heard a noise like a muffled explosion, not loud, but more like a 'whoosh', quiet but powerful. I stepped back, either pushed by the blast or on an instinct to move away. I saw Claire look behind her slowly, still smiling until the moment she saw flames engulfing the back of the garage. I was shocked and disorientated, but could already feel the heat of the fire on my face. Vast quantities of black smoke immediately began to swirl around and I watched people run past me as they made a beeline out of the garage towards the pit lane. Claire was gone. I think she went looking for her father.

I stumbled over a tyre pistol as I backed away from the fire and fumes. I saw Uli quickly disconnect the microphone cable and detach the monopod from the camera. Then Juan walked calmly in front of me as I turned away. The thick dark smoke took only seconds to fill the enclosed space before it began to pour out into the pit lane. I couldn't take in what was happening and retreated a little more. I glanced sideways and Uli was on his way, hurdling the few scattered items on the floor as he made his rapid retreat. I couldn't see anything inside the garage now as the smoke began to intensify. I didn't know whether to stay and try to help or get out as fast as possible.

The wind was beginning to blow the smoke down the pit lane behind me and to my right as I still faced into the garage. I distanced myself a little further. Then the wind must have changed direction for a moment because the smoke briefly cleared and I saw several mechanics with fire extinguishers in hand, before the cloud swirled and again I could see nothing. The mechanics seemed to know what they were doing but I dithered.

My mind was made up when two things happened. First, I saw Sir Frank Williams in his wheelchair being pushed at speed by his carer downwind and away from the garage. Then, I heard someone shout, 'Run for your lives!' The voice was authoritative but also somewhat panicky. It then occurred to me that, with the fuel barrels still in the garage, a bigger explosion could happen at any moment. I now know it wasn't Sir Frank or his carer who shouted those words, but in the confusion, I honestly thought it was and concluded that if the owner of the Williams team or his staff says to run for your life, it's probably best. Though why I thought he would know any better than anyone else is no longer clear to me.

Uli had disappeared. I followed Sir Frank's wheelchair as it sped down the pit lane to the right as you looked in, chased by the smoke that continued to pour from the Williams garage. Juan was now nowhere to be seen, so he must have been on the other side of the smoke cloud, doubtless the best place to be in the circumstances.

Brave mechanics and engineers mostly from Williams but also from Caterham and Force India (the two teams either side of the fire) and a few people from other teams came to help, pulling their colleagues out from the smog, while others, armed with fire extinguishers and wall hoses, risked their lives to put out the blaze and remove the 50-litre fuel containers to prevent a bigger explosion. By the time the local fire services arrived, the blaze was under control thanks to the prompt action of the pit crews, who prevented far more substantial damage and any further casualties.

Also upwind, doing their job brilliantly, were Sky TV's pit reporter Ted Kravitz and his cameraman, who kept their heads and continued reporting while the incident was happening.

Juan had also assessed the situation calmly and clearly and had headed upwind to the left of the garage. He was also ready to report the big story, but when he reeled in his microphone cable, he found that it was no longer attached to the camera and both the cameraman and producer had run for their lives.

I admit, when I found Uli taking a few shots of the smoking pits from a safe distance, I wished I had reacted differently. If only we had gone upwind, we could have either caught some fantastic shots for our own audience or been in a position to help people who were perhaps still in danger. Perhaps I would have been more heroic if I hadn't been terrified that the garage was going to explode at any second.

One thing was preying on my mind, however. Could the cigarette that Uli was smoking outside of the garage have been the cause of the fire? I had to ask.

'Uli,' I said while gesturing towards the chaotic scenes in the Williams garage. 'You did put your cigarette out before you went into the garage, right?'

'*Boludo! Por supuesto!*' (You idiot, of course!) he cried and then burst into his trademark peals of laughter. I have to say, the relief was tremendous.

Pastor Maldonado demonstrated more of his character during the fire when he piggybacked his 12-year-old cousin, Manuel, away. The small boy had a broken ankle at the time. A total of 31 people were taken to the medical centre following the incident with three Williams mechanics helicoptered to hospital in Barcelona after suffering smoke inhalation and burns. Four from Caterham and one from Force India were also injured, needing a trip to the hospital.

The fire caused extensive damage to Williams' equipment, particularly Bruno Senna's car, but once again their rival teams helped them out by lending items so they could compete in the next race in Monaco. The cause of the fire was later established to be a leakage from the rig used to drain fuel from Senna's car, ignited by a spark from the Kinetic Energy Recovery System (KERS) unit.

Although the fire certainly put a dampener on Williams' historic victory, the reaction of the rival teams showed that however cut-throat Formula One is on track, in moments of danger camaraderie will shine through.

When we met Juan back in the paddock, he was standing with the rest of the press outside the Williams motorhome with the three-pin XLR connector microphone dangling in front of him and an expression that didn't need any words. But he said them anyway.

'So, what happened to you two?'

The incident still leaves me feeling slightly guilty for blindly following a legend of Formula One down the pit lane to safety and not assessing the situation a little better, moving upwind to see if there was anything I could do. But in my defence, running for my life seemed like an unusually sensible decision at the time.

Never Lift, Never Give Up

2022 Abu Dhabi

I AM jogging alongside Sebastian Vettel down the main straight of the Yas Marina Circuit on the eve of his final race, the 2022 Abu Dhabi Grand Prix. After 15 years in the highest category of motorsport, winning four Drivers' World Championships and twice being runner-up, the German superstar is bowing out gracefully.

I'm not dressed for physical activity, wearing heavy shoes, long trousers and a thick ESPN polo shirt under the event T-shirt worn by nearly everyone. It spells out *'Danke Seb'* on the front and 'Never Lift, Never Give Up' on the back. Sebastian is wearing the same T-shirt, except his says *'Danke F1'*.

Sweating heavily, I snap a selfie with Sebastian, thank him and wish him luck. He pats me on the shoulder and smiles kindly. I like running and, despite my inappropriate attire, I would normally have joined the German legend and the hundreds of other paddock folk on his farewell lap. But I had played a two-hour football match with journalist friends the night before and, like Batigol at the end of his career, my legs are killing me.

So, I slowed to walking pace and Sebastian and his entourage disappear around the first corner. I wander back down the main straight where he had won the Grand Prix on three occasions and spot the Brazilian pit reporter and presenter Mariana Becker from the Rede Bandeirantes Channel.[85] She was sat at the start/finish line by herself and I can tell she is upset, so I sit down beside her

---

85 Often known simply as 'Band'.

and give her a hug. She was not the only person who will miss Sebastian Vettel.

Seb's retirement had perhaps been on the cards once he moved from Ferrari to Aston Martin in 2020, but it still came as a shock when it was formally announced at the 2022 Hungarian Grand Prix before the summer break. When a driver of Sebastian's calibre leaves the fold, you expect his fellow competitors to have nice words to say, but rarely have the comments been so heartfelt. Some spoke of his ability as a driver, but most referred to his character and things he had done for them over the years.

Carlos Sainz summed up his feelings:

'I was privileged to be a simulator driver when he was at his peak in Red Bull. I remember those years very well. He always had kind words for me. He would stop, chat, and give me advice. Always getting on well with all the teams, with everyone. Everyone in the paddock loves him, you know. You will not hear someone speaking bad about Seb.'

As I sat with Mariana in silence, I took a moment to reflect on what I remembered of Sebastian. I didn't think about the time I first saw him in 2011 when he was dominating the sport; nor any of his brilliant and brave overtaking manoeuvres during closely fought races; nor the time he stayed behind to clean up the litter left in the grandstands after the 2021 British Grand Prix at Silverstone; nor the time he rolled up his sleeves to help his mechanics get the car ready for qualifying after he crashed in free practice three, two days after he announced his retirement. Nor did I think of his trademark salute after every victory, nor the way he tried to use his platform to raise awareness about climate change, even though he knew he was in a business that was part of the problem. I didn't even think about his patience and kindness when it came to engaging with his fans. What came to mind was his smile and his laughter. A 'highlights reel' flashed through my mind of his beaming face at press conferences or paddock chats whenever he found something amusing. He chuckled to himself, or he shared a joke with other drivers, or best of all, reduced a large crowd to helpless laughter. That's what came to mind when I thought of Sebastian Vettel.

'I can't believe the season's almost over,' I said to Mariana.

'Oh yes, finally! One more day,' she said, praying her thanks to the sky. It had been a difficult season for her after she tore ligaments in her ankle in a skiing accident and had to do her reports and interviews first from a wheelchair, then perched on a knee scooter, and finally on crutches before she fully recovered. But it had been a long season for everyone in the circus.

I had travelled hundreds of thousands of miles from Buenos Aires and back, including a 45-hour one-way trip from Ezeiza to Melbourne Airport via Dallas and Los Angeles and a 46-hour stint from Ezeiza to Singapore Changi Airport via Houston and San Francisco. I shudder to think about my own carbon footprint. Sebastian would be horrified.

All 20 drivers came together for a farewell dinner for Sebastian on Thursday in Abu Dhabi and two of them showed up to Seb's farewell run, his friend Mick Schumacher and Charles Leclerc, who was his team-mate at Ferrari in 2019 and 2020. Charles, like me, had pulled the *'Danke Seb'* shirt over his regular clothes.

It had been a long year for Charles, too. The 2022 season was never going to deliver the controversy and excitement of 2021, but Charles had started it looking like a serious rival to the reigning world champion, Max Verstappen. Early on there was some great wheel-to-wheel racing between them. But it wasn't to be the Monégasque's year. Ferrari's engine was fast, but had reliability problems, causing Charles to crash out in Spain, retire in Baku and start at the back of the grid in Canada. Then the Ferrari team got the race strategy wrong in Monaco and Silverstone, being slow to make necessary tyre changes.

Charles also had his share of rank bad luck. In the Belgian Grand Prix on lap three, another driver's visor tear-off[86] improbably

---

86 The visor on F1 helmets carries layers of transparent strips that the driver can peel off if something sticks to it and obscures his view.

found its way into his brake duct, forcing him to pit, compromising his race strategy and dropping him to sixth place, while Verstappen won. It later emerged that the tear-off belonged to none other than Max Verstappen himself.

But Charles made mistakes. At the French Grand Prix momentum was back in his favour after a win in Austria and qualifying on pole. Charles built a comfortable lead, but then made an error and spun out on lap 18, handing an easy victory to his rival. You could hear Charles's bitter cry of despair and frustration over the radio.

Uli and I were waiting for Charles to come into the interview pen and tell us what happened. I wondered how to word my questions. You don't expect a driver, clearly fuming from what has just happened, to be talkative or to accept responsibility for their actions. You certainly don't expect them to engage with fans in the paddock as they make their way to confront the press.

But Charles Marc Hervé Perceval Leclerc is not like most drivers. Before he came through the turnstiles into the interview pen below the media centre, an excited father and his young child asked him for a photograph. Not only did he patiently pose for one, but he also spent time helping the nervous father, who was struggling to take the shot, by calmly showing him how to use the phone's camera. Not many drivers would have done that having just handed 25 points to their main rival.

Charles then came in and talked to all the world press, explaining to us all, one at a time, that if he kept making such mistakes, he didn't deserve to win the World Championship.

Born in Monaco to affluent parents, Charles certainly has the pedigree, as his father, Hervé Leclerc, and his grandfather were both racing drivers. The latter, Charles Manni, was founder of Mecaplast, later the Novares Group, one of the world's leading automotive parts providers. It would be easy to assume that Charles was destined to drive in Formula One and there is no doubt he has had opportunities granted only to a few.

Yet while privilege can make some people arrogant, it is certainly not the case with Charles. He is mature for his age but also humble and constantly trying to improve himself as a driver and a person. Above all, I think Charles deserves credit for a simple act of kindness which meant a lot to me, and even more to Juan. When Juan's mother passed away, Charles, who only knows Juan through the interviews they have done together, took the time to send a private message offering his condolences. That gesture, as far as I am concerned, speaks louder than racing records, rich and powerful friends, intelligence, sense of humour or anything else.

When I look at Charles, I often think of something Niki Lauda said:

'You have to be a bastard if you want to win in Formula One. No question. You cannot win being a nice guy.'

I hope that Charles will prove Niki wrong sometime soon.

The serious runners who went out with Sebastian were now completing their laps, so I stood up and waited for him to appear with his peloton of supporters. The screens above the podium in the pit lane were displaying images from his illustrious career.

The last time those large monitors had grabbed my attention was the previous year when Max Verstappen was the centre of attention after winning his first title. In 2022, however, his second successive World Championship was confirmed with four races still to go at the Japanese Grand Prix in Suzuka. When the much-shortened, rain-delayed race ended after only 28 laps with Verstappen in first place, everyone in the paddock, including the winner, expected reduced points would be awarded, leaving him short of the total required to confirm his second title.

While I was interviewing Sebastian Vettel, the 'WORLD CHAMPION 2THEMAX' graphic flashed up on the monitor beside us.

'So, he is the world champion? How does that work?' Sebastian asked me, looking back from the screen.

'Well, Sebastian, the FIA have clarified that full points have been awarded, even though the race was shortened to less than 75 per cent of the total race distance because of the three-hour rule. In previous years, as you know, that would have meant reduced points, but on a strict reading of the new rule introduced in 2022, the reduction only applies when a race is suspended and cannot be resumed. But in this case the race was restarted following a red flag, so that means the winner is awarded full points, which is sufficient to guarantee his second world title.'

Actually, that's what I would have liked to have said. What I did say was:

'Um. Er. No idea.'

Anyway, Sebastian was, as usual, smiling. He could afford to be generous. Max still had work to do to catch him up.[87]

When I think of Max I see a cascade of images, but I find it hard to select one that effectively encapsulates him. He was trained, you might even say programmed, from infancy to be a racing driver and there were few doubts where he was going. I first interviewed the Dutch whizz-kid when he was just 17 years and three days old, before he had his road driving licence, after he replaced Jean-Eric Vergne for free practice at the 2014 Japanese Grand Prix.

It had already been announced that he would drive for Toro Rosso for the 2015 season and so would be the youngest ever driver to race in a Formula One Grand Prix. He seemed completely unfazed as the press bustled to interview him, displaying an air of aloofness and unwavering self-confidence. And since that day he has remained the same. Win or lose, he is economical with his words, but has always been most respectful when dealing with me.

He does, however, sometimes show his ruthless side when talking to his race engineers during a race or dealing with other drivers. On one occasion he pushed and unpleasantly insulted Esteban Ocon after the Frenchman (who was a lap behind) made contact during the 2018 Brazilian GP and cost him the race. Some drivers and pundits have questioned his 'kamikaze' driving style and

---

[87] At the end of the 2023 season, Alberto Ascari, Graham Hill, Jim Clark, Emerson Fittipaldi, Mika Häkkinen and Fernando Alonso have won two World Championships. Only ten F1 drivers have won more: Jack Brabham, Jackie Stewart, Niki Lauda, Nelson Piquet and Ayrton Senna and (almost certainly) Max Verstappen with three, Sebastian and Alain Prost with four, Juan Fangio with five and, of course, Lewis Hamilton and Michael Schumacher with seven each.

Max may well envisage his Formula One car as fitting into smaller gaps than anyone else's. But it's hard to argue with his abundant success.

There was an incident, however, during the 2022 Formula One season that did get reporters and journalists (and a few million Mexican F1 fans) to mount their high horses. It happened at the penultimate race, at Interlagos in Brazil.

Red Bull had already won the driver's and the constructors' titles, but there was still the battle for second place in the Drivers' World Championship to be decided. While Ayrton Senna famously said 'second is to be the first of the ones who lose', there was still plenty at stake; hefty contractual payments and, more important, the honour and prestige of being runner-up in a Formula One championship.

Checo Pérez was leading Charles Leclerc by five points before the 2022 Brazilian GP and with a sprint race as well as the Grand Prix scheduled, a maximum of 34 points were available for a driver who could win both races and claim the fastest Sunday lap. Remarkably, George Russell did just that and claimed all those points after a faultless weekend. By the end of the race, Charles had picked up 15 points and Checo ten, sending them into the final race of the season level on 290.

However, Checo could, and perhaps should, have gone to Abu Dhabi with an all-important two-point lead. During the race, which was dominated by Mercedes and Ferrari, Checo, in sixth position, let his team-mate pass with five laps to go to see if Max could catch Fernando Alonso who was in fifth chasing Charles Leclerc, on the understanding that the place would be returned if Max could not catch Fernando. But Max was unable to get close enough to the Spaniard and so was asked three times by Red Bull to give Checo the place back. But he didn't and so finished in sixth place, depriving Checo of two valuable points in the race for second place in the championship, even though they had little value to Max with his world title already in the bag. Christian Horner was quick to apologise to Checo over the radio.

'He shows who he really is,' the Mexican fired back from his cockpit.

When Verstappen was questioned about his behaviour over the radio, he responded aggressively.

'I told you already. Don't ask that again to me. Okay, are we clear about that? I gave my reasons and I stand by it.'

Rumour has it that Max's reason for not yielding the position went back to an incident in Monaco when Checo allegedly crashed during qualifying to deny his team-mate a shot at pole. Checo went on to win that race, which gave rise to the scenes at the Red Bull Energy Station described at the beginning of this book. Only Max knows the real reason, but I do know that he lost the support of at least one fan by failing to let Checo through. Uli, a diehard Verstappen fan until that day, has not forgiven him.

To win a Formula One World Championship is to perform consistently at the very highest level of competition under extreme pressure. Nico Rosberg just managed to beat Lewis Hamilton to the championship in 2016, but has since spoken candidly about the debilitating pressure he endured and his bouts of self-doubt. It took so much out of him that he astounded the world of F1 by announcing his retirement just five days after he was crowned.

When Sebastian Vettel was fighting for his second title, he too ignored a clear message from Red Bull during the 2013 Malaysian GP in a notorious episode that became known as 'Multi-21'. This code meant Vettel should hold position behind his team-mate Mark Webber (who had led throughout the race) and let the Australian take the chequered flag. Instead, Sebastian ignored this team order and passed an angry Webber on the last lap to take the victory for himself.

Sebastian's defiance also arose from a perceived injustice. At the season-ending 2012 Brazilian Grand Prix, Vettel was in a title battle with Ferrari's Fernando Alonso. At the start of the race Vettel felt Webber had squeezed him against the wall, causing him to lose momentum and so get caught up in an incident a few corners later that dropped him to the back of the field, stationary and facing the wrong way. That day Sebastian heroically fought his way back to fourth and went on to win the drivers' title from Alonso by just three points, but Webber's actions, which Sebastian thought were deliberate, were not forgotten.

Sebastian was not penalised by Red Bull in the 'Multi-21' saga and nor was Max sanctioned for disobeying team orders at Brazil in 2022. When a driver is winning championships, they hold all the cards.

When Sebastian jogged past the finish line on his final lap of honour, he said his last goodbyes to his many friends and colleagues, posing for yet more selfies and photographs. I asked him to sign my season pass and he happily scribbled his autograph. Perhaps Sebastian thought he was no longer in a team where he could compete for victories, as he had done for so much of his career.[88] And when racing drivers who have tasted victory realise they can no longer win, they often decide to leave. But I wonder if he had any regrets when he saw how competitive the Aston Martin was in 2023.

Perhaps we will see Sebastian Vettel again in Formula One. Maybe he will return, like Michael Schumacher and Fernando Alonso did after announcing their retirements. But in the meantime, I wish him well on his new journey.

---

88 Despite Sebastian's less competitive car, he still performed brilliantly in qualifying and finished his final race in the points in tenth position.

Frankenstein's Baby

Abu Dhabi 2021 – race day

FIVE MINUTES and 16 seconds before the start of the Abu Dhabi Grand Prix, the one and only camera available to cover the pit and paddock action for millions of Spanish-speaking fans across the Americas, the Sony camera under my sole supervision, had completed its slide out of the housing from the tripod I was holding in the air and was in freefall, out of my reach.

It must be said that my camera was already a long way from mint condition. I had broken the hinge of the plastic panel that protected the audio dials and it was hanging off the camera like a bird's broken wing. A piece of metal had fallen out of the audio input plug, so it no longer clicked satisfyingly into place and instead wobbled around alarmingly. I had left the brand-new camera light, that Juan bought on his way through Miami, on a bench in the paddock in Saudi Arabia. The Abu Dhabi race began in daylight and ended under floodlights so film crews needed to be able to shine away the shadows with their own luminosity. So, a replacement was urgently required.

Fortunately, my good friend Roy 'Gooshbumpsh' Janssen found one, but there was a problem. The connectors on the light and the camera were all 'female' and so did not interlock, but I fixed them together with numerous cable ties. They looked most untidy, the excess waving around like the tendrils of a jellyfish, so I cut them down with a pair of pliers that I borrowed from the on-board camera maintenance workshop. But for some reason, or rather no reason at all, I cut them off at a 45-degree angle, which created countless stiletto-sharp daggers around the camera handle. Every time I picked the camera up or even when I just panned or zoomed, one cable tie or another stabbed me viciously in the back of my hand. After a few days my right paw had accumulated more puncture wounds than poor old Julius Caesar on the Ides of March.

The improvised attachment worked for a day or two, but by Saturday, the eve of the biggest race in Formula One history, the cable ties had loosened and the light began to tilt upwards, giving the top of Juan's blond head a glow like a renaissance saint, but leaving his body in the shade. He complained that the tilted-back light was casting an unflattering shadow beneath his chin and repeatedly tried to pull the light back to its correct position before recording his pieces to camera. But it refused to stay put.

So, on Sunday morning, when we arrived at the track, I went back to the kind folk in the on-board camera maintenance workshop and procured the longest cable tie they had, one about 50cm long. Confident I could make Juan's unflattering neck shadow a thing of the past, I went back to the paddock to find the camera. I used two of the smaller cable ties left over from my first operation to fix the long cable tie to the front of the camera handle. Then I looped it around the base of the light and tightened it, pulling it back to the desired position.

Success! However, it did leave a good 40cm or so of cable tie sticking out towards me. Predictably, I had no pliers with me to cut it off, so to avoid adding an eye injury to the multiple stab wounds on my hand, I tied the end of it into a clumsy knot and proudly went in search of Juan to show off my handiwork. When he saw the light restored to its correct position, he gave me a nod, but it crossed my mind he might not be as impressed as I was.

So, the camera, which had started its journey to the Middle East in pristine condition had, under my care, become more and more like Frankenstein's baby, with multiple porcupine-like cable ties, incompatible borrowed accessories, flapping broken parts and missing bits. Now, projecting from the top, was the bobbing cable tie, like the weird antenna of some mechanical insect, terminating in the bulbous knot bouncing ponderously on the end.

But, like the mother of even the ugliest infant, I still loved it. It was, after all, my camera. Or at any rate, it was the only one we had to bring the action from this sporting extravaganza to our viewers in the Americas. So, its continued existence was pretty crucial to any hopes I had of a future life worth living.

As the crowds left the Fanzone in search of their seats in the grandstands and the mechanics in the garages made their final adjustments to the cars, the worldwide audience settled themselves down for 58 laps of intriguing racing by the best drivers on the planet. The protagonists would shortly be exiting their hospitality suites, heading for their cars. In about two hours, everyone would learn whether Max Verstappen or Lewis Hamilton would be crowned world champion and then the post-race interviews, ceremonies and celebrations could be savoured.

But the Spanish speakers in the Americas were going to be disappointed, because my camera was on a collision course with the unyielding asphalt below and there was absolutely nothing I could do to prevent it from hitting the floor and exploding into 100 pieces.

Standing in for Uli the cameraman had been a steep learning curve. Mistakes were most definitely made. Batteries were a constant challenge. The wrong camera switches were pressed. Lenses were smeared. The original camera light was lost. The concept of 'white balance' had eluded me. Indeed, I had found that just moving myself around the paddock was a challenge because of all the bulky equipment I had to carry. On my back was the LiveU video transmission pack, streaming the pictures back to Buenos Aires and Mexico City and in my hands were either the tripod or monopod, as well as the camera.

On my head were the headphones, one wire from each earcup joining together below the breastbone to make a V-shape and forming the longer, thicker single wire that plugs into the camera. Microphone cables and mini camera-stands hung from the shoulder straps of the backpack on Velcro ties. Microphones stuck out of my back pockets. A GoPro nestled in my left side leg pocket, its mini tripod sticking bulkily out of the right. A Red Pod bean bag camera support (yes, a small bean bag to put a camera on) bulged in my front right trouser pocket. The lapel microphone kit was (I optimistically hoped) in the left.

I had become a human version of Buckaroo, the plastic toy mule popular in the seventies, upon which children would take turns to hang what today would no doubt be considered choking hazards: a little red saddle, shovels, a hat, blankets, a pan, a lantern, a bedroll, rope, a stick of dynamite and so on … until the bad-tempered burro decided it had had enough and bucked it all off.

But I did not get the option to throw anything off my back. The items were all essential and expensive. I tried to move slowly and smoothly to avoid dislodging the various bits, like a leopard stalking its prey, as I followed Juan to wherever the action was hottest. But numerous items got dropped anyway.

Twice, my dangling coaxial cable caught on the turnstile at the paddock entrance causing mayhem as I struggled to free myself, but only managed to get more snarled up, the people behind me clucking and tutting in impatient disbelief. Then as Juan went to interview the 6ft 1in Alex Albon, I unwittingly stood on the microphone cable, so when Juan finished his question and moved the microphone towards Alex to capture the reply, there was not enough free cable and it was jerked embarrassingly out of his hand, leaving him holding the black foam sponge windbreaker. Countless times I'd walk away from the camera on the tripod forgetting that my headphones were still plugged in, self-administering whiplash before the headphones fell off and smashed to the ground.

But right now, my problem was 1,000 times more serious. My hands were full holding the rear legs of the tripod and the camera had slid out of the housing. I was doomed. Only divine intervention could save me.

What I didn't know was that as I went to pick up the tripod, I had, as usual, managed to snag a wire, the one which ran from the right-hand earcup of my headphones, around the little finger of my left hand. It left the little V, where the wires from the earcups on my headphones joined together, jutting out to the left of my left hand.

Panic flooded through me as I saw that my ugly but oh-so-precious camera had now fallen about halfway to the ground, lens first, and hideous visions of the future flooded into my paralysed mind. When that camera hit the floor, I was done for.

What happened next may be difficult to believe, but on my children's lives I swear it's true. That bulbous knot, the one at the end of the new cable tie, the one I had tied just an hour or so beforehand, fell neatly into the V in the headphones wire and miraculously, if only for a moment, locked. I felt the weight pull on the wire between the little and ring fingers of my left hand and on the right earcup of my headphones.

With no idea what was happening, I dropped the tripod, a mistake because it was the headphone wire caught between my little finger and the tripod leg that momentarily arrested the camera's fall. Now with nothing to restrain it, the wire slipped through my fingers and pulled my headphones off. The camera resumed its fateful course towards the concrete. But now at least my hands were free and I moved my right hand despairingly towards the camera to try and catch it.

But it was too late. The camera was now below the level of my hands and falling too fast for me to catch. It was just 50cm from its demise.

But then, by another miracle, the trailing camera shoulder strap hooked over the thumb of my right hand as my arms flailed desperately in the air. My faulty brain registered the leather belt and, instead of continuing to follow the camera down, some instinct told me to raise my arm. The camera pivoted as the strap tightened and changed its course once more. But this time, like a puppeteer, I had some control over its trajectory. As the camera arced downwards like a pendulum pirate ship ride at a fairground, I raised my right hand again just enough to ensure that at the nadir of the camera's swing, the lens cover only brushed the ground. The camera spun as it swung upwards on the other side. But now I was in control and clamped my right fist shut, pulled my arms towards me, twisted my body and squatted so my legs were between the camera and the ground. At last, the precious camera was safely in my lap.

I hugged my prickly baby tightly to my breast, adding, through my thin shirt, another half dozen stab-wounds and scratches to accompany my hand injuries. But I didn't care. I felt a tsunami of relief and a wash of maternal emotion. Ugly and spiky though it was, had my baby wanted to feed, I would certainly have done my best to oblige.

After a full ten seconds I broke my love-locked gaze and looked around to see who had witnessed the miracles, but nobody was looking in my direction. There was, in fact, no camera, other than the one I was nursing, in the vicinity and no lens pointing at me. How disappointed Oprah would have been.

'We're Going to Need a Miracle'

AND SO the Grand Prix was run and the Spanish speakers across the Americas were not, after all, deprived of the fabulous entertainment. Instead, they followed the compelling action in the paddock and heard the words of their heroes on the way to their cars and watched them climb in and roar off to the race start. There was plenty more drama to come and my own miracle was not the last that afternoon.

Although Max Verstappen had claimed pole in qualifying, when the five red lights went out it was Lewis Hamilton, on medium tyres, who got the better start, even though Max was on the softer compound and should have had the better grip. To the relief of the millions of viewers who wanted the title settled on the track, there was no crash at the first corner and the British driver cleanly took the lead into the first left-hander. Behind Max was Checo Pérez, perfectly positioned to help defend his team-mate from the drivers behind him. But the world's attention was on the championship contenders. What would Max do now? The pressure was on to make use of his softer tyres before they began to deteriorate. When would he try to overtake? What lap? The answers to these two questions were, of course, 'immediately' and 'lap one'.

Max does not hang around and he seemed too far behind going down the back straight into turn six to make a move. But as he has proved many times, his understanding of a closable gap is different from most drivers'. Out-braking the seven-time world champion on the inside line into the left-hander, he forced Lewis to take a shortcut off the track to avoid contact. Max and the other cars following him, took the chicane on the track as Hamilton drove across the run-off area, so cutting out turn seven and re-joining the circuit still ahead.

'Lewis Hamilton [is] in the lead, but will he have to give that place back?' asked David 'Crofty' Croft on the World Feed commentary.

'Yes, of course he will,' replied Martin Brundle immediately. And indeed most of those not blinded by their love for Mercedes and Lewis Hamilton thought the same.

'He has to give that back!' said a fuming Max Verstappen over the team radio.

But Martin, Max, Red Bull and countless fans glued to their screens around the world were to be reminded their opinions did not count. The stewards confirmed there was 'no investigation necessary'. The Red Bull pit wall roared its indignation. The race was less than a lap old but already there was controversy.

It was the practice, at that time, for the racing teams to be able to talk directly to the race controller. The Red Bull team principal Christian Horner was quick to complain to Michael Masi, but the stewards' decision had been made.

Unable to pass his rival, Verstappen was called in to the pits on lap 14 for new hard tyres that ought to see him through to the end of the race. Mercedes responded and Hamilton pitted one lap later to change his tyres for the harder compound. Meanwhile, Red Bull kept Checo out on the track, now leading the race, putting the Mexican in a good position to help his team-mate. Pérez's role was crystal clear.

'Hold Lewis up,' was the team's succinct order to Pérez over the radio.

And that's exactly what he did, showing not only his sublime driving skills but also confirming what an excellent team player he is, giving no quarter to the Mercedes driver. Lewis overtook Checo on lap 20 but was unable to make it stick and Checo cut back across to reclaim the lead.

The international press 'oohed' and 'aahed' around me.

Then Lewis overtook again on lap 21, but once again Checo showed his resilience and went back in front.

'He's like a dog on a bone,' said Christian Horner, all admiration for his driver. 'He never gives up.'

'*Nein!*' screamed Toto Wolff, the normally calm Mercedes team principal.

'This is racing!' averred someone beside me. 'Fantastic!'

Red Bull's tactics were working and the back-and-forth contest with Pérez wiped out the 11-second lead Hamilton had had over Verstappen when he left the pits. Now Verstappen appeared in Hamilton's rear-view mirror. But, as if that were the spur he needed, Hamilton found a way past Pérez again and this time held on to the lead. Checo was even able to give his Dutch team-mate the final gift of a speed boost from DRS, Max's rear wing opening to provide a surge of speed to overtake Checo's Red Bull and take on the race leader.

But that was as close as he got. The seven-time world champion now had a clear road and gradually, corner after corner, lap after lap Lewis Hamilton pulled away from Max Verstappen. Here was the greatest driver of his times showing why that was so. The Mercedes with Lewis Hamilton at the wheel was the faster car and soon he was overtaking the back-markers. By lap 53 of 58 the 11-second gap was restored and there were five lapped cars between the two front-runners.

It was all over. All was quiet dejection in Red Bull control. Even the normally irrepressible Christian Horner was downbeat.

'Mercedes are just too fast for us today,' he said. And then, 'Max is driving his heart out … [but] we're going to need a miracle.'

Meanwhile, right at the back of the race, Mick Schumacher, driving an uncompetitive Haas, was duking it out with Nicholas Latifi to avoid the indignity of finishing in last place. Schumacher was in front and the pressure was on Latifi to overtake him. His race engineer Gaëtan Jego was geeing his driver up.

'It has to be this lap, mate. Give everything.'

Latifi, though doubting it was possible to catch, let alone overtake the Haas driver, dutifully complied. The engineers tried to squeeze everything out of the car using the mode settings to maximise the power output and minimise battery recharging. It worked and at turn nine of the 53rd lap Latifi drew alongside the Haas on the outside of the bend, but was forced wide and off the main track, doubtlessly dirtying his tyres in the run-off area. But he hadn't lost too much ground and Gaëtan kept pushing his driver to get past.

'Stay with him. Stay with him. Put him under pressure.'

At turn 14 Latifi, still in pursuit, though not close enough to pass, turned into the left-hander, but as he did so, his rear wheels lost their grip, probably due to a combination of dirty tyres and the turbulent air from Mick's car. The back end of his car slid away, crashing his right rear wheel into the barrier and destroying his suspension. The in-car camera showed Latifi trying vainly to steer out of the slide, his helmet rattling around alarmingly on impact.

The wreckage would have to be cleared away before the race could continue, so race director Michael Masi called for the safety car. This meant that the cars had to reduce their speed and no overtaking was allowed. More to the point, the field would now close up behind Lewis Hamilton, wiping out his hard-earned advantage. But there were five lapped drivers between Hamilton and Verstappen which would surely provide enough of a buffer to keep Hamilton safe even if the race was restarted, which appeared unlikely as the cars counted down the remaining few laps while the debris was removed.

Red Bull, ready to pounce on any opportunity, brought Verstappen in to change to fresh tyres, an option not open to Hamilton, who would have had to concede race position to do so. Masi issued a notice saying 'lapped cars will not be allowed to overtake', which confirmed the buffer of the five cars would remain in place. The world champion was safe.

Time and distance were running out for Red Bull. But poor Michael Masi was now under the most intense pressure. No one wanted to end the season with a procession behind the safety car, but the track was still unsafe and there was the question of how to deal with the lapped cars, of which there were five between the leaders, and more further down the field. To add to his difficulties Masi had the team principals and sporting directors, literally, in his ear, with Red Bull in particular urging him to clear the lapped cars out of the way by letting them pass the safety car and re-join at the back of the field. But there was not enough time to complete that manoeuvre before the 58 laps would be complete.

Then Red Bull's sporting director Jonathon Wheatley made a crucial suggestion to Masi.

'Those lapped cars. You don't need to let them go right the way around and catch up with the back of the pack. You only need to let them go and then we've got a motor race on our hands.'

To which Masi responded, 'Understood, give me a second.'

Soon after that exchange, Masi privately messaged just the five cars between Hamilton and Verstappen to overtake, removing Hamilton's safety buffer. The safety car then left the circuit with one lap remaining (although according to the rules it should have stayed out for another lap) and now with Verstappen right behind Hamilton on fresh soft tyres against Hamilton's old hard compounds, the game was up. Max Verstappen's overtaking move on Hamilton wasn't unchallenged and certainly looked exciting on TV and at trackside, but with the huge tyre advantage Verstappen ducked inside Hamilton at the first opportunity and passed in a flash. Max went on to take the chequered flag and win his first Formula One World Championship.

Indignant protests and challenges followed, which kept the press at the track for many hours, but all to no avail. Max Verstappen was confirmed in his well-deserved, if dubiously achieved, drivers' title. Months later, the FIA concluded an inquiry which said that, while everyone had acted in good faith, the rules had not been followed correctly. Michael Masi was replaced in his role and the absurd practice of allowing the teams to communicate directly with the race director during the race, enabling them to apply pressure, was stopped. But the result stood.

As Juan was still on air, I interviewed the drivers outside of the top three as they came into the pen. We would need their quotes for the news and highlights shows. I set up the camera frame to accommodate both the 6ft 1in giants Esteban Ocon and Alex Albon and the tiny Yuki Tsunoda, just in case I didn't have time to look into the viewfinder while I asked my questions. I could always adjust the framing later when I was editing.

Most of the drivers were stunned by what had happened. Lando Norris said, 'it was for the TV of course' and Charles Leclerc found it 'weird'. Carlos Sainz called it 'very strange'. But however weird or strange it was, Christian Horner had his miracle. That day the aces fell to him and Max Verstappen (and every other member of the Red Bull team). The jokers went to Michael Masi and Nicholas Latifi. The Canadian most unfairly received a lot of attention from internet trolls complaining about his decision to try and overtake Schumacher, but he later responded by saying: 'Whether I am racing for wins, podiums, points or even last place, I will always give it my all until the chequered flag.' And fair play to him. Nicholas Latifi is a Formula One racing driver and to expect him to do anything other than race his heart out is like hoping an alcoholic will resist a second drink.

But for all the hoopla, controversy and razzamatazz, my highlight from Abu Dhabi (apart from catching the camera before it smashed to pieces), was that I was able to interview my hero Kimi Räikkönen for the last time after his 349th and final Formula One appearance.

Kimi is a quite unique personality. Something of an introvert, he is renowned for his reluctance to give interviews, particularly before he has had a chance to drive his car around the circuit. Indeed, one of his more famous quotes is 'Formula One would be a paradise without the media.' But he is genuine, which is why everybody loves him. And whenever I really needed an answer from him, even if I turned up late and he was on the point of leaving the interview area, even if I was shaking and unprepared and the cameraman was taking too long to set up, Kimi was always kind enough to wait and oblige. Perhaps he can see desperation in a man's face, but his response was always to show empathy and compassion.

Despite a forgettable last race, spinning off into the barriers, Kimi was smiling when he looked me in the eye and waited for my questions. It seemed a huge weight had been lifted from his shoulders. I thanked him for all the wonderful moments he had given us over the years. I had really enjoyed some of his comments, particularly when replying to the usually banal and foolish instructions the drivers get over the radio, such as 'drive faster' or 'give it everything', which rather implies they are currently out for a pleasant spin admiring the countryside.

'Leave me alone. I know what I'm doing,' was one of his pithier ripostes.

Then I asked him what he was most looking forward to away from the crazy Formula One circus. He sensed that I was sincere and gave me a long answer about how important his family was to him and how he was looking forward to spending more time with them.

I really like Kimi Räikkönen, because of everyone in racing, he is perhaps the most genuine of them all. I won't miss him, because I know he is doing something that he loves more than racing motor cars. Being with his family and his friends and still being true to himself. Although I wouldn't mind betting that, like any racing driver, it won't be long before he is back behind the wheel somewhere or other.

The Ace and the Joker

TRULY OUR destiny can hinge on the turn of a card or the beat of a butterfly's wings, fleeting moments that lead us to triumph or disaster. The random chance that left me holding the business card of Danny McGill from a pile of over 300. A faintly written dot on a Rolodex card that transformed F! to F1. A clumsy knot on the end of a flailing cable tie, falling neatly into the V-notch of the headphone wire.

Nicholas Latifi driving wide during his skirmish with Mick Schumacher and picking up the tiny particles of dirt on his rear tyres that caused him to slide into the race barrier. An opportunistic suggestion from Red Bull's sporting director leading to a pressurised decision by Michael Masi to send the lapped cars forward, hoping to give the fans a great season finale, but costing him his job and more importantly, denying Lewis Hamilton his eighth World Championship. But then again perhaps it's not all that important. Lewis already has seven and his stellar place in the history of the sport is already assured. And Max Verstappen, of course, is a worthy champion.

So what is it that drives these people, day in, day out, to devote their lives to winning races in motor cars? To dedicate and even risk their lives just to get their car first across the finish line. There are, of course, rational reasons. A career in motorsport can be a good living and is certainly more fun than the daily grind that most people endure. You work with talented and committed people in a tight team committed to achieve the clearest of goals. You travel to exotic locations. You can contribute to the design and build of the fastest racing cars in the world. For many there are generous salaries and for some life-changing prizes and sponsorship deals which bring the countless benefits that go with wealth, glamour and prestige.

And there is the visceral thrill of racing the cars. The smell and sound of the engines, the acceleration, the exhilaration of split-second decision-making, the euphoria of the competition and the sheer speed.

But that is not it. That is not it at all.

To some extent, drivers race cars to the limit because they fear failure. For the vanquished Lewis Hamilton, on that extraordinary day, it didn't matter that he was, by popular consent, robbed of the title. That he was mugged. Never mind that in any remotely fair world, where there was a scintilla of justice or rightness, he would have been world champion for the eighth time, elevating his name to an unreachable height in the history of motor racing and world sport. In that moment there was only dejection, anger, isolation and despair. How could it happen? What more could I have done?

But the real reason people race motor cars is for glory. To win points, to stand on the podium and ultimately to fulfil the dream of becoming world champion.

When Max Verstappen crossed the line to win his 2021 title, the Red Bull team erupted into a volcanic orgy of celebration. The ecstasy of victory. The unbridled joy of at last beating their rivals Mercedes, who had dominated the sport for the last seven years. The primitive fist-clenched, arm-pumping, chest-thumping alpha displays. The hugs, the shouts and the wide, wide smiles. The outpouring of love for their team-mates with whom, in that exact moment, they create a lifelong bond that no one else can ever share.

They basked in the adulation of the crowd. At last, they had indisputable affirmation that all the months and years of disappointment, sacrifice, dedication and practice were worth it after all. Vindication. Fulfilment. The crushing pressure of the expectations of owners, team principals, engineers, mechanics, investors, sponsors, colleagues, parents, families and friends, exquisitely relieved. And the precious licence to do it all again, for at least another year.

And among it all, brief, silent moments of introspection. Max Verstappen, emotion welling, lingering, crouched by the rear wheel of the now silent and always soulless machine that propelled him to victory.

But for me it was time to take off my clown's costume and wipe off the tear-stained make-up. The season was over and I looked forward to Christmas with my family and friends. Actually, I'm scared to death of clowns, with their freaky face-paint, fluorescent wigs, baggy trousers, flapping footwear and big red noses. I certainly don't want to be one.

But I do sometimes dream of being a Formula One racing driver, standing high on the podium with my arms aloft, sipping a champagne shoey and celebrating in front of my adoring fans. I dream of becoming 'one with the car' like Michael Schumacher, or just 'going, going, going' with Ayrton Senna around the circuit at Monte Carlo. But dreams are just dreams and life's not always fair. You can only play the cards you are dealt.

And my cards are an ace and a joker. I wouldn't have it any other way.

Acknowledgements

THE AUTHORS would like to thank the people who gave their support to this most unlikely project. They are: Mark Rebindaine, Adrian Scott, Sue Filby, Ian Filby, Simon MacDonald, Ben Lethbridge, Sarah Pringle, Nick Vyse, Matt Ward, Aaron Deckers, Katie Field, Dean Rockett, Duncan Olner, David Tremayne, Matt Dryden, Lee McKenzie, Sam Hague, Ian Cassidy, Laurence Edmondson, Toby Trotman, Diego Mejia, Mervi Kallio, Albert Fabrega, Nick Murray, Will Buxton, Nick Durrant, Jim Brandon, Gonzalo Storni, Andy Cawte, Johnny Green, Matthew Marsh, James Moy, Peter Fox, Jose-María Rubio, Steve Etherington, Mark Sutton, Steven Tee, Peter Fox, Darren Heath, Joshua Paul, Jiří Křenek, Beto Issa, Jess McFadyen, Cathy Runciman, Claire Williams and particularly Lawrence Barretto, Stuart Morrison, Nick Walters, Vladimir Rys, Peter Nygaard, Juan Fossaroli, Chris Medland, Nigel Kirkham, Matt Chesterton, Jess McFadyen, Derek Chelley, John Murray, Simon Chelley, Richard Milner, James Allen, Ulises Panizza, Simon Strevens and Guenther Steiner, who went far beyond what we dared to ask.

Any mistakes are our own.